D1508921

METATHEORY AND CONSUMER RESEARCH

GERALD ZALTMAN

CHRISTIAN R. A. PINSON

REINHARD ANGELMAR *Northwestern University*

METATHEORY AND CONSUMER RESEARCH

DRYDEN PRESS
HINSDALE, ILLINOIS

We acknowledge the use of excerpts from the following sources:

David Harvey, **Explanation in Geography,** London: Edward Arnold Ltd., 1969.

Mario Bunge, **Scientific Research,** Vol. 1. Berlin: Springer-Verlag, 1967.

Gerald Zaltman, "Marketing Inference in the Behavioral Sciences," July, 1970. Reprinted from the **Journal of Marketing** published by the American Marketing Association.

Ernest Nagel, **The Structure of Science.** New York: Harcourt Brace Jovanovich, Inc.

Copyright © 1964 by Chandler Publishing Company, Reprinted from **The Conduct of Inquiry** by Abraham Kaplan, by permission of Intext Educational Publishers, publishers.

TO JOSHUA COHEN
     GEORGES AND MARIE-ROSE PINSON
     MATILDE RADL

Editors' Foreword

For years, marketing scholars have tried to build up theory in marketing for the purposes of explanation, prediction, and control. The result has been a great number of interesting but partial (and often conflicting) contributions. In the field of consumer behavior alone, there are several grand theories claiming to hold the key to explaining consumer behavior. These theories employ different variables and frameworks in their pursuit of scientific explanation.

Those who attempt to build theory unfortunately often are unaware of their use of arbitrary assumptions and concepts. In marketing particularly, there has hardly been any discussion of the process of theory building itself. It is with this in mind that Messrs. Zaltman, Angelmar, and Pinson undertook to develop their METATHEORY AND CONSUMER RESEARCH. Their book presents the most cogent and contemporaneous discussion within marketing of the philosophy and methods of science.

The authors examine the scientific nature of explanation, prediction, and control. They present an incisive discussion of the use of concepts, hypotheses, and theories in advancing scientific inquiry and knowledge. Throughout their discussion they utilize abundant examples drawn from the marketing literature to provide a rich motivation and illustration of the requirements of scientific process.

We welcome this book as a distinguished addition to the Holt, Rinehart and Winston's Editors' Series and believe that it will have an enduring influence on future marketing theory. There cannot be marketing science until marketing scholars are well trained in the philosophy of science and conduct their investigations in the best traditions of scientific research.

Paul E. Green
Philip Kotler

Preface

In recent years, a number of researchers have made substantive contributions to the understanding of buyer behavior (for example, Nicosia—1966; Howard and Sheth—1969; Engel, Kollat, and Blackwell—1968; and Hansen—1971). Indeed, we have come a long way from the days when, at the conceptual level, we had only long lists of possibly relevant variables to rely upon, and, at the empirical level, we were limited by simplistic uses and misuses of statistical inference.

These new contributions have assumed different forms. Some are verbally stated hypotheses, also frequently represented in the form of charts. Other contributions are hypotheses represented in flowcharts which can readily be translated into econometric specifications. And a couple of contributions are encoded into mathematical forms, which enable us to deal with problems such as identification, parameters' dimensionalities, and dynamic characteristics. While this variety is the best evidence of the progress we have made, it also necessitates monitoring our progress on some objective basis, possibly beyond the well-known test: it works. As one of us recently pointed out, what we badly need is one or more sets of criteria to evaluate existing conceptualizations and theories of buyer behavior (Sheth—1972).

Metatheory and Consumer Behavior is an excellent example of a set of criteria, drawn from philosophy of science, with which we can begin to assess objectively the process of theorizing in the discipline of consumer behavior. The book is very timely and will doubtlessly become a standard reference. Further, not only have the authors exhausted much of the literature in philosophy of science, but they have also judiciously identified the relevant and integrated it in a way meaningful for our discipline. We think the chapters on explanation and prediction provide some of the best illustrations of metatheory and its applications.

The greatest contribution of the book must be the chapters on the nature of theorizing in our discipline and the critical evaluation of some of the extant flowcharts and models on buyer decision processes. While the reader may or may not agree with the book's analysis and conclusions, we believe that the book deserves recognition for taking a new and bold approach— taking the bulls by their horns, so to speak. We are pleased to see such a thorough and thoughtful comparative review, and to see the birth of a critical and constructive attitude which has been so conspicuously lacking in our discipline. This makes it more evident that the discipline is becoming mature.

The rigorous and scientific manner in which Zaltman and his coauthors have attempted to evaluate existing conceptualizations of the consumer from the point of view of metatheory should set future standards. We hope that others will follow this pioneering example, because not only researchers but also managers of firms and public policy makers need to know the limitations and thus relative strengths of our evolving knowledge.

Francesco M. Nicosia
University of California
at Berkeley

Jagdish N. Sheth
University of Illinois
at Urbana-Champaign

Acknowledgements

We are indebted to a number of people in helping us throughout this adventure. For their thorough and insightful critique of the manuscript we particularly want to express our deep appreciation to Professor Paul Green, the University of Pennsylvania, Professor Philip Kotler, Northwestern University, and Professor Jagdish Sheth, the University of Illinois. Professor Richard Clewett of Northwestern also provided a valuable critique of the manuscript and was a source of constant encouragement and support. We would also like to thank the Graduate School of Management, Northwestern University and the Fondation Nationale pour l'Enseignement de la Gestion des Entreprises—France, for their general support. Mr. Donald Knudsen performed admirably in providing assistance in tracking down references. Our main obligations, of course, are to those numerous scholars in the philosophy of science whose seminal works provided us with the raw material for this book. We hasten to add that any errors made in this book are entirely our own. All of us participated fully in the preparation of all chapters. While this approach is not conducive to a speedy preparation of a book it does provide for a stimulating intellectual experience of a high order. We hope the reader will also capture some of this stimulation.

G. Zaltman
C. R. A. Pinson
R. Angelmar

Evanston, Illinois
1972

Contents

CHAPTER 1

METATHEORY AND RESEARCH

INTRODUCTION

An essential step in the development of any field of study is the successful utilization of a rigorous thinking methodology in the theorizing and basic and applied research of that field. As we have noted elsewhere, there have been remarkable efforts made during the past few years toward the advancement of knowledge in the behavioral sciences.[1] Although important and impressive steps toward this goal have been recorded, the actual accomplishment in the behavioral sciences has not been consistent with the magnitude of the effort. The applicability of this observation, of course, varies considerably among disciplines and among specialties within disciplines. One important reason underlying the failure of actual achievement to keep pace with effort expended is the seeming absence of a rigorous thinking methodology.[2] Certainly, consumer behavior is not exempt from this statement.[3] This has very important implications for the use and conduct of marketing research in consumer behavior. The consumer behavior researcher needs a thinking methodology to evaluate the material he tries to build upon and, equally important, he needs a thinking methodology to guide his own theoretical and applied research to ensure the greatest value for his efforts. The philosophy of science in general, and metatheory in particular, offers such a thinking methodology. It provides fruitful guidelines for using and conducting research in marketing. It is hoped that if the reader is exposed to some of the topics and issues involved in metatheory he will achieve a more selective and more critical ability to develop, test, and apply behavioral science in consumer behavior research.

Only recently has there been any significant widespread acknowledgment of the need for a much more careful scrutiny of the procedures or thinking methodologies used by marketers in their knowledge building and knowledge utilization activities. Various authors focusing on one or another aspect of metatheory have directly or indirectly suggested that it would be desirable to introduce metatheory in marketing. One early indication is Joseph Newman's observation concerning the lack of attention given "to the topic of *developing* potentially fruitful hypotheses to guide operations."[4] Another early but not explicit call for metatheory can be found in Michael Halbert's book, *The Meaning and Sources of Marketing Theory*, especially Chapters 1 and 10.[5] Robert Bartels in his *Marketing Theory and Metatheory* deals with the subject, though not in a consumer behavior context; nor does he address the formal metatheory literature. He points out, however, that "the term metatheory appears only once in marketing writings, in the preface of John

[1] Gerald Zaltman, Reinhard Angelmar, and Christian R. A. Pinson, "Metatheory in Consumer Behavior Research."

[2] National Research Council, *The Behavioral and Social Sciences*.

[3] For two good assessments of the state of consumer behavior in research the reader is directed to Thomas S. Robertson and Scott Ward, "Consumer Behavior Research: Promise and Prospects" and Chapter 27 in James Engel, David Kollat, and Roger Blackwell, *Consumer Behavior*.

[4] Joseph W. Newman, *Motivation Research and Marketing Management*, p. 40, cited in Francesco M. Nicosia, *Consumer Decision Processes*, p. 18.

[5] The reader is also directed to George Schwartz, *Development of Marketing Theory*, and Reavis Cox, Wroe Alderson, and Stanley J. Shapiro, *Theory in Marketing*.

Howard's *Marketing Theory*, wherein he says merely that 'a metatheory of marketing is needed,'" p. 2.

In much of Francesco Nicosia's book, *Consumer Decision Processes* (particularly in Chapter 1), the reader sees the call for metatheoretical activities and the actual undertaking of metatheory processes. Perhaps the first explicit confrontation with metatheory in a consumer behavior context is to be found in Chapter 1 in *The Theory of Buyer Behavior*.[6] In this seminal work Howard and Sheth discuss several aspects of theories and introduce in marketing some of the philosophy of science literature. David Kollat, James Engel, and Roger Blackwell have, although they don't use the terms, called for a metatheoretical approach to the study of concepts.[7] Gerald Zaltman has also pointed out metatheoretical problems in conducting consumer behavior research.[8] Zaltman discusses scientific inference in using behavioral theory in the study of consumer behavior and mentions briefly several criteria for evaluating theories. Shelby Hunt has also discussed some metatheoretical criteria in his critique of Bartels' theory.[9] Christian Pinson, Reinhard Angelmar, and Eduardo Roberto have also introduced metatheory into the marketing literature in their response to Hunt.[10] Gerald Zaltman, Reinhard Angelmar, and Christian Pinson have presented what is probably the most concise overview of metatheory in marketing.[11] Many of the themes in that paper are presented as chapters in this book. In the concluding chapter of their book James Engel, David Kollat, and Roger Blackwell also discuss the need for introducing more metatheory in the study of consumer research.[12] Similarly, Robertson and Ward also call for more metatheory sensitivity in the study of consumer behavior.[13]

Thus, in all the items cited above there is an acknowledged need for a systematic exploration of metatheory with illustrations of its relevance to the study of consumer behavior. This and subsequent chapters undertake such an exploration.

Let us turn now to an examination of what is meant by metatheory. Following this will be a discussion of various models of scientific processes and a treatment of various criteria for guiding the scientific process. The

[6] John Howard and Jagdish Sheth, *The Theory of Buyer Behavior*.

[7] David T. Kollat, James F. Engel, and Roger D. Blackwell, "Current Problems in Consumer Behavior Research."

[8] Gerald Zaltman, "Marketing Inference in the Behavioral Sciences."

[9] Shelby Hunt, "The Morphology of Theory and the General Theory of Marketing," and Robert Bartels, "The General Theory of Marketing."

[10] Christian Pinson, Reinhard Angelmar, and Eduardo Roberto, "An Evaluation of the General Theory of Marketing."

[11] Zaltman, Angelmar, and Pinson, "Metatheory in Consumer Behavior Research."

[12] Engel, Kollat, and Blackwell, *Consumer Behavior*, Chapter 27.

[13] Robertson and Ward, "Consumer Behavior Research: Promise and Prospects."

logic of scientific research in marketing will be the next topic followed by a discussion of different types of research in marketing.

METATHEORY

Metatheory is the science of science or the investigation of investigation. Metatheory involves the careful appraisal of the methodology of science and the philosophical issues involved in the conduct of science. It is concerned with such topics as the operationalization of scientific concepts, the logic of testing theories, the use of theory, the nature of causality, and procedures for making predictions. Broadly defined, metatheory is *the investigation, analysis, and the description of (1) the technology of building theory, (2) the theory itself, and (3) the utilization of theory.* This definition holds over all sciences. Thus metatheory is not concerned with the context of scientific activity but rather with the conceptual procedures of science.

Although metatheory is still in its infancy, it is valuable in many ways.[14]

1. It helps correct and systematize existing philosophical outlooks.
2. It provides the scientist with greater conceptual clarity, helping him avoid such confusions as equating precedence with causality and helps weigh empirical evidence.
3. It helps sensitize the researcher to make specific his assumptions.
4. It minimizes dogmatism in scientific thinking.
5. It helps the scientist appreciate the limitation of his instruments.
6. It sharpens research strategy; that is, it sensitizes the scientist to methodological problems.
7. It keeps the scientist intellectually restless and dissatisfied.

In sum, metatheory "helps in raising fundamental scientific and philosophic questions, it helps in asking them in right ways, it discloses conceptual sickness and prescribes treatment for it, and it widens the horizon of research."[15]

MODELS, STEPS, AND CRITERIA OF SCIENTIFIC PROCESSES

Perhaps the first issue to be raised is what does a scientist do? The following answer is perhaps the most concise yet inclusive response to this question to be found in the literature. With regard to real world phenomena a scientist "endeavors to *describe*, to *order*, to *record* (measure) them, to *understand* and to *explain* them; in these activities he is motivated particularly by a desire to be able to *predict* new phenomena, so that their predictability shall enable him to *control* his sector by *influencing* the phenomena."[16] These processes

[14] Mario Bunge, *Metascientific Queries*, pp. 22–25.
[15] Bunge, *Metascientific Queries*, p. 26.
[16] Adriaan D. de Groot, *Methodology: Foundations of Inference and Research in the Behavioral Sciences*, pp. 18–19.

accurately describe the activities of marketers, although most marketers are typically engaged in only one or two of the processes. Furthermore, most marketers (practitioners at least) are interested in the processes of prediction and control. However, because accurate prediction and effective control depend heavily upon prior knowledge, other marketers engage in description, explanation, and so on, for the purpose of providing sound knowledge bases for action.

A scientific method is a set of prescribed procedures for establishing and connecting general laws about events and for predicting events yet unknown. Although numerable scientists have tried to make explicit such prescribed sets of procedures, it has proved difficult to model the scientific method.[17] It is not within the purpose of this chapter to discuss the many reasons that account for this. It must suffice to say simply that controversy exists about what constitutes the appropriate procedures of a scientific method. The position adopted here is essentially the one assumed by Kaplan.[18] This acknowledges that there are alternative ways of conveying meanings of scientific methodology. Moreover, as Feigl observes, the various models or approaches are "ideals to be approximated, but never fully attained."[19]

We shall look briefly at alternative models of scientific methodology and then present a set of procedures consistent with a definition of research that is particularly appropriate to marketing. The procedures and interpretations presented, however, incorporate the most important considerations offered by the various schools of thought on the scientific method even though we avoid espousing any one school of thought.

The "Baconian" Model

The classic image of how a scientist proceeds as visualized by Francis Bacon is presented in Figure 1.1.[20] This model is essentially of an inductive procedure. Initially, sensory data or sense perception data provide the lowest and often the initial level of information for purposes of developing scientific understanding. These data are placed into sentences or statements and assume the character of unordered facts. These unordered facts, through a process of definition, classification, and measurement, are organized into meaningful categories. Upon study of these categories it may be possible to develop, through induction, certain generalizations. Some generalizations may be sufficiently rigorous to warrant the status of an empirical law, although

[17] David Harvey, *Explanation in Geography*, p. 31.
[18] Abraham Kaplan, *The Conduct of Inquiry: Methodology for Behavioral Science*, pp. 27–31.
[19] Herbert Feigl, "The Scientific Outlook: Naturalism and Humanism," p. 11.
[20] See Harvey, *Explanation in Geography*, p. 33, and C. G. Hempel, *Philosophy of Natural Science*, pp. 11 ff.

Figure 1.1   The "Baconian" route to scientific explanation.

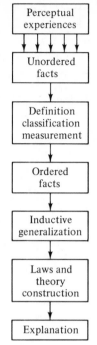

Source: David Harvey, *Explanation in Geography*, p. 34, © 1969 by Edward Arnold Ltd. Reprinted by permission of Edward Arnold Ltd.

there is controversy over the actual scientific validity of laws of this nature. Finally, the empirical laws may provide a basis for explaining phenomena.

The Harvey Model

The model presented by Harvey is shown in perhaps an oversimplified form in Figure 1.2. This model is more explicit in its recognition of the *a priori* nature of much of the knowledge present in science. We develop images of real-world structures based partly on perceptual experiences and related cognitive processes. These images are formally expressed as models representative of some theory or possibly some set of theories. Out of the model we derive hypotheses testable through appropriate experimental designs. Data are collected within the scope of the experimental design. Verification procedures are undertaken. If the outcome of the test is deemed successful, the original hypothesis may be accorded the higher "status" of a law and become a part of an existing theory, which is then used for explanation and other purposes.

It is important to take notice of a caveat: "We may view scientific knowledge as a kind of *controlled speculation*. The control really amounts to ensuring that statements are logically consistent and insisting that at least

Figure 1.2   An alternative route to scientific explanation.

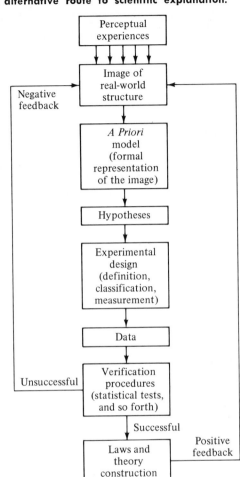

Source: David Harvey, *Explanation in Georgraphy*, p. 34 © 1960 by Edward Arnold Lt. Reprinted by permission of Edward Arnold Ltd.

some of the statements may be successfully related to sense-perception data."[21] In harmony with the notion of controlled speculation, Bunge cautions: ". . . it is best to keep in mind what is perhaps the sole golden rule of scientific work: *Audacity in conjecturing, cautiousness in testing.*"[22]

[21] Harvey, *Explanation in Geography*, p. 35. Italics added.
[22] Mario Bunge, *Scientific Research*, Vol. I, p. 12.

Bunge's formulation

Mario Bunge has suggested eight operations as being the main steps involved in the application of the scientific method. These are presented below:

1. Ask well-formulated and likely fruitful questions.
2. Devise hypotheses both grounded and testable to answer the questions.
3. State assumptions.
4. Derive logical consequences of the assumptions.
5. Design techniques to test the assumptions.
6. Test the techniques for relevance and reliability.
7. Execute the tests and interpret their results.
8. Evaluate the truth claims of the assumptions and the fidelity of the techniques.
9. Determine the domains in which the assumptions and the techniques hold, and state the new problems raised by the research.

These eight steps can be arranged schematically as shown in Figure 1.3.

Figure 1.3   A research cycle.

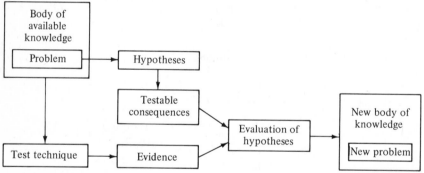

Source: Mario Bunge, *Scientific Research*, Vol. I, p. 9. Berlin: Springer-Verlag, 1967. Reprinted with permission of Springer-Verlag, New York.

Bunge also suggests a few rules to follow for the adequate execution of the research cycle shown in Figure 1.3.[23] Specifically, these are:

1. *"State your problem precisely and, in the beginning, specifically."* Ask not why consumers purchase luxury items but rather why some particular consumers purchase certain luxury items.
2. *"Try definite and somehow grounded conjectures rather than non-committal or wild hunches: risk hypothesizing definite relations among clear-*

[23] Bunge, p. 10.

cut variables. . . ." Do not be content with just the idea that frequency of exposure to advertising messages affects recall of their content, but hypothesize that this may only be true within a specified range of exposure and then only for particular consumer groups.

3. *"Subject your assumptions to tough tests rather than to soft ones."* The example above should not be tested by using simple advertising messages but by varying messages according to complexity.

4. *"Do not pronounce true a satisfactorily confirmed hypothesis: regard it as, at best, partially true."* Any finding concerning relationships among complexity of advertising messages, a given frequency, and particular consumer groups ought to be regarded as modifiable by subsequent investigation.

5. *"Ask why the answer should be as it is and not otherwise. . . ."* Ask what factors (for example, psychological mechanisms) account for the relationships observed among the variables mentioned above. Moreover, ask why the relevant mechanism and obtained relations should be operative and not others; that is, what conditions were conducive to our findings.

The Baconian model, it can be seen, is the position of the raw empiricist. The Harvey model introduces the concepts of an initial image of the real-world structure and the notion of experimental design. It also is more explicit than the Baconian and Bunge models in its treatment of positive and negative feedback. The model presented by Bunge emphasizes the notion of testable hypotheses somewhat more than the other models and stresses the importance of a scientific investigation being gauged by the changes it induces in our body of knowledge and the new problems it poses.

In the discussion to follow we note briefly phases in the empirical cycle of scientific inquiry that summarize some of the common features of the above three models. Criteria for scientists to have in mind when pursuing any model of scientific research are then presented.

De Groot's cycle of empirical scientific inquiry

The empirical cycle of scientific inquiry has approximately five phases. We shall comment briefly here upon these phases.[24]

Phase 1: Observation: "collection and grouping of empirical materials; (tentative) formation of hypotheses."

Phase 2: Induction: "formation of hypotheses."

Phase 3: Deduction: "derivation of specific consequences from the hypotheses, in the form of testable predictions."

[24] De Groot, *Methodology*, p. 28.

Phase 4:   Testing: "testing of the hypotheses against new empirical materials, by way of checking whether or not the predictions are fulfilled."

Phase 5:   Evaluation: evaluation "of the outcome of the testing procedure with respect to the hypotheses or theories stated, as well as with a view to subsequent, continued or related, investigations."

In subsequent parts of this volume we shall have occasion to examine in detail the meaning and procedures of such concepts as induction, deduction, and testing, among others. It is enough at this point to indicate simply that De Groot's five phases do correspond roughly to the different activities involved in empirical science.

Feigl's criterion for scientific activities

Feigl suggests several criteria or regulation ideals that characterize scientific inquiry in what he terms "factual" science—for example, physics.[25] It appears nevertheless (Feigl also acknowledges) that these criteria constitute good guidelines for scientific activities in the applied sciences (such as marketing).[26]

The first criterion is *objectivity*, sometimes technically referred to as *intersubjective testability*. Two elements are involved. One is the minimization of personal or cultural bias in the scientific activity. Note the use here of the term "minimization" in lieu of "elimination." No scientific activity at least in the social or behavioral sciences is ever value-free.[27] The researcher should try to minimize this by making explicit the types of biases he may be expressing or is assuming. He can only pursue objectivity and make known where, according to his own insight or introspection, he falls short.

The second element—namely, testability—imposes the requirement that scientific observations be amenable to empirical test.[28] Nagel is quite specific on this point: ". . . the quest for explanation in science . . . is a quest for explanatory hypotheses that are genuinely testable . . . the hypotheses sought must therefore be subject to the possibility of rejection, which will depend on the outcome of critical procedures, integral to the scientific quest, for determining what the actual facts are."[29] Intersubjective testability requires that the empirical test be capable of replication by other scientists.

A second criterion involves the distinction between opinion and well-

---

[25] Feigl, "The Scientific Outlook," p. 11.

[26] See Harvey, *Explanation in Geography*, p. 46.

[27] See, for example, Donald Warwick and Herbert Kelman, "Ethical Issues in Social Intervention," and Alan Guskin and Mark Chesler, "Partisan Diagnosis of Social Problems."

[28] Marx W. Wartofsky, *Conceptual Foundations of Scientific Thought.*

[29] Ernest Nagel, *The Structure of Science*, p. 12.

substantiated belief. This is the criterion of *reliability* or "sufficient degree of confirmation." The first criterion of testability is relatively easy to establish. The criterion of reliability, however, involves matters of degree. Where do we draw the line between well-substantiated knowledge and hunches? That is, when does a given proposition or a given theory move from "hunch" to "knowledge?"[30] Here the element of probability enters the picture and we ask ourselves how likely it is that a given test result would happen by chance. In this instance the scientist relies upon experimental and statistical tools. Nevertheless, the criterion of reliability is difficult to meet. Apart from establishing that a particular observation is not very likely to have occurred on a random basis, there is the more demanding question concerning the reliability of a particular explanation or interpretation. There will frequently be a competing explanation for the phenomenon observed that has not been ruled out by the particular test. This might be called the problem of *interpretative reliability:* The larger the number of plausible alternative interpretations, the lower the degree of reliability.

Definiteness and precision is a third criterion, which "requires that the concepts used in the formulation of scientific knowledge-claims be as definitely delimited as possible."[31] In other words, the theoretical nature of the units of theories, concepts, should be clearly spelled out and the most appropriate operational measure of that concept be obtained. Appropriate measures of a given theoretical concept may vary from context to context and the investigator must be wary of utilizing inappropriate operational measures, particularly when he is trying to draw inferences from one context to another, as is common in marketing. The topic area of concepts, including their precision, validity, and so forth, is elaborated upon in Chapter 2 and will not be dwelt upon any further here.

A fourth criterion suggested by Fiegl is *coherence or systematic structure.* Thus information gathered or knowledge acquired should not be found in random relationships. Instead, items of knowledge should be grouped together in some logical way. Thus, related concepts should be grouped to form hypotheses and related hypotheses grouped to form theories.[32] (This is discussed in Chapters 2, 3, and 4). The investigator should identify the body of knowledge he is drawing upon and to which he is attempting to contribute. His activities should be addressed to filling gaps in knowledge or in replicating previous work where that is desired. Preferably, too, he should attempt to dispel conflicts or shed light on conflicting viewpoints in his area of endeavor.[33]

---

[30] For an excellent discussion of the related measurement problems see Morris S. Cohen and Ernest Nagel, "Measurement."

[31] Feigl, "The Scientific Outlook," p. 12.

[32] Kaplan, *The Conduct of Inquiry*, pp. 27–31.

[33] Arthur L. Stinchcombe, *Constructing Social Theories.*

The pursuit of a unified system of explanation as a characteristic of science enables the researcher to confront inconsistencies and explore the causes and consequences of inconsistencies. In many instances, in contrast to common-sense approaches, inconsistencies stimulate investigation. Conflicting data or conflicting explanations spawn still further data-generating and explanatory activities. Common-sense approaches merely tolerate inconsistencies.

Finally, *comprehensiveness or scope of knowledge* is a desirable criterion. It is a goal of science, and ultimately an unachievable one in most instances, to develop statements or laws having wide applicability. The larger the number of different contexts a given theory or subtheory can encompass, the more powerful—that is, the more comprehensive—it is. This flows from the criterion of systematic coherence whereby unifying hypotheses link previously unconnected theories or subtheories. At the same time it is necessary to keep open the possibility of additions, alterations, and, importantly, deletions as new insights in the events or phenomena of concern are uncovered by the broadened scope of knowledge. Nagel has commented on this in his contrasting common sense with science: "The essential point to be observed is that, since common sense shows little interest in systematically explaining the facts it notes, the range of valid application of its beliefs . . . is not of serious concern.[34]

THE LOGIC OF SCIENTIFIC RESEARCH IN MARKETING

Here we shall examine a research process fundamental to marketing and other contexts. There is no basic difference between research methodology in marketing and research involved in other situations. The same metatheoretical considerations apply with more or less equal force in all areas of social research. Marketers, however, in their formal and informal ongoing education typically receive less exposure to philosophy-of-science types of issues. The purpose here of raising some of the basic processes of research one usually finds implicit and explicit in the philosophy-of-science literature is to sensitize the reader to—and thus make him more aware of—certain steps involved in conducting research in marketing. The value of such a sensitization is that it leaves behind it a more rigorous thinking methodology. This in turn produces more rigorous research.

Scientific research defined

Scientific research may be defined as *the effort to assess existing relevant knowledge and to extend it to concepts and testing integrated hypotheses through the acquisition and analysis of meaningful data, and the critical evaluation of the original concepts and premises.* A representation of this process is presented in Figure 1.4. First we shall elaborate somewhat upon the

---

[34] Nagel, *The Structure of Science*, p. 6.

process represented in the paradigm and then address the question of whether or not the term "research" can acceptably be applied to activities concerned with only one of the components in this figure.

Figure 1.4   A paradigm of research processes.

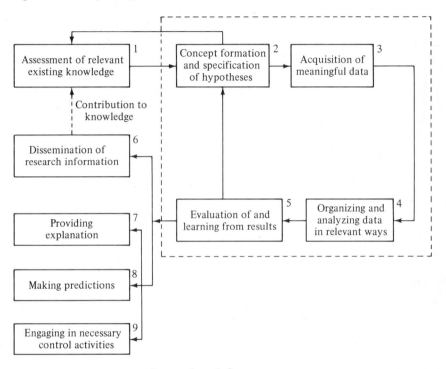

Assessment of existing relevant knowledge

The first step or stage is to review existing information pertaining to the problem at hand, assuming that the important task of defining the problem has been performed. Although it is neither necessary nor mandatory in research to assess existing information, it is highly desirable since it facilitates the formation of concepts and hypotheses and the development of research designs. Furthermore, it helps avoid needless replication of research. Assessing existing relevant knowledge is essential to meeting Feigl's fourth criterion of coherence or systematic structure.

Concept formation and specification of hypotheses

Concept formation is achieved by grouping material observed intuitively and by assessing existing data, and, through a process of induction, formulating (1) the basic concepts to be used in the research, (2) the propositions relating concepts, and (3) the relations among propositions. As in the other stages, the quality of activities are of great importance. The way in which concepts are defined theoretically and operationally and the way propositions are stated have great bearing on the ability to confirm or refute the theory or subtheory one is working with. This has bearing on the criteria of intersubjective testability, comprehensiveness, and precision. Chapters 3 and 4 discuss this subject.

It is important here to distinguish two important reasoning methods: induction and deduction. The deductive method involves a set of initial conditions, a set of laws, and the inevitable conclusion that when these particular sets of premises or conditions—assumed to be true—are present with the specified law(s) then a particular event must necessarily occur; the event is a logical certainty. Inductive inferences imply no such certainty; rather, they involve probability statements. "Induction is the process by which the scientist forms a theory to explain the observed facts."[35] Thus it is possible to draw false conclusions from correct premises. For this reason inductive logic has been criticized by many philosophers at least to the point of excluding it from any distinct association with scientific methodology.[36] Some, such as Braithwaite, defend the use of the inductive method because "it yields hypotheses from which testable consequences can be deduced which are found to be true."[37] Thus induction plays an important role in the discovery of theories.[38] Induction may be viewed as the initial part of the scientific research process and deduction the final part; they are not mutually exclusive forms of reasoning.[39]

The acquisition of meaningful data

Meaningful data are derived from specific *tests* of *deductively* derived hypotheses. Through a process of logical deduction from theory, one or more hypotheses are derived and tested empirically. Again we see the importance of intersubjective testability as the criterion of definiteness and precision. The research design employed should permit falsification of the hypotheses. The data should be collected in such a way as to constitute an empirical test that clearly allows for the possibility of the hypothesis being shown false and not simply unsupported. Ideally, too, and this is a subject of controversy,[40] the test should be so designed that if the hypothesis is supported, alternative competing theories are at the same time and by the same data

---

[35] John G. Kemeny, *A Philosopher Looks at Science*, p. 93.
[36] Karl R. Popper, *Conjectures and Refutations: The Growth of Scientific Knowledge*.
[37] R. B. Braithwaite, *Scientific Explanation*, p. 264.
[38] John R. Platt, "Strong Inference."
[39] For an important discussion related to this point see Hempel, *Philosophy of Natural Science*, pp. 10–18.
[40] Stinchcombe, *Constructing Social Theories*.

demonstrated to be false. This relates to interpretative reliability. Of course, data should also be meaningful in the conventional sense of being relevant to the problem at hand and interpretable. This is the requirement of explanatory relevance: that "the account of some phenomenon provided by an explanation would constitute good grounds for expecting that the phenomenon would appear under the specific circumstances."[41] The importance of carefully designed and tested research instrument, though not elaborated here, cannot be understated.

Organizing and analyzing data in relevant ways

The organization process involves the theory of measurement. In an operational sense it consists of the selection and application of appropriate statistical techniques.[42] Measurement of basic concepts as manifest in their real-world existence are undertaken at this stage. Preferably, analytical techniques relevant to causal analysis would be employed and causal imageries used.[43] Causal imageries are conceptualizations of cause and effect among two or more variables.

Evaluation

Ultimately the application of technical tools in tests of deductively derived hypotheses is for the purpose of assessing some theory or hypothesis and asserting empirical generalizations. Two types of outcomes are frequently expected or desired. One outcome of the evaluation process satisfies a control function (see Chapter 8). "Control is the systematic manipulation of some element related to or contained within a system so as to effect a change in one or more elements in that system."[44] Marketers are concerned with manipulating their own activities to be in accord with essentially unalterable customer system states or, where possible, to intervene and alter psychosocial customer states. Thus evaluation provides a basis for intervention. A second outcome is the contribution of new material for concept formation and hypothesis specification by the same or other researchers.

A usual consequence of any research effort is the dissemination of the results of the evaluation process. In addition, particularly in marketing, specific actions are often undertaken on the basis of the final evaluations.

---

[41] Zaltman, Angelmar, and Pinson, "Metatheory in Consumer Behavior Research." See also Hempel, *Philosophy of Natural Science*, p. 48.

[42] For two good treatments of multivariate statistics see Jagdish Sheth, "The Multivariate Revolution in Marketing Research," and Thomas C. Kinnear and James R. Taylor, "Multivariate Methods in Marketing Research: A Further Attempt at Classification."

[43] For a good source book on the measurement aspect of causal analysis see Hubert M. Blalock, Jr., *Causal Models in the Social Sciences.*

[44] Zaltman, Angelmar, and Pinson, "Metatheory in Consumer Behavior Research," p. 485.

Although both the dissemination and action activities are important, they are not of central concern now and will not be discussed here. The action activity, however, is the major subject of Chapter 8.

TYPES OF RESEARCH IN MARKETING

Obviously, a considerable volume of research in, and outside of, marketing does not encompass the entire process shown in Figure 1.4. There appear to be five basic types of investigation relevant to marketing, each of which is implicit or explicit in Figure 1.4.[45] The basic types of investigation are discussed briefly below.

Resource reviews

Investigations of resources, represented by box 1 in Figure 1.4, involve the analysis and codification of existing information to be found in the written literature and the minds of resource persons. The usual product of such investigations in marketing are review articles and case studies. The contribution to knowledge made by review articles is partly one of information dissemination and partly one of formulating new concepts and explanations. Literature reviews are also of value to the extent that they highlight areas of neglect, although this is not a direct contribution to knowledge.

Hypothesis testing

"Characteristically, a single or few related hypotheses, as a rule theoretically derived, are tested against empirical data. . . . *in general*, an invaluable advantage of antecedent formation of (falsifiable) hypotheses, and hence of hypothesis-testing investigations, is that the investigator compels himself to be explicit and objective, to avoid contaminations, and to take a risk."[46] Hypothesis testing is a commonly found research activity in marketing. Most hypotheses in marketing appear to be middle-range in nature; that is, they apply to a limited set of phenomena found in relatively narrowly defined circumstances. This appears to be a very fruitful level of analysis in marketing. A simple example of a widely tested middle-range hypothesis is: Consumer innovators are more cosmopolite than noninnovators.

Instrumental investigations

Here concern is with data-gathering instruments, such as questionnaires, psychological tests, statistical techniques, and the like. Efforts are made to validate the instrument for the purpose of minimizing the so-called operational research epistemic gap.[47] This gap refers to the lack of correspondence

[45] See De Groot, *Methodology*.
[46] De Groot, pp. 302–303.
[47] Zaltman, "Marketing Inference in the Behavioral Sciences."

or isomorphism between a theoretical concept and its operationalization. The intent is to achieve a high degree of isomorphism between the data generated and the theoretical concepts involved in the research. Instrumental investigations, though crucial to the advancement of knowledge, play an indirect role by enabling the researcher to gather more exact data in the process of concept formation and hypothesis testing. The better the instruments, the more confidence one can place in the final conclusions drawn about hypotheses. Also, the analytical techniques employed influence the amount of opportunity allowed for gaining insights into the data collected. The better the research instruments and techniques, the greater the likelihood of generating explanations not specifically conceived prior to the investigation.

Descriptive investigation

Descriptive investigations attempt to provide profiles for a population or subgroup with respect to preselected criteria. Information is not dynamic but, rather, static. Explanations for relationships among variables—if relations are in fact posited—are not provided. This type of study is desirable chiefly "whenever, in preparation for explicit theory or hypothesis formation or in preparation for the instrumental realization of constructs, a survey is needed of what objects and events are on hand or are relevant . . . in a given area of the phenomenal world."[48] Descriptive investigations are also useful for developing ideal-type constructs. For example, the development of adopter categories in diffusion research was the product of largely descriptive studies.

Exploratory research

Located between hypothesis testing and descriptive analysis is exploratory research,[49] which is essentially concerned with the selection and clarification of hypotheses. The researcher typically has in mind a theory or set of hypotheses and thus certain expectations about what might be found. Even so, the nature of the exploratory mission is to clarify existing ideas about relations among concepts and perhaps discover new hypotheses. This is useful when the state of available evidence is internally contradictory or insufficient to permit the statement of formal hypotheses or the detection of new concepts. Exploratory research ranges from pilot studies to laboratory experiments to statistical reanalysis (for example, factor analysis and automatic interaction detection) of existing data.

Hypothesis testing—involving as it does concept formation, the specification of hypotheses, and the acquisition of meaningful data—is what is often termed pure research or "real" research by philosophers of science. In reality, all the investigations discussed above have some direct or indirect special

[48] De Groot, *Methodology*, p. 305.
[49] De Groot, p. 306.

contribution to make to the development of knowledge. The major issue seems to be not which is best but rather which is most useful, given the state of the art in a problem area at a given moment in time. Different problem areas will have different optimal combinations of resource allocations among the different types of investigations.

RESEARCH ACTIVITIES RECONSTRUCTED

The four research activities bracketed by dashed lines in Figure 1.4 are the necessary or the most basic in scientific research. Again, these need not all be performed by all investigators in each of their studies; but for progress to be made in a field of inquiry or for a given problem area these activities must be performed, albeit by different researchers communicating the results of their efforts to each other. These four basic activities can be arranged as shown in Figure 1.5.

Figure 1.5   Basic research activities.

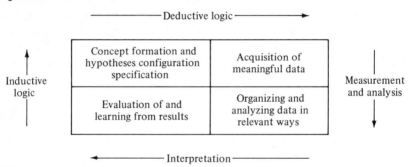

Figure 1.5 is a fuller representation of the process of scientific research. The process of theorizing involves both the construction of theories through concept development and hypothesis specification and, through a process of deduction, the application of theories in such a way that meaningful data (as previously defined) can be acquired. Theory application also involves careful measurement—both in the sense of experimental design and choice of quantitative tools. This is expressed in the lower-right-hand cell of Figure 1.5. Given proper measurement in the test of a theory or some component thereof, one then interprets the data collected. This involves the evaluation and learning from the results of the test. Notice that these are empirical research activities. The research process then proceeds through inductive logic from the empirical plane to the theoretical plane. The inductive logic process involves the integration of the final evaluations of the test into the existing theoretical state, making such changes in the existing concepts and theories as seem warranted by the data.

PLAN OF THE BOOK

The concern of this book is not limited to theory simply as a goal to be achieved but also as a means to different but related ends. These ends are explanation, prediction, and control. Thus the plan of the book can be shown schematically as in Fig. 1.6.

Figure 1.6   Overall plan of this book.

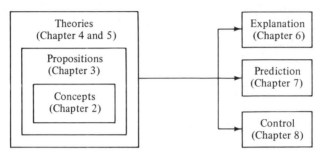

Part II of this book starts with Chapter 2, which focuses on concepts, the building blocks of theories. Concepts are characteristics that can be grouped together; they are the subject matter of science. Chapter 2 considers the relationship between concepts, terms, and objects and discusses the different types of concepts.

Chapter 3 concerns propositions, which are sequences of concepts having stated relationships between them. The notion of sentences, propositions, hypotheses, and laws are treated along with the dual criteria of confirmability and refutability. The chapter concludes with a discussion of the various forms that relationships between concepts can assume. The subject matter of Chapter 4 is theory. Several alternative definitions of theory are presented. Most simply, a theory is a set of interrelated hypotheses or propositions. Various technical aspects of theories are discussed. Chapter 5 is concerned with criteria for evaluating theories. A major section of the chapter applies many of these criteria to three well-known theories of consumer and buyer behavior.

In Part III attention focuses upon the three uses of information. The first of these is explanation, which is the ascription of causes to an event. Thus Chapter 6 discusses various types of scientific explanations, the levels of understanding in explanation, and the evaluation of explanation. Also treated is the role of explanation in developing marketing strategy. The nature of prediction is the subject matter of Chapter 7. Prediction refers to a stated expectation about a particular aspect of behavior or some particular set of circumstances that may be verified by subsequent observation. This chapter compares scientific and nonscientific prediction and the structure of the former. Levels of understanding in prediction and prediction techniques are also treated. Chapter 7 concludes with several criteria for evaluating predictions.

Chapter 8 is concerned with the nature of control—that is, the systematic manipulation of some element related to or contained within a system so as to effect a change in one or more elements in that system. The chapter discusses the interventionist, theory implementation criteria, types of strategies, and levels of understanding in control. It concludes with a discussion of the task of translating practical problems into theoretical issues and the evaluation of control efforts.

Thus one develops concepts, propositions, and theories for the purpose of being able to explain, predict, and control events.

CHAPTER 2

THE NATURE OF
CONCEPTS

INTRODUCTION

The subject matter of this chapter concerns concepts. Concepts are the fundamental units that marketers employ in their thinking about marketing problems and in their approaches to solving those problems. Examples of frequently used concepts in marketing include product positioning, market segmentation, brand loyalty, innovation, retailing, and loss leaders. It is appropriate, then, to choose the subject of concepts as the starting point in our exploration of metatheory. The discussion will focus first on the distinction between concepts, terms, and objects. Following this is a treatment of formal and nonformal concepts. The chapter concludes with a treatment of observational and theoretical concepts. Although concept formation is an important topic, it cannot be treated here. However, the reader is encouraged to consult some of the interesting literature available on this subject.[1]

A concept refers to certain characteristics or phenomena that can be grouped together. Alternatively, a concept represents similarities in otherwise diverse phenomena. For example, the concept "consumer" as it is used in most marketing contexts identifies and groups together at least three characteristics, namely the (1) consumption of (2) nonindustrial (3) ideas, goods, and services. Some authors add a fourth phenomenon, purchasing, to their treatment of the concept consumer. Other frequently used marketing related concepts include brand loyalty, personality, habit, convenience goods, product life cycle, and channel.

Concepts are of fundamental importance in science. "Scientific knowledge is entirely *conceptual*: it consists of systems of concepts interrelated in different ways."[2] Thus concepts are those items which refer to the subject matter of science: "In normal scientific discourse we use phrases like_____is the antecedent of_____, or if_____then_____with a probability of X."[3] The terms that would go in the blanks are examples of concepts or units of a theory.

Whereas concept formation is basic to theory formation, good theory is also necessary for good concept formation. Kaplan refers to this as the *paradox of conceptualization*[4]: "The proper concepts are needed to formulate a good theory, but we need a good theory to arrive at proper concepts." The paradox is resolved somewhat by approximation: "The better our concepts, the better the theory we can formulate with them, and in turn, the better the concepts available for the next, improved theory."

CONCEPTS, TERMS, AND OBJECTS

Concepts have to be distinguished from both objects and terms. Concepts are located in the world of thought rather than in the world of actual things

---

[1] J. S. Bruner, J. J. Goodnow, and G. A. Austin, *A Study of Thinking*; L. E. Bourne and F. Restle, "Mathematical Theory of Concept Identification;" E. B. Hunt, *Concept Learning: An Information-Processing Problem*; H. S. Kendler, "Concept Formation;" C. E. Osgood, G. J. Suci, and P. H. Tannenbaum, *The Measurement of Meaning*; and W. E. Vinacke, *Psychology of Thinking*.

[2] Mario Bunge, *Scientific Research*, Vol. I, p. 46.

[3] Robert Dubin, *Theory Building*, p. 29.

[4] Abraham Kaplan, *The Conduct of Inquiry: Methodology for Behavioral Science*, pp. 53–54.

referred to here as objects, including linguistic objects commonly referred to as terms. They are abstracted forms and do not reflect objects in their entirety but comprehend only a few aspects of objects. Those aspects of the objects that are comprehended in concepts are called their *intension*. To illustrate the distinction between concepts, terms, and objects, consider the case of "attitude." First of all, we may think of the concept of attitude. This is likely to elicit a number of aspects, properties, or attributes such as (1) a mental and neural state (both affective and cognitive) (2) of a readiness to respond (3) in organized ways, and so forth.[5] Next, there is the *term* attitude, which was responsible for eliciting our mental response in the first place. Finally, we can think of people who behave in a consistent way toward social objects or who fill out questionnaires concerning these objects, and this may constitute the "real" attitude, the *object* whose properties are reflected in our concept of attitude.[6]

Concepts, objects and terms are related as shown in Figures 2.1a and 2.1b. Figure 2.1b is taken from Harvey, who substitutes percept for object: "We may therefore think of a set of connections running from sense perceptions (*percepts*), through mental constructs and images (*concepts*) to linguistic representation (*terms*). 'Percepts,' 'concepts,' and 'terms,' cannot be regarded as truly isomorphic. They possess, in some degree, an independent existence."[7] The *s* in Figure 2.1b represents a perspective from which perception, thought, and language can be viewed. It is important to note Harvey's observation that the relations among percepts or objects and concepts and terms are never truly isomorphic and that concepts are expressions of organized percepts and are in turn expressed by terms. In the discussion to follow we shall examine these relationships.

CONCEPTS AND TERMS

The relationship between terms and concepts is called *designation*; a concept is designated by a word or group of words. It may be useful to think of this relationship in terms of mapping: On one hand there is a set of concepts, and on the other hand a set of terms, with the designation relationship establishing the connection between the two sets.

As just noted there is not a one-to-one correspondence between concepts and terms: for example, the term "balance" corresponds to one concept in ordinary language and to another concept in the psychological literature. Another example is provided by the term "market." In some instances market refers to a set of potential customers, whereas in another instance it may refer to a place where vendors congregate. For example:

5 William J. McGuire, "The Nature of Attitudes and Attitude Change," p. 142.
6 Lewis W. Brandt and Wolfgang Metzger, "Reality: What Does It Mean?"
7 David Harvey, *Explanation in Geography*, p. 19.

Figure 2.1a   Objects, concepts, and terms.

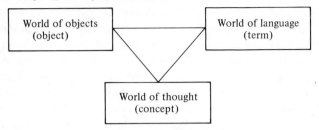

Source: Adapted from *The Philosophy of Science* by Peter Caws, © 1965 by Litton Educational Publishing, Inc. Reprinted by permission of Van Nostrand Reinhold Company.

Figure 2.1b   Percepts, concepts, and terms.

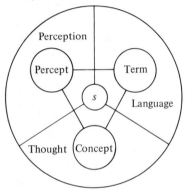

Source: David Harvey, *Explanation in Geography.*

To a stock broker, the market is the place where stocks are traded. To a produce merchant, the market is a location in the city where produce is received, sorted, and sold. To a sales manager, the market is a geographical unit, such as a city or region, for which decisions are made with respect to distributors, advertising effort, salesmen, and possibly prices. To an economist, the market is all the buyers and sellers interested or potentially interested in a product group. Finally, to a marketer, the market is *all individuals and organizations who are actual or potential customers for a product or service.*[8]

The frequently used concept of a reference group as employed in the consumer behavior literature also has a multiplicity of meanings.[9] It may or may not involve a group in which the consumer is a member, can ever be a member, or ever wants to be a member. Moreover, the reference of whatever standing may perform different functions—for example, provide measures for self-assessment or standards or codes of conduct.

[8] Philip Kotler, *Marketing Management*, p. 89.
[9] Lyman Ostland, "Role Theory and Group Dynamics."

Second, it is important to keep in mind that "rules of designation introduce symbols by convention."[10] Rules of designation stipulate names in a very arbitrary way and definitely do not constitute analyses of the properties of the concepts. An example of rules of designation: Let P $[A(t)]$ represent the choice probability of product A in time t,[11] or let A stand for new products. The statement or designation that A represents new products is not a proposition and cannot be tested for truth. It is simply a "ground rule," established for convenience. In some few cases it may happen that a rule of designation may be missing. This means that either there is no term corresponding to a given concept or that there is no concept corresponding to a given term.

The first situation may be exemplified by the lack of French and Spanish terms corresponding to the concepts of "marketing" and "merchandising." One could think of three remedies to that situation: (1) the "importation" of the English terms; (2) the use of existing terms, which badly designate the defined concepts, such as "commercialisation" and "mercadotecnia," which are in fact the solution adopted by some French and Spanish purists (the term marketing was banned from the "Academie Française" dictionary); or (3) the creation of a new term, which is the usual procedure taken in any language when new objects or percepts and their corresponding concepts are born. An example of an instance where a concept does not exist for a given term is provided by the many types of snow for which Eskimos have individual names or terms. However, for many individuals in more temperate (but snowy) climates whose activities are less dominated by snow, the individual terms the Eskimos have for snow are not differentiable into separate concepts.

Barring those rather exceptional instances, the search for rules of designation is a problem frequently encountered during the process of growth in a science. Suppose, for example, that one wants to characterize antecedents of consumer behavior by adapting Ackoff's distinction between necessary and sufficient conditions of an event. Four possibilities exist in this regard (see Figure 2.2): The antecedent conditions may be necessary but not sufficient; sufficient but not necessary; neither sufficient nor necessary; or sufficient and necessary for the event to occur. Ackoff calls the first three possibilities response, reaction, and act.[12] He does not designate a term for the fourth concept, for the necessary and sufficient conditions. As an exercise the reader is invited to develop a term for the underlying concept of his percept of the upper-left cell in Figure 2.2.

---

[10] Bunge, *Scientific Research*, Vol. I, p. 151. Italics added.
[11] David B. Montgomery and Adrian B. Ryans, "Stochastic Models of Consumer Choice Behavior."
[12] R. L. Ackoff, "Toward a System of Systems Concepts," p. 664.

Figure 2.2   Example of a lack of designation.

Necessity

		Yes	No
Sufficiency	Yes	?	Reaction
	No	Response	Act

DEFINITION

A brief discourse on definition will be useful before proceeding further. At the linguistic level, definition is an operation that introduces a new term on the basis of already existing terms. Definitions establish an equivalence relation between the term to be introduced, the *definiendum*, and the expression used to define it, the *definiens*. There are two types of such definitions, namely explicit and contextual definitions.

Explicit definitions are stipulations to the effect that a specified expression, the definiendum, is to be synonymous with a certain other expression, the definiens. An explicit definition may therefore be put into the form: "Let the expression E_2 be synonymous with the expression E_1."[13] For example, let E_2 stand for "brand loyalty" and E_1 for "proportion of a household's purchases of a product class devoted to the most frequently purchased brand."[14] If we now stipulate "Let E_2 be synonymous with E_1," we can use the short expression E_2 rather than the long expression E_1.

Contextual definitions introduce a term s by providing synonyms for certain expressions containing s but not for s itself.[15] An example of this kind of definition in marketing is: "Consumer A has a preference for brand Y = consumer A chooses brand Y when offered brands Y, X."

It should be noted that the type of definition covered by explicit and contextual definitions is referred to as a *nominal* definition.

Often psychological concepts are both nominally and operationally defined . . . The operational definition leaves out the subtle psychological forms (of the concept) that are implied in the nominal definition. Although there are serious problems in obtaining meaningful operational definitions that adequately

---

[13] Carl G. Hempel, *Fundamentals of Concept Formation in Empirical Science*, pp. 3 ff.
[14] For the definition of brand loyalty see David B. Montgomery "Consumer Characteristics Associated with Dealing: An Empirical Example."
[15] Hempel, *Fundamentals of Concept Formation in Empirical Science*, p. 4.

reflect (are isomorphic with) the nominal definitions, linking a concept to the empirical world is crucial to the development of science.[16]

The notion of nominal definitions can be used to develop two logical types of terms, namely *primitive* and *derived* (or defined) terms. We have assumed that the definiens in nominal definitions contains only terms that have been defined previously in the same way. Now we must acknowledge that this is not the case. To avoid the pain of infinite regress we must decide upon certain primitive terms that then can be used to define the derived terms, but that themselves remain undefined in the system under analysis.[17] (They may be defined in another system.) For example, if we define homophilly in an interpersonal selling situation as the degree to which salesmen and prospective clients show common traits and perceive themselves to be similar, we rely on the undefined or primitive terms contained in the definiens such as "traits" and "perceive." Similarly, if we define empathy in a mass media advertising situation as the degree to which the audience identifies with the source of the message, we use the term "identifies" as a primitive term. In Kotler's definition of the marketing concept as "a consumer orientation backed by integrated marketing aimed at generating customer satisfaction as the key to satisfying organizational goals," the terms customer orientation, integrated marketing, and customer satisfaction are primitive terms.[18]

Because of the theoretical isomorphism between terms and concepts, definitions, in addition to establishing equivalence of use among terms, are also said to establish equivalence of meaning among concepts. Analogously to the logical types of terms, one can also speak about derived and primitive concepts.

CONCEPTS AND TERMS RELATED TO OBJECTS

Now having discussed the relationship between terms and concepts we are still left with two more links, namely between terms and objects, and between concepts and objects. We shall deal with the two at the same time and label the relationship as "reference." (We say "a term" (concept) *refers* to an object.) The reference relationship can be thought of as composed of two arrows pointing in opposite directions (Fig. 2.3). One arrow originates with the objects and points to the terms and concepts; the other arrow leads from terms and concepts to objects. The latter arrow can be said to represent the process of interpretation, whereas the former represents the process of abstraction.

[16] Sanford Labovitz and Robert Hagedorn, *Introduction to Social Research*, p. 22.
[17] Carl G. Hempel, *Aspects of Scientific Explanation*.
[18] Kotler, *Marketing Management: Analysis, Planning and Control*, p. 17.

Figure 2.3   The processes of abstraction and interpretation.

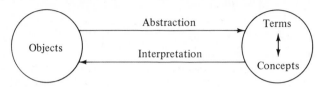

The process of *abstraction* can be described in the following way:

> When we consider the common form of various things, or various events, and call it by a name that does not suggest any particular thing or event, or commit us to any mental picture . . . we are consciously, deliberately abstracting the form from all things which have it.[19]

The common form of things are those properties that constitute the *intension* of concepts. As an example of the process of abstraction, consider the concept of attitude. The term "attitude" abstracts at least three basic orientations toward objects: affect, cognition, and predisposition to act. Consequently, particular attitudes toward soap, cars, freedom, and pollution all involve the same orientations of the basic concept of attitude.

Phillips has suggested a ladder of abstraction for concepts for viewing the range of concepts from observation to theory.[20] This ladder, presented in Figure 2.4, involves the concept of choice behavior. As one moves up the ladder the basic concept becomes more abstract, wider in scope, and less amenable to measurement although some form of measurement is still possible even at the highest level of abstraction. The ladder approach is useful, for it is important to define clearly what level of abstraction is involved in the formulation of a given concept. This is necessary for it helps determine measurement procedures and sensitizes the researcher to problems involved in relating different concepts that are at different levels of abstraction.

Table 2.1 is another form of illustration showing the range from general to specific psychographic concepts involving opinion leadership.[21] Note that there are different alternative statements operationalizing the constructs at each of the three levels. There is a basic issue as to whether or not two different operationalizations can represent a single object or the exact same attributes of a given object. For example, Tucker and Painter[22] and Boone[23] studied the personality trait of sociability as it relates to consumer behavior.

[19] Susanne K. Langer, *An Introduction to Symbolic Logic*, 3d rev. ed., p. 36.
[20] B. S. Phillips, *Social Research: Strategy and Tactics*, p. 28. Phillips patterned this approach using S. I. Hayakawa, *Language in Thought and Action*, p. 169.
[21] Fred D. Reynolds and William Darden, "Construing Life Style and Psychographics."
[22] W. T. Tucker and J. J. Painter, "Personality and Product Use."
[23] L. E. Boone, "The Search for the Consumer Innovator."

Figure 2.4   A ladder of abstraction for concepts.

The choice behavior of human beings
The choice behavior of living human beings
The choice behavior of living Americans
The choice behavior of John Smith
The choices John Smith makes during a series of interviews, as well as under periodic observations, over a period of one year
John Smith's answer to a question about his preferences among product brands
REALITY

Source: Adapted from Bernard S. Phillips, *Social Research: Strategy and Tactics*, p. 28. New York: The Macmillan Company, 1966. © Copyright Bernard S. Phillips, 1966. Reprinted with permission of the Macmillan Company.

However, Tucker and Painter studied the concept by using the Gordon Personal Profile test and linked the test findings with the use of vitamins and acceptance of new fashions. Boone, on the other hand, used the California Psychological Inventory as his measure of sociability and linked this with the adoption of CATV. The question raised is whether Tucker and Painter and Boone actually studied the same concept? Are the concepts of sociability as measured by the GPP the same as that measured by the CPI?

Let us consider now the process of *interpretation*. Given that we have constituted a concept (attitude) and a corresponding term (the word "attitude"), we go back to the world of objects and events, examining each one in order to ascertain whether they embody the properties listed in the intension of the concept. If an object does possess these properties we say that it is an instance, or an interpretation of the concept. Thus if a product is one purchased frequently by its consumers with a minimum of effort in comparison and buying, we say it is an instance or example of the concept of a convenience good. Equivalently, we can say that the object is a member (element) of the class (set) X, where X designates the concept.[24]

There are various kinds of interpretation procedures; the three most important will be discussed here. *Ostensive* interpretation of a concept is done by pointing out something to which it applies. It usually takes the form of an utterance such as "this is a so and so" accompanied by some gesture with "so and so" indicating the name of the object.[25] As an example, one can

[24] Langer, *An Introduction to Symbolic Logic.*
[25] See Bunge, *Scientific Research*, Vol. I, pp. 146 ff and Peter Caws, *The Philosophy of Science*, p. 43.

Table 2.1   Example Measures Illustrating the General-Specific Continuum of Psychographic Constructs

General		Specific
Self-Designated Opinion Leader	Self-Designated Fashion Opinion Leader	Self-Designated Midi Opinion Leader
1. My friends or neighbors often come to me for advice.	1. My friends and neighbors often ask my advice about clothing fashions.	1. Several of my friends asked my advice about whether the midi would become a fashion or not.
2. I sometimes influence what my friends buy.	2. I sometimes influence the types of clothes my friends buy.	2. I told my friends that the midi was a recurrent style from yesteryear and that it would be unflattering and make most women look older.
3. People come to me more often than I go to them for information about brands.	3. My friends come to me more often than I go to them for information about clothes.	3. At coffee breaks my friends tended to ask my opinion of the midi more often than I initiated the conversation about it.
	4. I feel that I am generally regarded by my friends and neighbors as a good source of advice about clothing fashions.	
	5. I can think of at least two people whom I have told about some clothing fashion in the past six months.	

Source: Reynolds and Darden, "Construing Life Style and Psychographics."

think of pointing to a waterbed and uttering: "This is an innovation." This statement, however, leaves considerable room for misunderstanding. One might be led to believe that "innovation" refers to a particular shape of the waterbed, or to its bedlike character, or any number of things. Accordingly, only after a certain number of examples of the application of the term "innovation" to various objects would it become clear to any degree what particular combination of properties was meant. A variation of this type of interpretation is called *quasi-ostensive* interpretation. It consists of enumerating objects that are proper interpretations of the concept. For example, consider the following interpretation of the concept of innovation:

> Examples of innovations . . . would be electric typewriters, language laboratories, a new brand of soap, smoking pipes for women, charge accounts, stainless steel razor blades, sauna baths, and Cinerama.[26]

Another example is the following:

> (demographic characteristics) . . . include the kinds of things one learns about people from published statistical sources such as the census. Among the most important of these are age, national origin, location, size of family, family status and religion.[27]

Still another type of interpretation procedure is *operational* interpretation. It establishes correspondences between concepts (terms) and controlled operations or their results. Operational interpretations not only ascertain the possession of properties by objects but also measure the degree to which they possess them. Particular operations of measurement produce ordered pairs, each having as one element a member of a class of physical properties and as the other a member of a class of mathematical entities, usually a number. Thus, we can distinguish two component parts of operational interpretation. The first one can be called *observation* (identifies the property to be measured) and the second consists of *operations*, which generate the values of this property.[28] Consider as an example of an operational interpretation the following interpretation of the concept of attitude: "Attitude is . . . measured (either verbal or self-administered) on a set of bipolar scales reflecting salient purchase criteria. . . ."[29] Different operational interpretations of attitude may be given, such as the type and intensity of pupillary response upon presentation of the social object,[30] and the direction and amount of bias on an information test.[31] It might be noted here that it is important not to confuse the operational definition of a concept with a dependent variable to be

[26] Kotler, *Marketing Management*, p. 506.
[27] Alfred R. Oxenfeldt, *Executive Action in Marketing*, p. 102.
[28] See Bunge, *Scientific Research*, Vol. I, p. 148, and Caws, *The Philosophy of Science*, p. 47.
[29] John Howard and Jagdish Sheth, *The Theory of Buyer Behavior*, p. 193.
[30] John J. Woodman, "The Pupil Response as a Measure of Social Attitudes."
[31] Louise H. Kidder and Donald T. Campbell, "The Indirect Testing of Social Attitudes."

explained by that concept. Cronkhite raises an interesting example of such confusion.

> To ask whether "attitudes" predict "overt behavior" is to ask a rather strange question, because we have no measure of "attitudes" except "overt behavior." An attitude test response is certainly behavior, and is certainly overt as well, although it may not require quite as much energy as a lynching. On the other hand, to participate in a lynching can certainly be interpreted as a response to an attitude test, in that an observer is certainly likely to infer that the participants hold certain attitudes toward their victims and toward law enforcement. That is, "overt behavior" may be viewed as an attitude test response.[32]

INTENSION, DENOTATION, CONNOTATION, EXTENSION

To conclude our discussion of the reference relationship let us introduce a few notions that may prove useful. First is the already mentioned *intension* of a concept. The intension of a concept is the list of all the properties it possesses, such as reversibility, demonstrability, complexity, and so forth.[33] The *denotation* of a concept is the class of objects and events embodying the properties of a concept. Given the denotation, we may be interested in finding out all the properties that are common to the elements of the denotation. These properties, including those comprised by the concept's intension, constitute the *connotation* of the concept. Finally, we can extend the notion of denotation to all possible objects, past or future, known or unknown, that if they existed would belong to the concept's denotation. We shall call this set the *extension* of a concept.

TYPES OF CONCEPTS

FORMAL AND NONFORMAL CONCEPTS

Given the nature of concepts, what are the various types of concepts? The first distinction required is between *formal* and *nonformal* concepts. The basis of this distinction is the reference of these concepts. Formal concepts are defined within formal systems that are not intended to refer to any objects of the real world. Nonformal concepts, in contrast, always refer to some aspect of the real world.[34] Formal and nonformal concepts, however, are intertwined in the study of real systems. In such contexts, formal concepts most often are related to the scientist's methodology and, in particular, to the treatment of data. As an example, consider again the concept of brand loyalty as defined by the *proportion of a household's purchases of a product class devoted to the most frequently purchased brand*. The nonformal con-

---

[32] Gary Cronkhite, *Persuasion: Speech and Behavioral Change*, p. 9.

[33] For a discussion of properties related to innovations see, Nan Lin and Gerald Zaltman, "Dimensions of Innovations."

[34] Bunge, *Scientific Research*, Vol. I, p. 59.

cepts in this definition consist of "purchase," "household," "product class," and "brand." The formal concepts are "proportion" and "most frequently." Both of these formal concepts refer to the treatment of data—data that have been gathered through the interpretation of the nonformal concepts. Let us note one important difference between these two types of terms. The formal terms have *little vagueness* and a *high consistency of use*, whereas the nonformal terms are generally vague and their use is often inconsistent. If we presented the same set of data to a number of researchers with the instruction to compute the brand loyalty, as we have chosen to define it, there would be perfect correlation between the results, assuming no computational mistakes. Compare this with the results that we would obtain if we performed the same experiment not for the treatment of the data but for their gathering. What correlation among researchers would occur for the brands included in the product class? Howard and Sheth pose this problem in the form of a question: Should one place freeze-dried Maxim coffee in a product class containing only other freeze-dried brands, or should one include brands of all types of instant coffee, or even group all types of instant coffee together with regular coffee, to form a comprehensive product class?[35] Different researchers might well follow different approaches with differing results and interpretations. If different researchers differ in what they perceive as similarities or common elements in otherwise varied phenomena then we are, for all practical purposes, dealing with different concepts. Some variation is of course inevitable, but care should be exercised when comparing research utilizing the same term. Do the researchers mean essentially the same thing? Exactly what are the elements viewed as being common to different phenomena?

The same problem exists in data collection. Do respondents interpret or decode the stimulus (the concept) in similar ways? Some definitions of innovation, for example, have stressed the importance of potential user's perception as a determinant of whether an idea or thing should be classified as an innovation. To the extent that there are different perceptions, and hence conceptualization, there are correspondingly different concepts. The product concept or "image" will vary. That newness is common to the different images held by a consumer group enables us to use the term "innovation" with reference to that group.

DEGREE OF OBSERVABILITY OF NONFORMAL CONCEPTS

The next distinction among concepts concerns only the nonformal concepts. These concepts can be ranked along a dimension of observability. The degree of observability of a term or concept can be defined as the extent to which its use is prompted by environmental events as compared to intraverbal contexts. Verbal utterances of consumers during an interview are part

---

[35] Howard and Sheth, *The Theory of Buyer Behavior*, p. 283.

of the environment of the researcher and, thus, constitute data. Verbal utterances referring to these data, however, can be considered to occur within a
scientific intraverbal context. For example "I do not like brand A" as
uttered by an interviewee belongs to the researcher's environment. "The interviewee said, 'I do not like brand A,' " however, is a scientific statement, containing the two relatively observational concepts "interviewee" and "said."[36]
Now consider the statement "the interviewee dislikes product A," which
contains the concepts "interviewee," "dislikes," and "product A," all nonformal concepts. Now imagine that we perform the kind of experiment that
we performed with the concepts "proportion," "most frequently," and "product class." This time we want to compare the uses of "said" and of "dislikes."
Few researchers will disagree over the use of the term "said" when they can
observe mouth movements and hear sounds coming from the direction of the
interviewee. Less agreement can be expected, on the other hand, for the use
of the term "dislikes." One researcher may argue that the interviewee *said*
that he disliked the brand but he really did not mean it since the tone of voice
and nonverbal behavior suggested sarcasm. Another researcher might say that
the interviewee must really like the brand, contrary to what he said, because
of past or recent purchases as evidenced by his having a whole carton of the
item in his home. A third researcher might argue that the interviewee did not
mean what he said because the interviewee was simply trying to please him.
Thus the use of the term "dislikes" is subject to greater inconsistency than
that of "said." It might be inferred that "said" is relatively more observational than "dislike." However, someone might argue that "dislikes" is really
not less observational than "said," for it is easy to define "dislikes" contextually as "the interviewee dislikes brand A is the definitional equivalent
of: "the interviewee said 'I do not like brand A.' " Consequently, because
"said" and "interviewee" are observational, "dislikes" is also observational.
For the definiendum of a nominal definition is in principle as observational
as the terms in its definiens. Note the caution expressed by "in principle." It
is to be emphasized that the observability of a concept's constituents (that is,
its intension) is necessary but not sufficient for the observability of the concept itself. The argument is essentially right. It is *possible* to define "dislikes"
in such a way as to remove its ambiguity. The question is whether it is useful
to do this. We shall return to this problem, which is an example of the normative aspect of metatheory, after a more detailed investigation of the implications of the varying degree of observability of scientific concepts.

OBSERVATIONAL CONCEPTS

First, what are the characteristics of *observational* concepts? Following
Hempel, they can be defined as referring to

[36] See G. Mandler and W. Kessen, *The Language of Psychology.*

certain directly observable characteristics of objects, i.e., properties or relations whose presence or absence in a given case can be intersubjectively ascertained, under suitable circumstances, by direct observation.[37]

Let us look at the constituents of this definition.[38]

Consider first the expression "characteristics of objects, i.e., properties or relations. . . ." It is important to note that Hempel does not talk about the objects, but about their characteristics. Behind this is the rationale that researchers never deal with objects *qua* objects but rather with their characteristics. This distinction between objects and their characteristics is reflected in the logical types of concepts.[39] In logic, one distinguishes proper (individual) concepts and generic (class) concepts. *Proper or individual concepts* refer to the characteristics of one object only and are applicable only to it. Names of individuals are examples of such concepts—for example, Gerald Zaltman, Christian Pinson, and Reinhard Angelmar. Clearly, while the goal of science is the construction of general statements, individual concepts also have an important place in scientific language. *Generic concepts* also refer to objects, but they are based on the possession of certain characteristics by these objects, characteristics that are in principle also applicable to other objects. Hence, whenever we utter a certain term in response to an object it is by virtue of its possessing a number of attributes—namely, the intension of the generic concept.

The next constituent in Hempel's definition is "directly observable," which he also rephrases as ". . . whose presence or absence can be . . . ascertained." Thus demonstrability as a product characteristic is directly observable from an inspection of the product. The term in this case is a descriptive one. Hempel's use of the term "directly" implies that concepts may also be "indirectly" observable. *Indirect observables* involve inferences, usually causal, "between what is directly observed and what the term signifies." For example, we don't actually see a consumer's attitude toward a salesman but infer it from particular verbal and nonverbal expressions by the consumer. Similarly, "satisfactory experience" with a product is not a visible term but inferred from its repeated purchase. "Diffusion" is a construct measured directly over time and social-system space, but it is not observable nor can it be inferred in a given instant. The diffusion rate at a particular point can be calculated but not directly observed.

---

[37] Hempel, *Aspects of Scientific Explanation*, p. 22.

[38] For other treatments see Richard S. Rudner, *Philosophy of Social Science*, pp. 18–23; Kaplan, *The Conduct of Inquiry*, pp. 54–56; Peter Achinstein, *Concepts of Science: A Philosophical Analysis*, pp. 157–178; and John G. Kemeny, *A Philosopher Looks at Science*, pp. 122–125.

[39] For a very good discussion of this general topic, see W. S. Torgerson, *Theory and Methods of Scaling*.

The next element in the definition of an observable concept is "under suitable circumstances" or "in a given case." This implies that the observable character of a concept is not absolute but relative. There are two aspects to the relative observability of concepts. First, it may be "relative to the current development and to the sophistication of the observers."[40] For example, perceptual processes have become more and more observational with the development of new experimental devices (such as the tachistoscope technique).[41] Second, it may be relative to the context of application such that a term is observable in certain situations but not in others. The concept of cost effects on purchase behavior may be more readily observed among low-income consumers than among high-income consumers. Deal proneness, for instance, may be readily observable in a laboratory situation where many variables intervening between this deal proneness and overt response to a stimulus may be held constant. In the real world it may be very difficult to observe deal proneness. It might be added that certain elements of concepts are more readily observed than others. For example, the behavioral component of attitudes is more readily and reliably observed than are their affective and cognitive components. Similarly the concept of "information-gathering behavior" will be far easier to observe when product adoption is viewed as a risk-taking decision than when it does not. The element of risk causes consumers to be more deliberate in their actions and hence their behavior to be more readily monitored.

The final part of Hempel's definition is "intersubjectively." The purpose is to ensure that the same concept is being "observed" not only by one researcher but by most researchers in one discipline. We have illustrated this characteristic in our thought experiments involving "proportion" and "product class," and "said" and "dislikes." The problem here is that a concept will be said to be "observable" when "observed" by several observers, but there is no clear criterion as to the required number and/or quality of those observers.

CONCEPTS DEFINED IN TERMS OF OBSERVABLES

Thus far we have attempted to describe the characteristics of concepts that are relatively observational. It is necessary now to go one step further and look at the concepts that are not observational but that are introduced into scientific system or theories by way of nominal definitions involving directly observational concepts. We shall distinguish several varieties of such concepts.

One common type of nonobservational concept definition is in terms of

---

[40] Mary Hesse, "Laws and Theories," p. 405.
[41] See James Engel, David Kollat, and Roger Blackwell, *Consumer Behavior*, 1968, pp. 96–111.

the manipulations performed by an experimenter. This is a special case of what is frequently called operational definition, wherein the use of a term is specified by a set of operations. For instance, innovators have sometimes been defined as the first 3–10 percent of a population to adopt an innovation.[42] Cosmopoliteness is operationally defined in various ways, including travel to communities larger than one's own place of residence, variety of media exposed to, membership in formal organizations, and so on.

One other type of concept is what is called an "intervening variable,"[43] which Labovitz and Hagedorn view as a factor occurring between and connecting the independent and dependent variables.[44] The distinguishing characteristic of this type of concept is that it involves the treatment of data. Consequently, the definiens can usually be represented as a mathematical formula. (For the preceding types only a logical representation could be achieved.) Examples of this type of concept include brand loyalty and opinion leadership.

Finally, the last concept type is the so-called "disposition concepts." According to Hempel, disposition concepts refer to a tendency "to display specific reactions . . . under certain specifiable circumstances. . . ."[45] This can be interpreted in a more behaviorally oriented terminology as follows: "These [concepts] describe the disposition of an object or organism to display a certain characteristic or response, under certain given conditions of stimulation."[46] An example is the concept of attitudes. We can define consumer A as having a favorable attitude toward brand X if and only if his score is "higher than. . . ." Similarly, we could define "If consumer A is presented with brands X, Y, Z, then A prefers X if and only if A chooses X." The concept of innovativeness could be defined in a similar way: "If A and B are exposed to information about the innovation X at the same time, then A is innovative if and only if A adopts X earlier than B." Or X is an innovation if and only if it is perceived as new.

THEORETICAL CONCEPTS

Theoretical concepts (also referred to as hypothetical constructs) are those that derive meaning from their role in the theory in which they are embedded and the purposes of the theory. For example, the concept "consistency" derives one meaning when used in the phrase "consistent brand choice."[47]

---

[42] Thomas S. Robertson, *Innovative Behavior and Communication.*

[43] K. MacCorquodale and P. E. Meehl, "On a Distinction between Hypothetical Constructs and Intervening Variables." See also Howard and Sheth, *The Theory of Buyer Behavior*, for a good treatment of the notion of intervening variables in a consumer behavior context.

[44] Labovitz and Hagedorn, *Introduction to Social Research*, p. 106.

[45] Hempel, *Aspects of Scientific Explanation*, p. 24.

[46] Mandler and Kessen, *The Language of Psychology*, p. 115.

[47] See, for example, M. Venkatesan, "Cognitive Consistency and Novelty Seeking."

Similarly, personality as a concept takes on different attributes depending upon context and hence the theory within which it is being used.[48]

Theoretical concepts "are not introduced by definitions or reduction chains based on observables; in fact, they are not introduced by any piecemeal process of assigning meaning to them individually. Rather, the constructs used in a theory are introduced jointly, as it were, by setting up a theoretical system formulated in terms of them and by giving this system an experiential interpretation, which in turn confers meaning on the theoretical construct."[49] Let us look at the three main components of this definition in more detail.

The first characterization of hypothetical constructs is a negative one: They "are not introduced by definition or reduction chains based on observables." This characteristic distinguishes them from all of the previously discussed types of concepts. These other concepts could ultimately all be reduced to relatively observational concepts by replacing each concept by its definiens.

Now that we know how theoretical concepts are *not* introduced, how do they actually enter our scientific system? Again following Hempel, they "are introduced jointly, as it were, by setting up a theoretical system formulated in terms of them." As an example of such a system, consider the fragmentary theory that is depicted in Figure 2.5. In such a system the meaning of each concept is not given by a definition of the nominal variety but by the relationships into which the concepts enter. It is "defined" by the relationship that it entertains with "choice criteria," "brand comprehension," and "intention." Thus, *attitude* is the result of an evaluation according to *choice criteria* which is performed on social objects that have been identified and described by *brand comprehension*.[50] In the absence of any "inhibiting" variables, *intention* is identical to *attitude*.

Figure 2.5   Example of how theoretical concepts enter our scientific system.

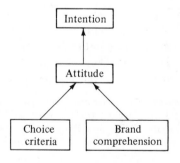

[48] See for example William D. Wells and Arthur Beard, "Personality and Consumer Behavior."

[49] Hempel, *Aspects of Scientific Explanation*, p. 32.

[50] For more perspective on consumer choice criteria, see Steven H. Chaffee and Jack M. McLeod, "Consumer Decisions and Information Use."

The foregoing example should render more clear the assertion made previously concerning the degree of observability of a term. It was said that the "observability of a term (concept) can be defined as the extent to which its use is prompted by environmental events as compared to intraverbal contexts." The concept of attitude above has been given a primarily intraverbal definition.

This brings us to the third component of Hempel's definition, namely where he speaks of "giving this (theoretical) system an experiential interpretation, which in turn confers meaning on the theoretical concept." Because a system of concepts that are without linkage to observational concepts would have no value for explanation, prediction, and control. Such systems would have a purely formal character, just like pure mathematics, for example.

CONCEPT VALIDITY

In an article devoted to the problems in consumer behavior research, Kollat *et al.* pointed out that "future progress in consumer behavior research will depend on overcoming several problems with commonly used variables and constructs, including the need for standardized definitions and categories. . . ."[51] Their request implies two evaluative judgments. First, a judgment has to be made as to the standard. Second, it is implied that the lack of standardization is bad. Whenever such an evaluative judgment of concepts is required, the problem of concept validity is raised. This means that the question "How valid is this concept?" has to be answered. We shall present general answers to this question given by philosophers of science and behavioral scientists. Following this, an approach that considers the objectives of consumer behavior research is proposed.

SEVERAL APPROACHES TO CONCEPT VALIDITY

There are a variety of answers to the question, "What is a valid concept?" The *first* and most traditional approach considers that only observational concepts are valid. In its extreme form it requires the *exhaustive* reducibility of all concepts to observations.[52] This school of thought has been called operationism. Hempel notes that the "central idea of operationism is that the meaning of every scientific term must be specifiable by indicating a definite testing operation that provides the criterion for its application."[53] Concepts that are provided with such criteria are said to be operationally defined. Bridgman has added a further specification to this point of view by stipulating that different operations characterize different concepts and that these

[51] David T. Kollat, James F. Engel, and Roger D. Blackwell, "Current Problems in Consumer Behavior Research," p. 328.
[52] See Ernest Nagel, *The Structure of Science*, pp. 119–121; and M. Hesse, "Laws and Theories."
[53] C. G. Hempel, *Philosophy of Natural Science*, p. 8.

operations should be ideally designated by different terms.[54] This version of operationism has also been called "definitional" operationism.[55]

The basic motivation underlying operationism is to "emancipate science from any dependency on unverifiable 'metaphysical' commitments."[56] The extreme operationalist view has been criticized on several counts. One counter-argument notes that "if explicit definitions of all theoretical terms by means of observables could be carried out, theories would be incapable of growth and therefore useless."[57] Hempel argues that the definitional operationist maxim would lead to a proliferation of concepts "that would not only be practically unmanageable but theoretically endless, and this would defeat one of the principal purposes of science; namely, the attainment of a simple, systematically unified account of empirical phenomena."[58] Campbell advances a theoretical and a practical argument against definitional operationism. The theoretical argument says that any specific measurement reflects not a single parameter of a scientific theory but is "a joint function of many scientific laws."[59] The practical argument says that the doctrine does not take into account the ongoing effort to improve measurement devices: "While logical positivists were defining intelligence in terms of the Stanford-Binet, 1916 edition, Terman was already initiating revisions designed to make it a less biased and more accurate test of intelligence."[60]

A less extreme form of operationism has been advanced by Carnap.[61] He requires only *partial* reducibility of concepts to observations. If a concept is introduced into some scientific system one must be able to construct some proposition containing this new concept, which, together with one or several other propositions containing only already tested terms, entails observation statements whose truth can be directly tested. This approach avoids the disadvantages of the extreme operationist position while still guaranteeing the empirical significance of concepts.

A second, widely held approach defines concept validity as the degree to which an instrument can measure the concept under investigation. Three types of concept validity—namely content, criterion-related, and construct validity—are usually subsumed under this definition.[62] *Content validity* refers to "the degree that the score or scale being used represents the concept

[54] Percy W. Bridgman, *The Logic of Modern Physics.*
[55] Donald T. Campbell, "Definitional versus Multiple Operationalism."
[56] Nagel, *The Structure of Science,* p. 119.
[57] Hesse, "Laws and Theories," pp. 406–407.
[58] Hempel, *Philosophy of Natural Science,* p. 94.
[59] Campbell, "Definitional versus Multiple Operationalism," p. 14.
[60] Donald T. Campbell, "Prospective: Artifact and Control."
[61] R. Carnap, "The Methodological Character of Theoretical Concepts."
[62] Lee J. Cronbach, *Essentials of Psychological Testing,* and Claire Selltitz, Marie Jahoda, Morton Deutsch, and Stuart Cook, *Research Methods in Social Relations.*

about which generalizations are to be made."[63] *Criterion-related validity* is concerned with how well the concept enables one to predict the value of some other concept which constitutes the criterion. Criterion validity consists of the two subtypes of predictive and concurrent validity. In predictive validity the criterion measure is separated in time from the predictor concept, whereas for concurrent validity both concepts are measured at the same time.

The studies by Axelrod[64] and Assael and Day[65] provide examples of predictive validity studies. Axelrod was interested in finding a "measure that not only reflects the immediate effect of a stimulus on a consumer but also predicts his subsequent purchase behavior."[66] For this purpose Axelrod developed ten measures. The predictive validity of each measure was determined as the percentage of obtained market as compared to predicted market. Axelrod concluded that two of the measures, namely "First Brand Awareness" and the "Constant Sum" had the highest predictive validity as far as short-term trends in purchase behavior are concerned. For situations where one is also concerned with "providing diagnostic information—what beliefs are held by those who are going to switch to various brands, what do they like, want, etc.—the Constant Sum is superior."[67] The study by Assael and Day was concerned with the nature and strength of the predictive relationship between attitudes, awareness, and usage to subsequent market share. The predictive validity of each independent variable was indicated by r^2 (the coefficient of multiple determination), which represents "the percentage variance in market share explained by the particular independent variable."[68] The findings indicated that in general all of the independent variables were important factors in explaining the variance in market share. Their relative importance, however, varied by brand and product category. Consequently, Assael and Day concluded that "predictive models must be built by product and by brand in forecasting changes in aggregate market response."[69]

Cohen's study on interpersonal orientation includes concurrent validation among other validation procedures.[70] He developed a scale purporting to measure the interpersonal response traits of compliance, aggression, and detachment. Rosenberg[71] had previously related the same traits to occupational preference. Based on Rosenberg's work Cohen developed a set of

---

[63] G. W. Bohrnstedt, "Reliability and Validity Assessment in Attitude Measurement," p. 91.

[64] Joel N. Axelrod, "Attitude Measures that Predict Purchase."

[65] Henry Assael and George S. Day, "Attitude and Awareness as Predictors of Market Share."

[66] Axelrod, "Attitude Measures that Predict Purchase," p. 3.

[67] Axelrod, p. 4.

[68] Assael and Day, "Attitude and Awareness as Predictors of Market Share," p. 7.

[69] Assael and Day, p. 10.

[70] Joel Cohen, "An Interpersonal Orientation to the Study of Consumer Behavior."

[71] Morris Rosenberg, *Occupations and Values.*

different measures of the same response traits. Because of this prior empirical basis the latter measures could be considered to be somewhat validated—that is, actually to reflect the three traits of interest. Since Cohen's new scale purported to measure the same traits, he should have been able to predict from the new scale how subjects responded to the other scale. Thus Cohen correlated the responses to both scales, with the intercorrelations among the measures of compliance and detachment being significant at the 0.01 level, among the aggression measures at the 0.05 level.

Construct validity consists of convergent, discriminant, and nomological validity. Convergent validity is represented by the correlation between two attempts to measure the same concept through maximally different methods. Discriminant validity measures the extent to which a concept differs from other similar concepts.

Davis illustrated convergent and discriminant validation procedures for the concept of husband-wife influence in consumer purchase decisions.[72] He used four different measures of purchase influence and administered each to both husbands and wives. Convergent validity was examined by looking at the size of the correlation between husbands' and wives' answers to the same questionnaires. Only two of the measures testified to convergent validity, which in this context means to ask whether "husbands and wives within the same family agree in their perception of relative influence."[73] As far as discriminant validity is concerned, Davis investigated three relevant criteria: (1) The association between husbands' and wives' responses to the same questionnaires should be higher than the association between questionnaires as perceived by either spouse or between husbands' and wives' answers to different questionnaires. (2) The correlation between husbands' and wives' responses to the same questionnaires should be higher than the correlations between each spouse's responses to the different questionnaires. (3) The same pattern of interrelationship should be found between each spouse's response to different questionnaires, "that is, if the furniture and automobile purchase measures are the most highly correlated based upon husbands' responses, the same should be true in the wives' responses."[74] Among the four measures used, only two satisfied two of the three criteria of discriminant validity. Nomological validity, finally, validates an instrument by interpreting the obtained scores in terms of a theoretical concept and consequently generates predictions that, if confirmed, have a validating effect. Cohen's study on interpersonal orientations includes also nomological validation procedures.[75]

As previously mentioned, Cohen developed a scale, responses to which

---

[72] Harry L. Davis, "Measurement of Husband-Wife Influence in Consumer Purchase Decisions."
[73] Davis, p. 311.
[74] Davis, p. 310.
[75] Cohen, "An Interpersonal Orientation to the Subject of Consumer Behavior."

should reflect the interpersonal traits of compliance, aggression, and detachment. The underlying theory suggested that persons having any one of these traits should respond in a particular way to face-to-face influence. If the scale were a valid measure of the response traits, persons who scored as highly compliant should actually show compliant behavior in the experiment. Similarly, people scoring as highly aggressive on the scale should actually display aggressive behavior. The results of this particular validation of the scale confirmed the scale's validity for indicating the compliant and aggressive trait but failed to validate it for the detached trait.

Criterion-related validity, by its very nature, is concerned with explanation and prediction. Content and construct validity, by comparison, aim primarily at the description of some real referent although they may also entail prediction.[76] A *third* approach considers concepts to be more valid the more they "establish relations among concepts and contribute thereby to systemicity (theoretical fertility)."[77] We propose to call this type of concept validity, *systemic validity*. The emphasis is thus on the extent to which a concept enables the integration of previously unconnected concepts and/or the generation of a new conceptual system. A *fourth* approach, which we propose to refer to as *semantic validity*, requires that concepts have a uniform semantic usage.[78] This serves the objectives of comparing, synthesizing, and accumulating findings, objectives which are characteristic of paradigmatic research.[79] *Finally*, users of consumer behavior research, such as marketing managers and other change agents, judge the validity of a concept according to its manipulability and capacity to influence variables of interest. We propose to call this type of concept validity, *control validity*. Table 2.2 summarizes the various types of concept validity.

It can be seen that each of the foregoing approaches emphasizes a different dimension of the problem of concept validity. Each seems to judge a concept's validity in terms of its attaining some objective. The objectives to be considered here are description, explanation, prediction, and control, for consumer behavior research aims to "identify the basic properties of the consumer, to understand and explain, as well as perhaps to influence and predict, his behavior."[80] Description is primarily concerned with the *what* and *how* of phenomena.[81] A concept's validity for descriptive purposes is therefore determined by how well it describes real objects and events. Explanation is concerned with the *why* of phenomena.[82] Following Hempel and Oppen-

---

[76] Brandt and Metzer, "Reality: What Does It Mean?"
[77] Bunge, *Scientific Research*, Vol. I, p. 133.
[78] Melvin H. Marx, "The Dimension of Operational Clarity."
[79] Thomas S. Kuhn, *The Structure of Scientific Revolutions.*
[80] Francesco M. Nicosia, *Consumer Decision Processes*, p. 7.
[81] Kaplan, *The Conduct of Inquiry*, p. 72.
[82] Kaplan, p. 330.

Table 2.2   Types of Concept Validity

1. Observational validity	The degree to which a concept is reducible to observations.
2. Content validity	The degree to which an operationalization *represents* the concept about which generalizations are to be made.
3. Criterion-related validity	The degree to which the concept under consideration enables one to predict the value of some other concept that constitutes the criterion.
3a. Predictive validity	A subtype of criterion-related validity in which the criterion measured is separated in time from the predictor concept.
3b. Concurrent validity	A subtype criterion-related validity in which the criterion and the predictor concepts are measured at the same time.
4. Construct validity	The extent to which an operationalization *measures* the concept which it purports to *measure*.
4a. Convergent validity	The degree to which two attempts to measure the same concept through maximally different methods are convergent. It is generally represented by the correlation between the two attempts.
4b. Discriminant validity	The extent to which a concept differs from other concepts.
4c. Nomological validity	The extent to which predictions based on the concept which an instrument purports to measure are confirmed.
5. Systemic validity	The degree to which a concept enables the integration of previously unconnected concepts and/or the generation of a new conceptual system.
6. Semantic validity	The degree to which a concept has a uniform semantic usage.
7. Control validity	The degree to which a concept is manipulable and capable of influencing other variables of influence.

heim, explanation and prediction are considered to be a symmetrical.[83] A concept's validity with respect to these objectives is determined by how well it explains and predicts other phenomena. Control, finally, is concerned with the manipulation of a variable so as to effect a change in some other variable.

As criteria for the *descriptive* validity of concepts, we propose the follow-

[83] Hempel, *Aspects of Scientific Explanation*, 1965.

ing: reliability, convergent validity, nomological validity, content validity, and discriminant validity. All of these criteria, with the exception of discriminant validity, focus on the relationship between a concept and its real referent. Discriminant validity, by contrast, refers to the economy of the description by stipulating that intentionally identical concepts should be recognized as such and labeled in the same way. It represents the principle of parsimony as applied to description.[84] Reliability is usually treated separately from the validity types with which it is lumped together here. It can be defined as the degree of agreement between two efforts to measure the same concept through maximally similar methods.[85] Reliability is an intramethod convergence, while convergent validity is an intermethod convergence. Contrary to what one might think, both criteria apply not only to concepts with quantitative but also to those with qualitative attributes. For the latter concepts, the criteria become the criteria of intra- and intersubjective reliability of usage: "If different users employ a term in the same fashion then this observation confirms intersubjective reliability. A similar confirmation is sought for intrasubjective reliability. When such confirmations are absent, the term is rejected."[86] It can be seen that reliability is an important criterion for evaluating a concept's usefulness for description. While the separate treatment of reliability and the validity types may be justified in different contexts, for our purposes they belong in the same category since they both serve the objective of description.

For the *explanatory-predictive* validity of concepts, it will be useful to distinguish two evaluative discussions, namely the accuracy and the range of the explanation-prediction.[87] The dimension of accuracy refers to the extent of agreement between the predicted and the observed value for each dependent variable. The range refers to the number of dependent variables that can be explained-predicted with the help of the independent variable. For an observational concept, the accuracy is indicated by the criterion-related validity. Its overall explanatory-predictive validity then depends on the magnitude of the correlation with each criterion and the number of criteria explained-predicted, where the criterion is the dependent variable. In the case where the concept under investigation is a theoretical construct with multiple operationalizations, the concept's explanatory-predictive validity is a function of the validities of its operationalizations. An example of the distinction between the two types of concepts would be the explanatory-predictive validity of a particular instrument of attitude measurement and the concept of attitude itself.

Although interest usually focuses on the independent variable of explana-

[84] See Rudner, *Philosophy of Social Science*, p. 42.
[85] Donald T. Campbell and D. W. Fiske, "Convergent and Discriminant Validation by the Multitrait-Multimethod Matrix."
[86] Mandler and Kessen, *The Language of Psychology*, p. 46.
[87] Bunge, *Scientific Research*, Vol I, pp. 475 and 238.

tions and predictions, a look at the dependent variable—that is, the criterion —is equally justified. Here, the question becomes: "How valid is a concept for *being* explained and predicted?" Since the criterion-related validity indicates the correlation between independent variable and criterion, it is no surprise that the reverse of this correlation can be used to measure the degree of success of a criterion as explanandum. A criterion for which explanations and predictions are difficult to obtain may be poorly conceptualized, may be too complex, or may be the result of too many independent variables.[88] It is here that the boundary between explanation and prediction on one hand and description on the other hand becomes rather fuzzy.[89] A good description may greatly facilitate the finding of an explanation and prediction. After all, explanation can be understood as stating "what the explanandum *really* is and, hence, relating it to other systems which are then seen to be essentially similar to it."[90]

Finally, a concept's *control* validity is indicated by its effectiveness and efficiency. Prior to the determination of the effectiveness and efficiency has to be the determination of whether a concept enables control in principle. If this question is to be answered positively, in our opinion the following requirements will have to be satisfied: (1) The relationship between the concept and the criterion has to be causal. (2) The concept must be directly or indirectly manipulable. Attitudes, by comparison, are not directly manipulable. In the indirect case a third requirement has to be added: (3) Another concept must exist that is manipulable and has a causal relationship to the original concept. For example, a marketing manager must be able to control one or several causal antecedents of attitudes, if attitude is to have control validity. For concepts passing these tests, one index of effectiveness of control is given by the criterion-related validity. The criterion of efficiency is the output-input ratio. Further specification depends on which factors are included in input and output in each particular case.

INTERRELATIONSHIPS OF THE CRITERIA OF CONCEPT VALIDITY

The following relationships between the *descriptive* criteria and the criteria for *explanatory-predictive* validity can be noted. It has been demonstrated that reliability imposes an upper limit on criterion-related validity, because the correlation of some concept with the criterion can never exceed the square root of the reliability of the concept.[91] In other words, it is necessary to have descriptively valid concepts before attempting to obtain valid relationships between them.[92] As far as content and discriminant valid-

---

[88] Consider the discussion of the difficulties in defining innovators, in Robertson, *Innovative Behavior and Communication*, pp. 87–88.

[89] Kaplan, *The Conduct of Inquiry*, p. 329, and Nagel, *The Structure of Science*, pp. 117–129.

[90] Hesse, "Laws and Theories," p. 72.

[91] Bohrnstedt, "Reliability and Validity Assessment in Attitude Measurement," p. 97.

ity are concerned, we think that they have a direct effect on the accuracy and range of the explanation-prediction. Convergent validity, by establishing the existence of a concept of some generality, provides the necessary conditions for explanations-predictions of large range.[93] As an illustration, one may think of the increase in generality affected by interpreting the scores of a chewing-gum attitude test in terms of "oral fixation." Since this is a concept of great generality, the attitude test, if validated convergently, would lead to a number of predictions for products other than chewing gum. Nomological validity has the same effect plus an immediate contribution to explanation and prediction.[94] The effect of convergent and nomological validity on criterion-related validity, on the other hand, is in general thought to be negative: There is a tradeoff between magnitude of the correlation and the number of criteria explained-predicted—that is, between accuracy and range; the more criteria a given concept can explain-predict, the lower its correlation with each.

The relationship between *description* and *control* is similar to the previous one: High reliability is a necessary condition for high effectiveness of control. Convergent and nomological validity involve again the tradeoff between accuracy and range of control effectiveness.

Explanation-prediction and *control* are related as follows: On the basis of the foregoing discussion of control validity it can be concluded that a concept's criterion validity is a necessary, but not sufficient, condition for its control effectiveness. A high control effectiveness, in turn, is necessary and sufficient for a concept's high criterion-related validity. This corresponds to the principle that "correlation does not necessarily indicate causation, but a causal law . . . does imply correlation."[95]

SUMMARY

Concepts have been identified as the fundamental units marketers use in their everyday marketing activities; concepts are the building blocks of the propositions and theories that marketers use in explaining, predicting, and controlling marketplace phenomena. It is essential that a basic understanding of concepts be achieved. This chapter has attempted to provide such an understanding by first distinguishing among concepts, terms, and objects. Further distinctions were made between formal and nonformal concepts and between theoretical and observational concepts. Finally, various types of concept validity of relevance to the study of consumer behavior were examined.

[92] See Campbell and Fiske, "Convergent and Discriminant Validation by the Multitrait-Multimethod Matrix," p. 100.
[93] See L. J. Cronbach and P. E. Meehl, "Construct Validity in Psychological Tests," p. 285.
[94] See Donald T. Campbell, "Recommendations for APA Test Standards Regarding Construct, Trait, or Discriminant Validity," p. 547.
[95] Donald T. Campbell and Julian C. Stanley, *Experimental and Quasi-experimental Designs for Research.*

CHAPTER 3

THE NATURE OF PROPOSITIONS

INTRODUCTION

The preceding chapter dealt with the basic units of language (terms) and of thought (concepts). The present chapter discusses the elements of a *higher-order* level of language and thought, namely *sentences* (defined as sequences of terms) and *propositions* (defined as sequences of concepts). Propositions establish relations among concepts. The beginning of the chapter discusses the relationships between sentences, propositions, and facts. After this, the syntactical, semantical, and epistemological dimensions of propositions are investigated. The degree and number of predicates in a proposition are the *syntactical* dimensions of interest to us. As for the *semantical* and *epistemological* dimensions, we shall discuss the precision of propositions and their observational status. Of particular importance is the distinction between empirical propositions, generalizations, and nonobservational propositions. The first two types of propositions are observational, but the latter type is not. Therefore, correspondence rules, another type of propositions, are needed to connect nonobservational propositions to data. Next, the types of relationships that are obtained between the variables in a proposition are discussed

The final part of this chapter looks at the problems of testability, confirmability, and degree of corroboration of propositions. The concepts of a hypothesis and of laws are defined in this context.

SENTENCES AND PROPOSITIONS

Sentences establish relations among terms: for example " 'retail store image' is the total conceptualized or expected reinforcement that a person associates with shopping at a particular shop"[1] can be seen as merely a sequence of 20 terms—that is, of 20 signs. The *form* of the foregoing linguistic expression may be expressed as being a particular combination of signs. Not any sign combination is permissible: "permissible sign combinations are ruled by formation rules (or grammatical rules in an ample sense of 'grammar'): their meanings by designations rules."[2] A rule of designation is the rule by which a term is arbitrarily introduced. In short, a designation rule stipulates correspondence between a term and a concept.

It follows that a sentence *designates* a proposition and a proposition cannot be expressed except through a sentence—that is, a specific combination of basic linguistic symbols (terms). In other words, *a proposition is the meaning of a sentence.*[3]

It should be noted that the same proposition can be expressed by different sentences. For example, the sentences "buyer behavior is rational" and "buyers behave in a rational way" are viewed as expressing the same proposition. Another example of two sentences corresponding to a simple proposition

[1] John H. Kunkel and Leonard L. Berry, "A Behavioral Conception of Retail Image."
[2] Mario Bunge, *Scientific Research*, Vol. I, p. 49.
[3] This view is not uncontested. Among those who oppose it are Gilbert Ryle, "Meaning and Necessity," *Philosophy*; Bertrand Russell, *An Inquiry into Meaning and Truth*; Stuart Hampshire, "Ideas, Propositions and Signs." Among those who are in favor of this view are Gottlob Frege, "The Thought"; William Kneale and Martha Kneale, *The Development of Logic*; Alonzo Church, *Introduction to Mathematical Logic*, Vol. I; Rudolf Carnap, *Meaning and Necessity.*

is "Product A is more satisfying than product B" and "Product B is less satisfying than product A." On the other hand, the *same* sentence used in different contexts may give birth to different propositions. For example, the statement "information seeking is high under conditions of uncertainty" is a relevant proposition in both consumer and industrial settings. However, the functioning or operation of the sentence as a proposition differs in the two contexts. Sources and types of information sought, as well as what constitutes uncertainty, may differ. Moreover, elements of the same sentence may receive differential emphasis in different contexts. Uncertainty in the previous proposition may be manifest in different ways in the category of durable goods than in the category of convenience goods.

There is a second type of relationship between sentence and proposition in addition to that of designation, namely the *relationship of reference*. The relation of reference establishes links between the linguistic expression (sentence) and the conceptual level (proposition) on one hand and the physical level on the other hand. We say that sentences and propositions refer to facts when they have physical referents. For example, "The young blacks who expressed a more positive attitude than other respondents were not heads of households or spouses" refers to a fact.[4]

The "reference relationship" can be handled in two ways. First, we may start with some fact and move to the corresponding propositions. Second, we may begin with a proposition and try to find a corresponding fact. To begin with the first case, we assume that we have already a certain number of *isolated* concepts at our disposition. With these concepts in mind we gather facts; that is, we interpret our concepts and record the results. As an example take the concepts "life style" and "users and nonusers of commercial bank charge cards." To say that we interpret these concepts means that we define them operationally such that we can determine unambiguously in each case whether a person is a user of commercial bank charge cards and what his life style is. For example, Plummer used a 300 Activity, Interest, and Opinion statements measure of life style;[5] the concept of bank charge card usage was operationalized by the following question: "Thinking of all members of your family, how many times in the average month do all members of your family use a bank charge card?"[6] Then to each of the states of nature that we so encounter, there will correspond a proposition of the form "User A has life style X" "Nonuser B has life style Y" and so forth. Finally Plummer concluded that "the life style portrait of the users indicates an active,

[4] Dennis H. Gensch and Richard Staelin, "The Appeal of Buying Black," *Journal of Marketing Research*, 9, 1972.

[5] Joseph T. Plummer, "Life Style Patterns and Commercial Bank Credit Card Usage," *Journal of Marketing*; see also William D. Wells and Douglas J. Tigert, "Activities, Interests, and Opinions."

[6] Plummer, p. 36.

upper socioeconomic, urban-suburban life style with many interests outside the home."[7] Another example is Wiseman's propositions concerning how buyers of "new season" automobiles differ from buyers of "new leftover" automobiles during the period when both models are available for sale.[8] As another example, take the concepts "consumer," "innovator," and "brand loyalty." To say that we interpret these concepts means that we define them operationally such that we can determine unambiguously in each case whether a person is an innovator and to what degree he is brand loyal. To each of the states of nature that we so encounter, there will correspond a proposition of the form "Consumer A is brand loyal and not an innovator," or "Consumer B is brand loyal and is not an innovator," and so forth.

If we look at the reverse process, we start not only with a set of concepts but also with a proposition relating them, such as "Innovators are not brand loyal (in the context in which they innovate)." For example, Corey decided "first, to take the standard definition of opinion leaders, translate it into specific hypotheses about consumer topics, and then test those hypotheses with data from three market studies."[9] The standard definition referred to was taken from Berelson and Steiner[10] and the hypotheses were the following ones:

H_1: consumer opinion leaders will be significantly more involved in activities related to their topic than nonleaders.

H_2: consumer opinion leaders will be significantly more informed about new developments in their topic than nonleaders.

H_3: the extent to which consumer opinion leaders read in the media related to their topic will be significantly greater than among nonleaders.

H_4: consumer opinion leaders will have the same demographic characteristics as nonleaders, except for their higher socioeconomic status. However, to one extent or another, consumer opinion leaders will be found in all demographic groups.[11]

Then, we follow a procedure similar to the one described above; that is, we examine the states of nature that we encounter and form the propositions that correspond to them. A comparison of these propositions with our original propositions is then made to determine whether the original propositions

[7] Plummer, p. 41.

[8] Frederick Wiseman, "A Segmentation Analysis on Automobile Buyers During the New Model Year Transition Period."

[9] Lawrence G. Corey, "People Who Claim To Be Opinion Leaders: Identifying Their Characteristics by Self-Report," *Journal of Marketing*, p. 49.

[10] Bernard Berelson and Gary A. Steiner, *Human Behavior: An Inventory of Scientific Findings*, p. 550.

[11] Corey, "People Who Claim to be Opinion Leaders, p. 49.

refer to an actual state of nature or not. This then is the crucial difference between the two procedures: If we construct our propositions starting with facts, then the propositions are automatically "factually true." If, however, we start with some proposition, we cannot be sure *a priori* whether it actually refers to some existing state of nature or not. Note that the appearance of the sentence does not tell us this difference. Thus, the sentence "consumer opinion leaders are significantly more involved in activities related to their topic than nonleaders" can be arrived at either deductively or inductively. First, it may be the conclusion of a number of premises that belong to some theoretical system. This is the deductive derivation of the sentence. Alternatively, the sentence may be inductively derived not from a theory but as a result of an observation of facts.

It will be useful now to examine the various types of propositions. There are several dimensions of propositions that may be used for the construction of types; propositions can be compared in terms of their *syntactical, semantical,* and *epistemological* characteristics. Let us consider first the syntactical dimension.

SYNTACTICAL DIMENSIONS OF PROPOSITIONS

Propositions may first be compared with respect to the *number and degree of the predicates* they contain. A predicate is a syntactic unit expressing the action performed by or on the state attributed to the subject of the sentence.[12] For example, the proposition "this is a gatekeeper" contains one predicate whereas the proposition "some consumers are both opinion leaders and innovators" contains two predicates, namely "opinion leader" and "innovator." We recall that a predicate is a syntactic unit expressing the action performed by or the state attributed to the subject of the sentence. Thus, in the preceding proposition "some consumers" is the subject.

Secondly, one can consider the *degree* of the predicates contained in the proposition—that is, whether they are one-place or two-or-more-place predicates. A one-place predicate is a predicate that designates properties, not relations. For example, the predicate "is a consumer" is a one-place predicate, whereas the predicates "an opinion leader of" and "innovator" are two-place predicates. They imply a relationship with other individuals. Two-place predicates are also sometimes labeled "relational concept." Note, however, that "the degree of predicates . . . is contextual rather than absolute: it depends on the state of the body of knowledge in which they occur and on the analytic fineness that is required or possible."[13]

A second formal syntactical dimension of a proposition is its *degree of generality.* All propositions purport to refer to a particular segment of the

[12] Rudolph Carnap, *Introduction to Symbolic Logic and Its Applications.*
[13] Bunge, *Scientific Research*, Vol. I, p. 237.

world, their universe of discourse. The notion of "universe of discourse" is related to the notion of "denotation" and "extension" discussed in Chapter 2. The reader will recall that the denotation of a concept refers to the class of actual objects that possess the properties included in the intension of a concept. The extension of a concept, on the other hand, refers to the class of possible or potential objects, "past or future, known or unknown, which if they existed would belong to the concept's denotation."[14] Thus, the denotation is a subset of the extension of a concept. The size of the extension (or denotation, respectively) of all the concepts contained in a proposition, then, determines the generality of the proposition, since the universe of discourse of the proposition is the set of entities referred to by the whole proposition. Usually, one distinguishes two aspects of the extention of a concept: (1) the openness with respect to time-space (spatiotemporal universality); and (2) the openness with respect to the kind of objects (referential universality).[15] For example, the proposition "with few exceptions, it is reasonable to conclude that social class is basically inferior to income as a correlate of buying behavior *for the consumer packaged goods covered in this study*"[16] is remarkably well specified with respect to the above two types of universality. The spatiotemporal generality is rarely given explicit attention. Rather, it is an assumption that underlies most scientific activity. As such it can be formulated as a metastatement of the form "most propositions are independent of location in space-time," or "most propositions are neither dated or placed." The degree of referential generality of propositions is indicated by the quantifiers that are prefixed to the object variables (that is, the concepts) of propositions. Table 3.1 lists the most common quantifiers and shows the types of propositions that result when one uses these quantifiers as a criterion of classification.

Let us consider now the possible propositions that can be formed when we consider the above quantifiers and a single predicate $P(\quad)$, where $P(\quad)$, for example, might mean "is innovative." The kinds of propositions that result are shown in Figure 3.1 ranging from the lower level to the higher level of generality.

Some illustrations of the types of propositions shown in Figure 3.1 will be helpful. To begin with the singular proposition type, consider "consumer A is innovative." The next type of proposition, the existential proposition, is exemplified by the statement, "there is exactly one innovative consumer." Here there is also only one individual to which the proposition refers; the difference with regard to the preceding proposition, however, is that this proposition contains only generic (class) concepts, whereas the previous proposition

---

[14] See Chapter 2 of this text.
[15] See Bunge, *Scientific Research*, Vol. I, p. 328.
[16] James H. Myers, Roger R. Stanton, and Arne F. Haug, "Correlates of Buying Behavior: Social Class vs. Income," p. 14. Italics added.

Table 3.1   List of Quantifiers

Name	Symbol	Read
Indefinite existential quantifier	$(\exists x)$	There is at least one x such that. . . . *Example:* There is at least one innovator in any changing society
Definite existential quantifiers	$(\exists x)_n$	There are exactly n x such that. . . . *Example:* There is exactly 10% of any population who are innovators.
Bounded existential quantifier	$(\exists x)_U$	There are x in U such that. . . . *Example:* There are innovators in peasant societies who have well-developed abilities to identify with change agents.
Bounded universal quantifier	$(x)_x \in U$	Every x in U is such that. . . . *Example:* Every innovator in a peasant community is a high risk taker.
Unbound universal quantifier	(x)	Every x is such that. . . . *Example:* Every innovator has a perceptual process that differs from noninnovators.

Note: U designates the universe of discourse, $\exists$ reads "there is," and x is the variable under consideration. For example x can be equated to "consumer" and U to "the sample of consumers."
Source: Adapted from Mario Bunge, Scientific Research, Vol. I, p. 51. Berlin: Springer-Verlag, 1967. Reprinted with permission of Springer-Verlag, New York.

contained the individual concept "*A.*" An example of the next larger degree of generality is "there is at least one innovative consumer." Next, there is a statement like "there are exactly n innovative consumers; n greater than 1." Finally, we have bounded and unbounded universal propositions. The former are of the form: "All consumers in our sample are innovative" while the latter are as follows: "All consumers are innovative."

Another dimension of interest here is *precision*. A proposition, as stated earlier, relates attributes of concepts (that is, predicates, or properties of objects). The quantifiers refer to the size of the denotation of the concepts. The concepts appearing in a proposition may thus be either specified or left unspecified. For example, in the statement "the greater the psychological rigidity, the greater the likelihood of avoiding dissonant information," the attribute "rigidity" is not ascribed to either all consumers or some subset. Therefore, in order to render the proposition specific, we have to specify the population to whom the proposition involving "rigidity" applies.

Not only must the relevant domain of concepts be specified in a proposi-

Figure 3.1   Kinds of elementary propositions.

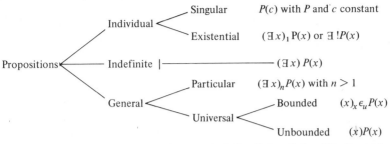

Source: Mario Bunge, *Scientific Research*, vol. I, p. 51. Berlin: Springer-Verlag, 1967. Reprinted with permission of Springer-Verlag, New York.

tion but so must the attributes of the concept. For example, we often find assertions to the effect that "the characteristics of salesmen affect adoption decisions by potential customers." Here, we may wonder exactly what characteristics of the salesman are referred to in the proposition: These may be his empathetic ability, his ethnic background, and so on. Another example is the proposition, "a shopping center's trading area is limited by the factor of drive time and . . . the most significant driving-time dimension for trade-area analysis is 15 minutes."[17] Such a proposition would be imprecise if the concept "most significant" were not further defined. For example, Brunner and Mason called the 15-minute driving point "the most significant driving dimension for trade-area analysis" because "three fourths of each center's shoppers resided within this range."[17] Hence, we can see that there are two elements of uncertainty in a proposition: the universe of discourse and the attributes. If either of these two components is left unspecified we say that we have a propositional function rather than a precise proposition.

SEMANTICAL DIMENSION OF PROPOSITIONS

The semantical dimension that can be used to classify propositions is the observational character of the constituents of the proposition. It should be noted that we refer to the observational status of the attributes contained in propositions and not to the object variables to which they are attributed. This implies that one and the same proposition may contain only observational constituents or only theoretical ones, depending on the variables (the universe of discourse) to which the proposition refers. For example, consider the proposition "imbalance creates forces that attempt to redress balance." In one case, the concepts of imbalance and balance may refer to some physical system, such as a scale that is held up on one side. Here, the statement refers to an observable state of nature. Consider, however, the same attributes as

[17] James A. Brunner and John L. Mason, "The Influence of Driving Time upon Shopping Center Preference," p. 59.

referring to the cognitive system of some individual. In this context, the proposition is clearly nonobservational.[18] Therefore, as was the case with concepts, *the criterion of observability has to be applied contextually*. With this constraint in mind, we can now distinguish three types of propositions. First, there are those propositions containing only observational concepts. Second, certain propositions may contain both observational and nonobservational concepts. Finally, there are propositions containing only nonobservational concepts. Each of these three types of propositions will be discussed now beginning with the most observational.

OBSERVATIONAL PROPOSITIONS

Observational propositions contain only relatively observational concepts and grammatical or logical connectives (that is, formal concepts). Consider the following proposition, "out-shopping [is] less frequent among lower-income families, and families with younger children or a large number of children."[19] Here in order for the proposition to be observational, the concepts "out-shopping," "lower-income families," and so forth must be operationally defined. For example "out-shoppers" were defined as "those who had shopped outside a five-mile radius of the downtown area one or more times during the previous year;" "lower-income families" was operationalized by introducing four income categories (under $5000; $5000 to $9999; $10,000 to $14,999; $15,000 and over); the concept of families with younger children "was operationalized by using two age categories: families with "youngest child 0–12" and "youngest child 13–24."[20] Within the observational type of proposition, two important subtypes can be distinguished, namely, *empirical propositions* and *empirical generalizations*.

Empirical propositions are derived from "facts" or "data" and their linguistic expression is called a "protocol sentence."[21] As such, they must satisfy two conditions. First, it must be possible to reach a decision as to their truth or falsity in a finite number of observations. Second, they must be intersubjectively corroborated, which means that the empirical truth or falsity of the proposition must be agreed upon by *different* observers.[22]

The first requirement amounts to stipulating that the universe of dis-

[18] By postulating certain observable effects of balanced and imbalanced cognitive systems (that is, by "operationally" defining these concepts), one obtains observational propositions that are easily confused with the original nonobservational (theoretical) propositions.

[19] Robert O. Herrmann and Leland L. Beik, "Shoppers' Movements Outside Their Local Retail Area."

[20] Herrmann and Beik, p. 47.

[21] Peter Caws, *The Philosophy of Science: A Systematic Account*, p. 73.

[22] Caws, p. 73; see also Herbert Feigl, "The Scientific Outlook: Naturalism and Humanism," and Johan Galtung, "An Inquiry into the Concepts of 'Reliability,' 'Intersubjectivity,' and 'Constancy.'"

course is a finite set rather than an infinite set. Thus, the universe of discourse, in this case, is the denotation rather than the extension; that is, the empirical proposition is either a singular proposition or a conjunction of such propositions. For example, Brunner's and Mason's proposition that "three fourths of each center's shoppers [reside] within [a 15-minute driving time] range"[23] in order to be an empirical proposition must refer to a well-defined universe of buyers. As such its test can be reduced to the final examination of n singular propositions such as "Shopper A_1 drives less than 15 minutes to patronize a shopping center," "Shopper A_2 drives more than 15 minutes to patronize a shopping center," . . . "A_n . . ." with n being finite.

The second aforementioned criterion for empirical propositions was the intersubjective corroboration. This is the criterion of convergent validity (with which we are familiar from our discussion of observational concepts) now extended to the propositions: The results of one observation must be verifiable by subsequent observations by different observers.

Empirical generalizations must also satisfy the criterion of intersubjective corroboration. In contrast to the preceding type of proposition, however, *their truth or falsity is not ascertainable in a finite number of steps.* This implies that the universe of discourse of empirical generalizations is an infinite set. Thus, it refers to the extension of object variables rather than their denotation. For example, consider again the proposition "three fourths of each center's shoppers [resides] within [a 15-minute driving time] range" and suppose that we are not referring to a particular sample of shoppers but rather to all buying behaviors that have taken place in the past, are taking place at present, and will occur in the future. Hence, empirical generalizations go beyond actual data. They constitute a "jump" from the collection of singular statements about the states of affairs $A_1, A_2, \ldots, A_n$ (n being finite) to a universal statement about the class of A's.[24] Well-known instances of broad and *explicit* attempts to generalize empirical findings are Rogers and Shoemaker; Berelson and Steiner; and Engel, Kollat, and Blackwell.[25]

NONOBSERVATIONAL PROPOSITIONS

These are propositions containing only nonobservational concepts. This does not imply that the object variables to which these concepts are attributed are necessarily unobservable. It is entirely possible to ascribe a nonobservational attribute to an otherwise observable entity. We can distinguish two cases of nonobservational propositions. First, the object variable is obser-

[23] Brunner and Mason, "The Influence of Driving Time upon Shopping Center Preference, p. 59.
[24] Caws, *The Philosophy of Science,* p. 76.
[25] Everett M. Rogers and Floyd F. Shoemaker, *Communication of Innovations: A Cross-Cultural Approach;* Berelson and Steiner, *Human Behavior,* p. 550; James F. Engel, David T. Kollat, and Roger D. Blackwell, *Consumer Behavior,* 1968.

vational even though the attribute is not; second, both the object variables and the attributes are unobservable. Let us illustrate the first case. Consider the proposition, "All branded products have images." A product is a very observable entity, whereas its image is a relatively unobservable attribute. As an illustration of the second case consider the following statement: "The subject's cognitive system is imbalanced." Here, neither the entity (that is, "cognitive system") nor the atttribute ("imbalanced") are observational. In this case, we operate on the basis of an analogy or of a model, which may be some familiar physical system.

CORRESPONDENCE RULES

These rules, also called "bridge principles,"[26] constitute the major and more interesting instance of propositions containing both observational and nonobservational concepts. Correspondence rules establish a linkage between nonobservational and observational concepts. They indicate "how the processes envisaged by the theory are related to empirical phenomena. . . ."[27] For example, if we want to test the hypothesis, "The greater the congruence of self with the brand image, the more positive is the attitude toward the brand" we need the following two correspondence rules: "instrument X is a measure of congruence, instrument Y is a measure of brand attitude."[28] Stated somewhat differently, correspondence rules are "interpretive sentences."[29] They link propositions to empirical phenomena and thus help define the domain of the proposition. A correspondence rule $(A = A')$ sets up equivalence between, say, the concept attitude A and the testing instrument A' used to measure attitudes. In another context, Wells and Tigert[30] developed a measure of price consciousness for use in a correspondence rule. Their measure in this case involved a composite score derived from the following test items: "I shop a lot for 'specials,' " "I find myself checking the prices in the grocery store even for small items," "I usually watch the advertisements for announcements of sales," and "A person can save a lot of money by shopping around for bargains." The correspondence rule implied is that price consciousness is the equivalent of the composite score derived from consumer responses to these items. Thus we may have the primary hypothesis (if A, then B) and the auxiliary hypotheses or assumptions or correspondence rules $(A = A'$ and $B = B'$, where the A' and B' are tests measuring A and B.[31]

[26] Carl G. Hempel, *Philosophy of Natural Science*; see also Herbert L. Costner, "Theory, Deduction, and Rules of Correspondence."
[27] Hempel, p. 72.
[28] Gerald Zaltman, Reinhard Angelmar, and Christian Pinson, "Metatheory in Consumer Behavior Research," pp. 476–497.
[29] David Harvey, *Explanation in Geography*, p. 88.
[30] Wells and Tigert, "Activities, Interests, and Opinions."
[31] Hempel, *Philosophy of Natural Science*, p. 23.

Thus if we find empirically A' to be the case then we infer A is the case and hence condition B is also the case which can be corroborated by test B'.

Let us look more closely at the way correspondence rules are derived. First, it may be that the correspondence rules are deduced from a set of theoretically relatively independent statements.[32] For example we could deduce the relationship of an "attitude" to an attitude measurement instrument as follows:

Statement 1: The direction and strength of attitudes induces a systematic bias concerning beliefs about a social object

Statement 2: The beliefs about social objects can be measured by an information test

Statement 3: The direction and strength of attitudes can be measured by the bias in an information test

In this kind of test we do not measure the concept directly but rather its effect. The inference from the measure to the construct can be done only after a transformation of the data has taken place that takes into account the various concepts determining the variance in the data. The truth of the auxiliary hypothesis, in this case, is a function of the truth of the theory from which it has been deduced, and it has to be tested within this context.

Another possibility is to use a direct measure. This is the alternative most often chosen by researchers. Howard and Sheth, for example, chose this option by linking certain of their hypothetical constructs or operational measures.[33] Farley and Ring, in their testing of the Howard and Sheth theory, have given operational definitions to the remaining hypothetical constructs.[34] It must be said that this kind of correspondence rule tends to confer on the correspondence rules the character of more or less independent empirical assumptions—that is, independent from the theory they are testing. The problem with such a procedure is that one could always deal with apparent refutations at the observation level by arbitrarily modifying the correspondence rules.[35] Consequently, a refutation of the theory is made very difficult. Farley and Ring provide an example of the tendency, albeit justified in their case, to question the correspondence rules rather than the theory when they suggest that "the model was useful for organizing this analysis of consumer behavior, but the test put extreme pressures on the data. *Con-*

---

[32] Mary Hesse, "Is There an Independent Observation Language?" p. 67; Paul F. Lazarsfeld, "Concepts Formation and Measurement in the Behavioral Sciences: Some Historical Observations" and Hempel, *Philosophy of Natural Science*, p. 23.

[33] John A. Howard and Jagdish N. Sheth, *The Theory of Buyer Behavior.*

[34] John U. Farley and Winston L. Ring, "An Empirical Test of the Howard-Sheth Model of Buyer Behavior."

[35] Hesse, "Is There an Independent Observation Language?" p. 68.

siderably improved data collection techniques and procedures will be needed before the full empirical potential of such models will be realized."[36]

A third view of correspondence rules regards such propositions as neither deducible theorems nor more or less independent empirical assumptions. Rather, the correspondence rule is the result of an "inductive or analogical inference from other accepted empirical correlations."[37] Thus, in this view, the relationship of the theoretical concept to the observational base is dependent on a model.[38] Accordingly, the use of attitude questionnaires as a measure of attitudes can be justified by noting that linguistic structures are analogous to mental structures. Figure 3.2 gives an overview of the various types of propositions discussed.

Figure 3.2   Kinds of propositions.

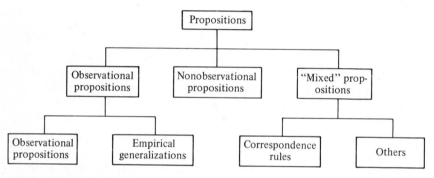

TYPES OF RELATIONSHIPS

Propositions involve statements of relationship between concepts. Either explicitly or implicitly we find statements describing interactions between or among the concepts contained in the proposition. The relationships may be stated with more or less specificity. Specificity may be relevant in several ways. First, there is specificity in terms of how explicit the mechanism assumed in the proposition is. This involves different levels of understanding in explanation (see Chapter 6). Second, there is specificity in terms of identifying other conditions affecting the propositional relationship. What exogenous or intervening variables can we specify as being relevant to the proposition? Among the most specific relationships are quantitative directional relationships assuming cause and effect. As the strength of some measured attribute of one concept changes so is there a change in the strength of a causally associated attribute of another concept. For example, consider the following hypoth-

---

[36] Farley and Ring, "An Empirical Test of the Howard-Sheth Model of Buyer Behavior," p. 427. Italics added.
[37] Hesse, "Is There An Independent Observation Language?" pp. 67 ff.
[38] Mary Hesse, "Laws and Theories," p. 406.

esis: "A consumer will distort (shift) his affective reaction to a specific product characteristic in the negative direction when that characteristic is linked to an unfamiliar (highly ambiguous) brand name."[39] Here degree of ambiguity is causally linked to changes in negative affect strength. Abell would point out that the connectives relating two concepts or variables (a variable being a measured concept) may be observational or theoretical.[40] Such connectives as "increase with" or "if A then B" are observational, and connectives such as "cause" or "function to" are theoretical in nature. In practical circumstances "cause" may be manifest by "increases with." The causality issue has been aptly described as an "extensive philosophical thicket."[41] Nevertheless it is important that the notion be raised and, following Abell, we shall present a few basic requirements for propositions where internal structures approximate the form "A causes B."[42] First, cause is a theoretical concept. It is inferred from observations made which are consistent with some causal account. Thus causation is not observed but inferred. Second, A and B must be defined or operationalized independently such that the indicators involved for each are mutually exclusive. A third but highly debatable point is that A must be temporally prior to B. This ignores, however, the fact that the anticipation of an event may bring about its own causes, which is not the same as reciprocal causation. Fourth, causal links cannot necessarily be inferred, even with perfect correlation between A and B. Fifth, a known causal link between two concepts does not always imply correlation between them. Sometimes, other variables may interact with the independent variable of interest so as to cancel its effect on the dependent variable. For example, Jacoby et al. have concluded that "brand image (as mediated by brand name) does affect perception of quality, *especially for brands with strong positive images*."[43] Presumably, the proposition concerning brand image and quality perception is relevant primarily under conditions of strong positive images and not relevant, or at least less relevant, under other circumstances.

Sheth and Talarzyk have also noted an unexpected finding in a recent study in which the impact of perceived instrumentality of a brand of products (beliefs about a product's ability to satisfy needs or attitudes toward that brand) are muted or dampened by value importance (the importance

[39] Stephen J. Miller, Michael B. Mazis, and Peter L. Wright, "The Influence of Brand Ambiguity on Brand Attitude Development," p. 456.

[40] Peter Abell, *Model Building in Sociology.*

[41] Abell, p. 116; see also Mario Bunge, *Causality: The Place of the Causal Principle in Modern Science*; Hubert M. Blalock, Jr., *Causal Inferences in Nonexperimental Research*; and Hubert M. Blalock, Jr., ed., *Causal Models in the Social Sciences.*

[42] Abell, pp. 116–134.

[43] Jacoby, J., "Price, Brand Name, and Product Composition Characteristics as Determinants of Perceived Quality." Italics added.

of motives related to the consumption and use of the brand).[44] *Sixth*, a distinction should always be made between a logical statement of the conditions supporting a causal notion and the actual causal link or mechanism itself. *Seventh*, under conditions supporting a causal image or notion, there are three possible logical interpretations of the causal link: A is a necessary and sufficient condition for B; condition A is necessary but not sufficient for B and A is sufficient but not necessary for event B. Here we consider necessary and sufficient conditions both for the dependent variable and for support conditions. First, "A *necessary condition* is a state of affairs that would justify the prediction of the nonoccurrence of an event."[45] If a necessary condition were not present there would be no event. Thus we would want to ask whether the particular attribute of the variable concept viewed as the causal factor is a necessary condition. Furthermore, we would want to ask whether there are other variables whose absence or presence constitute necessary conditions for the so-called causal factor to have its impact. For example, store images may have an impact on perceived product quality only in interaction with price.[46] Thus a relatively high price may be necessary before store image can have an impact on perceived product quality. Are these variables taken into account by the proposition? Second, we must consider *sufficient conditions*, which are states of affairs justifying the prediction of an event: ". . . if A is a sufficient condition then given that we have observed A we would automatically expect to observe B."[47]

The element of *monotonicity* is another important characteristic of the relationships between variables contained in propositions. We must always ask whether the relationship is monotonic or nonmonotonic at least in the relevant range of operation.[48] It is particularly necessary to ask about monotonicity when "U-shaped" relationships are possible. The relationship between fear and likelihood of behavioral response has long been considered to be U-shaped.

Nonmonotonicity is an especially important factor to consider, since it suggests the existence of different explanations for different observed relationships between any two variables. An excellent detailed discussion of this can be found in Howard and Sheth, and only the basic idea is presented here.[49] Consider a proposed relationship between arousal and stimulus ambi-

---

[44] Jagdish N. Sheth and W. Wayne Talarzyk, "Perceived Instrumentality and Value Importance as Determinants of Attitudes."

[45] Harvey, *Explanation in Geography*, p. 395.

[46] J. E. Stafford and B. M. Ennis, "The Price-Quality Relationship: An Extension," *Journal of Marketing Research*.

[47] Harvey, *Explanation in Geography*, p. 395.

[48] For a discussion of an instance where nonmonotonicity was unexpectedly found in an assumed linear relationship between prospect status and exposure to print advertising, see Alvin J. Silk and Frank P. Geiger, "Advertisement Size and the Relationship between Product Usage and Advertising Exposure."

[49] Howard and Sheth, *The Theory of Buyer Behavior*.

guity such as shown in Figure 3.3. Notice that if data gathering and measurement were restricted to the X_0–X_1 range, or, importantly, if the observations were made when X_0–X_1 was the relevant range, we would have a proposition to the effect that the greater the stimulus ambiguity (for example, the ambiguity of the advertising), the lower the level of consumer arousal. On the other hand, if data were collected from the X_1–X_2 range (or again, alternatively, when that range was the relevant market condition or was the range of stimulation used in the laboratory experiment), we would have a proposition saying that the greater the ambiguity of the advertisement the greater the level of consumer arousal. Conversely, as consumers learn more about a brand they have a lowered level of arousal with regard to it.

Figure 3.3   Relationship between arousal and stimulus ambiguity.

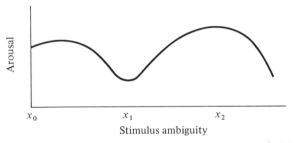

Stimulus ambiguity

Source: John Howard and Jagdish Sheth, *The Theory of Buyer Behavior*, p. 161, © 1969 by John Wiley & Sons, Inc. Reprinted by permission of John Wiley & Sons, Inc.

(Arousal is used here in the information-seeking sense rather than in an affective sense.) In both instances the propositions would be correct interpretations but neither would fully disclose the true nature of the relationships between the two concepts of concern. It is also particularly important to note that although the propositions based on data from X_0–X_1 and X_2–X_3 are the same sententially or verbally, rather different conditions may be inherent in two propositions. Moreover, as the consumer moves to the right on the segment of the curve between X_1 and X_2, stimulus ambiguity increases and hence arousal increases, and as ambiguity decreases arousal decreases; hence in a measurement sense these two propositions are identical. This is very misleading, however; clearly the cognitive state of the consumer is very different in the two situations. In the one case he presumably tries to structure a stimulus and in the other he has presumably already adequately structured the vague stimulus. Although these are not the points that Howard and Sheth are explicitly concerned with, the reader is urged to consult their work for explanations of consumer behavior that underlie the different slopes in Figure 3.3 and the observations made above concerning this figure.

In some instances nonmonotonicity is due to qualitative changes that occur as changes in strength take place. Rather different attributes of a concept may function at different levels of strength. For instance, as the perceived threat posed by an instance of social change increases in salience to an individual, different psychological mechanisms (attributes) of resistance (the concept) are called into play. It is not only a matter of the greater the perceived threat the greater the resistance but also a matter of a different kind of resistance.

The notion of *threshold* is also relevant to the problem of monotonicity: Does any degree of change in the causal variable produce a change in the dependent variable or does a critical threshold of change in the causal variable have to be reached before a measurable change in the dependent variable can be brought about? If so, does the statement of the proposition acknowledge this? A proposition that does acknowledge this has been suggested by Rogers and Shoemaker.[50] They propose that as the level of knowledge and adoption in a social system increases there is a cumulatively increasing pressure on the nonadopter to adopt. They refer to this as the "diffusion effect" and tie it directly to thresholds: ". . . as the rate of awareness-knowledge of the innovation increased up to about 20–30 percent, there was almost no adoption. Then once this threshold was passed, each additional percentage of awareness-knowledge in the system was associated with several percentage increases in the rate of adoption."[51]

THE SEARCH FOR TRUTH: FROM HYPOTHESES TO LAWS

In this section propositions will be considered in a more dynamic perspective: we will examine the conditions that a candidate proposition has to meet in order to qualify as a scientific hypothesis and the way hypotheses upgrade to laws. Following Bunge, a hypothesis will be defined as a specific type of proposition that (1) refers to facts that are unexperienced or perhaps in principle unexperientiable (for example, nonobservable events whose effects, however, are observable) and (2) is corrigible in view of fresh knowledge.[52] It follows that any hypothesis goes beyond the data it purports to account for and has a greater context than the empirical propositions it covers. A *scientific hypothesis* has the following additional characteristics.[53]

1. The hypothesis must be *well formed*; that is, it must be correct. It is remembered that permissible sign combinations are ruled by formation rules.
2. The hypothesis must be *meaningful*; that is, it must have a semantical content in some scientific context. It is remembered here that permissible sign combinations are also rules by designation rules.
3. The hypothesis must be *empirically testable*.

---

[50] Rogers and Shoemaker, *Communication of Innovations*.
[51] Rogers and Shoemaker, p. 163.
[52] Bunge, *Scientific Research*, Vol. I, p. 222.
[53] Bunge, p. 229.

4. Finally, the hypothesis must be *grounded* or *compatible* with previous knowledge.

Conditions 1 and 2 have been already touched upon in other chapters or sections and consequently will not be further elaborated upon here. Condition 4 will be considered as a weak requirement (that is, rather as a conservative warrant that the hypothesis is worth formulating). Scientific research presupposes some already *existing* scientific knowledge but should by no means be limited to it.[54] Consequently, the focus here will be primarily on condition 3, namely the problem of testability. This, of course, is linked to the semantical status of the candidate proposition.

TESTABLE-IN-PRINCIPLE PROPOSITIONS

The first distinction to be drawn is between analytic and synthetic propositions. *Analytic propositions* are propositions that can only be logically true or false.[55] They cannot be factually true or false. All propositions of formal science (except for the axioms) are analytic propositions. *Synthetic propositions*, on the other hand, can be factually true or false. In factual science, both types of propositions occur. Operational definitions, and, in general, all nominal definitions, are instances of analytic propositions. Thus, the statement "brand loyalty is the proportion of a household's product purchase devoted to the most frequently purchased brand" cannot be pronounced true or false. Rather, as we saw in the preceding chapter, it may be more or less useful, depending on the predictive power of brand loyalty so defined, and depending further on the concept's reliability. Compare this with the following synthetic proposition: "word-of-mouth influences subsequent intention to purchase."[56] It is obvious that this statement is subject to empirical validation; that is, it may be factually true or false. Consequently, the problem of testability applies only to synthetic propositions.

Among synthetic propositions one has to sort out next those that can be subjected to an empirical test and those that cannot. The latter will be said to have no "*empirical significance*."[57]

Empirical generalizations pose no problem in this respect, for the observational concepts guarantee "testability in principle." Testability in principle means that "it must be possible to derive from T (a hypothesis or set of hypotheses), . . . certain test implications of the form; if test conditions C are realized, then outcome B will occur. But the test conditions need not be

[54] On this point and the concept of a scientific paradigm, see Thomas S. Kuhn, *The Structure of Scientific Revolutions*.

[55] See D. W. Hamlyn, "Analytic and Synthetic Statements"; also Carnap, *Introduction to Symbolic Logic and Its Applications*, pp. 16–18, and Caws, *The Philosophy of Science*, pp. 135–136.

[56] Terrence V. O'Brien, "Tracking Consumer Decision Making," p. 39.

[57] Rudolf Carnap, "The Methodological Character of Theoretical Concepts."

realized or technologically realizable at the time when T is propounded or contemplated."[58]

Correspondence rules and, more generally, propositions containing observational and nonobservational concepts are by definition "linking up" with the observational plane and are thus more likely to be empirically significant.

The problem of testability arises with respect to *nonobservational propositions*: When they are not related to the realm of observation by correspondence rules they are *empirically* insignificant and cannot qualify as hypotheses in the sense defined here. If one sorts out the empirically meaningless nonobservational propositions, one is left with a set of propositions that are "testable in principle." One may now ask whether a truth value can, in principle, be assigned to such hypotheses—that is, whether they can be refuted or confirmed, or falsified or verified, respectively.

CONFIRMABLE AND/OR REFUTABLE HYPOTHESES

With respect to the confirmability of an hypothesis we can distinguish between (1) *purely confirmable*, (2) *purely refutable*, and (3) *both confirmable and refutable hypotheses.*[59]

All existential propositions are *purely confirmable hypotheses.*[60] For example, the hypothesis "there are opinion leaders within industrial firms . . ."[61] is a purely confirmable hypothesis. If a number of studies failed to discover opinion leaders in industrial firms this would still not refute the possibility of eventually discovering them at some future time. Such hypotheses, even though they are irrefutable, are of heuristic value. They are quite often fundamental assumptions underlying a research strategy and, as such, have more of a programmatic than empirical character (for example, the hypothesis that diffusion is essentially a communication process).[62]

Another major class of hypotheses that are primarily confirmable and only weakly refutable are propositions involving probability statements. In marketing, this can be exemplified by the various learning and Markov models that are being proposed. Here, the hypothesis is whether the particular model is "applicable" to consumer behavior or not. The procedure followed is to compare the model's predictions with the actual events and to compute a "goodness-of-fit" measure. Only if the "goodness-of-fit" measure is low is the hypothesis of applicability rejected, and only for the particular application tested.[63]

Next, there are those hypotheses that are *purely refutable*. These are the

---

[58] Hempel, *Philosophy of Natural Science*, p. 30.
[59] Bunge, *Scientific Research*, Vol. I, p. 266.
[60] See Karl R. Popper, *The Logic of Scientific Discovery*, p. 69.
[61] J. A. Martilla, "Word-of-Mouth Communication in the Industrial Adoption Process."
[62] Thomas S. Robertson, *Innovative Behavior and Communication*, p. x.
[63] See Frank M. Bass, "Testing vs. Estimation in Simultaneous-Equation Regression Models," p. 389.

universal propositions (see above). Although they can never be confirmed, a single negative instance suffices to refute them; this has been called the *asymmetry* between verifiability and falsifiability.[64] As an example of such a hypothesis, consider: "All innovators are cosmopolite." We need to find only one case of an innovator who happens not to be cosmopolite to refute this hypothesis. Because universal propositions have an infinite universe of discourse, they can never be confirmed even if all existing testing experience is supportive. Theoretically, there will always be a remaining uninvestigated context which potentially could disconfirm the proposition.

The testing of such hypotheses is not undertaken directly, but by deriving certain test implications from them: for example, "All innovators are cosmopolite" leads to the test implication, "*A* is cosmopolite" (with the help of the auxiliary assumption, "*A* is an innovator"). While the original hypothesis was only refutable, "*A* is cosmopolite" is a singular proposition and, hence, both confirmable and refutable. In the event the singular proposition is refuted, the hypothesis from which it was derived may be considered refuted. In the event the proposition is confirmed, we still cannot say that the original hypothesis is therefore confirmed, both for the reason just given above (the infinite universe) and for a different reason, called the "fallacy of affirming the consequent."[65] Although we are assuming some kind of necessary connection between innovativeness and cosmopoliteness, this connection may, in fact, be spurious—that is, caused by some third factor or by any number of variables. For example, consider the hypothesis: "Messages that are congruent with the values of the audience lead to positive attitude change." From this hypothesis, we can derive the test implication: "Message *A* will lead to positive attitude change with audience *B*." The auxiliary assumptions required are the following: "Message *A* is congruent with the values of audience *B*," "Attitude questionnaire *X* is a valid measure of attitudes at time t and $t + 1$." Now suppose that we perform the experiment and actually obtain positive results. The natural inclination would be to say that the hypothesis was confirmed. Suppose, however, that another hypothesis had also received considerable empirical support, namely: "The administration of attitude questionnaires at time t leads to an increase in scores on the same questionnaire at time $t + 1$." This hypothesis, in effect, says that our positive result could have resulted not from the effect of our message but from previous testing. This situation obviously calls for "control;" that is, if we ever want to test the value-congruence hypothesis we either have to resort to different methods of measuring attitudes or we have to "control" for the effects of testing. The latter strategy is quite familiar; it is the strategy of "control groups."[66] The results of an experiment using control groups,

[64] Popper, *The Logic of Scientific Discovery*, p. 7.
[65] Hempel, *Philosophy of Natural Science*, p. 7.
[66] Donald T. Campbell and Julian C. Stanley, *Experimental and Quasi-experimental Designs for Research*.

then, not only yields information about the hypothesis of primary interest but also on the hypothesis whose plausibility forced us to institute the control group in the first place. Therefore, our experiment may give some credibility to one, to both, or to neither, of the hypotheses. It is important to note that we are not forced to make a choice between the two hypotheses. Rather, they are complementary; that is, they are two different antecedents of the same effect. This situation differs quite clearly from that of a *"crucial test."* Whereas in the previous case the two hypotheses had more or less identical test implications, in the case of a crucial test the test implications of the two hypotheses are conflicting—that is, mutually exclusive; only one or the other may apply, but never both of them.

Finally, there are those hypotheses that are both *confirmable and refutable.* As an example, consider the following hypothesis: "High fear appeals will be more powerful in stimulating avoidant behavior (in a given test) than will low fear appeals."[67] Clearly, this hypothesis may be confirmed and refuted as well.

Figure 3.4 summarizes the preceding distinctions between the different types of hypotheses.

Figure 3.4   Types of hypotheses.

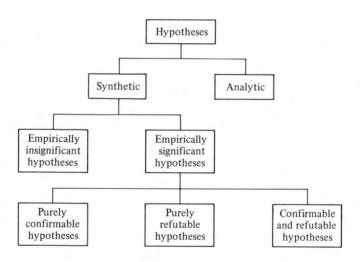

TYPE OF CONFIRMING EVIDENCE

By type of confirming evidence we refer to the variety in test settings and measurement procedures. The first maxim in this respect is that the increase in confirmation effected by an additional favorable test instance is less, the

---

[67] Michael L. Ray and William L. Wilkie, "Fear: The Potential of an Appeal Neglected by Marketing," and Howard Leventhal, "Fear Appeals and Persuasion: The Differentiation of a Motivational Construct."

greater the similarity of the new instance to the previous instances.[68] Stinchcombe argues that the more *different things* and the more *different kinds of implications* derived from a test situation the stronger the test of the theory.[69] This argument may be presented in the following way (adapted from Stinchcombe) where A is the hypothesis and B the test implication:

I	II	III
If A, then B	If A, then B	If A, then $B_1, B_2, \ldots B_n$,
B is false	B is true	where $B_1 \ldots _n$ are sim-
—	—	ilar
A is false	A is somewhat	$B_1 \ldots _n$ are true
	credible	—
		A is substantially more
		credible

If A, then $B_1, B_2, \ldots B_n$,
     where $B_1 \ldots _n$ are different
$B_1 \ldots _n$ are true
—
A is more credible

Thus in case I, if hypothesis A implies the test implication B and B is not found to hold, then we can conclude that A is false. On the other hand, in case II if B is found to hold or is true, then we may place at least some reliance upon A and consider it somewhat credible. Test situation IV is the strongest test, lending greater confirmability to hypothesis A than any of the previous test situations, in that it tests many things differing from one another. Consider the following hypothesis discussed by Ostland:[70] When high perceived risk is associated with a particular purchase decision, greater importance is attached to interpersonal communication (relative to impersonal sources, for example). Correspondence rules would be established for the concepts of perceived risk and interpersonal communication importance. If the hypothesis were substantiated with regard to a household appliance, we would establish a minimum level of confirmation or credibility. If two or more household appliances were involved and the hypothesis supported for each, we would have an even higher level of confirmation. Still stronger tests of the hypothesis would entail extending the test to durable goods other than household appliances and perhaps eventually to nondurable goods. The credibility in our hypothesis increases considerably and its range expands. This is to say that the universe of discourse to which the hypothesis has been successfully applied has increased. For example, when trying to confirm his four hypotheses about the personal characteristics of opinion leaders on consumer topics, Corey used three market studies each of a different consumer topic

[68] Hempel, *Philosophy of Natural Science*, pp. 33 ff.; Arthur L. Stinchcombe, *Constructing Social Theories*, pp. 17 ff.
[69] Stinchcombe, p. 20.
[70] Lyman Ostland, "Role Theory and Group Dynamics."

(food preparation, grocery products, and automobiles).[71] To conclude the discussion on this point, let us quote Hempel as saying that "the confirmation of a hypothesis depends not only on the quality of the favorable evidence available, but also on its variety: the greater the variety, the stronger the resulting support."[72]

One other point needs to be made concerning the universe of discourse covered by a hypothesis. Hypotheses are invented in order to account for a set of known facts or data (the denotation of the constituent concepts). It is now desirable that the hypothesis be confirmed by "new" evidence—that is, by facts that were not known or not taken into account when the hypothesis was formulated.[73] Webb *et al.* call these instances "outcroppings": "Any given theory has innumerable implications and makes innumerable predictions which are inaccessible to available measures at any given time."[74] New advances in measurement technology may provide an opportunity for testing the hypothesis where it previously had not been thought to apply.

GROUNDED HYPOTHESES

So far we have only considered the *evidential support* of hypotheses—that is, the support derived from comparing their predictions with the actual evidence obtained. In addition to evidential support, however, hypotheses must and can receive theoretical support (condition 4, page 65) in order to qualify as scientific hypotheses. As an example, consider the following statements: "When a response is followed by a reward (or 'reinforcement'), the frequency or probability of its recurrence increases" and "Satisfaction with a brand is positively related to brand purchase." The latter statement can be deduced (or subsumed) under the first statement. If we now presume that the first statement—the learning hypothesis—has received *independent* evidential support (that is, it has been tested in a variety of contexts excluding that of consumer behavior), then even before testing the product satisfaction generalization we have some confidence in the hypothesis already (a kind of *a priori* confidence).

In general, we can say that the credibility of a hypothesis depends "on the relevant parts of the total scientific knowledge at that time, including all the evidence relevant to the hypothesis and all the hypotheses and theories then accepted that have any bearing upon it."[75] No hypothesis can be

---

[71] Corey, "People Who Claim To Be Opinion Leaders," p. 49.

[72] Hempel, *Philosophy of Natural Science*, p. 34; for analogous arguments at the level of concepts see Donald T. Campbell, "Methodological Suggestions from a Comparative Psychology of Knowledge Processes."

[73] Hempel, *Philosophy of Natural Science*, p. 37.

[74] E. J. Webb, D. T. Campbell, R. D. Schwartz, and L. Sechrest, *Unobtrusive Measures: Nonreactive Research in the Social Sciences*, p. 28.

[75] Hempel, *Philosophy of Natural Science*, p. 45.

established or tested in isolation. The definition of constituent concepts requires the presence of some theoretical network, and so does its testing. For example, Seipel formulated the hypothesis that "the less demanded in return for a premium, the more positive the attitudes toward the company and its products"[76] and justified the formulation and testing of such an hypothesis by the fact that it is "founded on theories of attitudinal relationships stating that attitude objects (the company and its products) which are associated with a positively evaluated concept (the premium offer) will also be viewed positively."[76]

It should be recognized, however, that the requirement that an hypothesis be grounded is double-edged: On one side it certainly eliminated some non-scientific propositions; on the other side it may prevent or delay revolutionary hypotheses. In fact, it may happen that a change of *paradigm* is necessary.[77] In conclusion, the requirement of theoretical validation must be handled with extra care.

DEGREE OF CORROBORATION: THE EMERGENCE OF LAWS

Hypotheses may have varying degrees of corroboration. Naturally, those hypotheses commanding a high degree of corroboration have a somewhat special status in science. Those hypotheses are called "laws." *Laws*, therefore, are *hypotheses that are empirically corroborated to a degree regarded as satisfactory at a certain point in time.* As Harvey has it: "A scientific law may be interpreted most rigidly as a generalization which is empirically universally true, and one which is also an integral part of a theoretical system in which we have supreme confidence. Such a rigid interpretation would probably mean that scientific laws would be nonexistent in all the sciences. Scientists therefore relax these criteria to some degree in their practical application of the norm. The precise degree of relaxation remains very much a matter of individual judgment. . . ."[78] It is obvious that what is regarded as satisfactory at one time may turn out to be deficient at some later time.[79] The levels of tolerance for "satisfactory" corroboration are dependent on whether any alternatives to the existing laws and principles exist.[80] A slight discrepancy between predicted and observed results, which is considered as a corroborating instance in the absence of any rival hypothesis, may in other instances lead to the refutation of the same hypothesis.

[76] Carl-Magnus Seipel, "Premiums—Forgotten by Theory," p. 30.
[77] See Kuhn, *The Structure of Scientific Revolutions.*
[78] Harvey, *Explanation in Geography,* pp. 105–106.
[79] See Bunge, *Scientific Research,* Vol. I, p. 360; Caws, *The Philosophy of Science,* p. 83; and Donald T. Campbell, "Prospective: Artifact and Control.
[80] See Campbell, "Prospective," and Kuhn, *The Structure of Scientific Revolutions.*

CHAPTER 4

THEORIES

INTRODUCTION

The two preceding chapters dealt with the two basic units of language (terms and sentences) and thought (concepts and propositions). This chapter discusses the elements of a higher level of complexity, namely theories, which are broadly defined here as a set of connected propositions (or sentences). Just as propositions are connected concepts, so theories will be considered to be connected propositions (or sentences).

THE NATURE OF THEORIES 73

In the first section we will try to give the reader a preliminary understanding of the nature of theories. We will then examine, in a more rigorous way, the problem of defining theories. In the next section we will discuss the cognitive status of theories and in the sections following we will distinguish among different degrees of formalization of theories. The chapter will conclude with a comparison of models and theories. The next chapter presents a set of criteria for evaluating theories and applies these criteria to three major theories in the consumer behavior field.

THE NATURE OF THEORIES˙

The difference between theories and propositions is one of degree rather than of kind. As we move from empirical generalizations to nonobservational propositions a certain degree of systemicity develops, in the sense that we need auxiliary assumptions to test our nonobservational propositions directly and other nonobservational propositions to test them indirectly. Similarly, as our concepts evolve from operationally defined concepts through traits to theoretical concepts, a network is emerging that may bear the name "theory." Let us pursue this "network" analogy a little bit further in order to get an intuitive feeling for the structure of a theory. Hempel has given the classical account of the traditional view of this network:

A scientific theory might therefore be likened to a complex spatial network: Its terms are represented by the knots, while the threads connecting the latter correspond, in part, to the definitions, and, in part, to the fundamental and derivative hypotheses included in the theory. The whole system floats, as it were, above the plane of observation and is anchored to it by rules of interpretation. These might be viewed as strings, which are not part of the network but link certain points of the latter with specific places in the plane of observation. By virtue of those interpretive connections, the network can function as a scientific theory: From certain observational data, we may ascend, via an interpretive string, to some point in the theoretical network, thence proceed, via definitions and hypotheses, to other points, from which another interpretive string permits a descent to the plane of observation.[1]

Even though Hempel's account of a theory has not been spared from criticism by fellow philosophers of science,[2] it provides a convenient analogy. It integrates a number of metatheoretical concepts that we have been discussing in the preceding chapter. Figure 4.1 is a representation of this network, albeit in some modified form, and contains most of the discussed concepts. Next, let us suppose that we want to give a concrete example of a "minitheory" and see whether it can be represented in this way (see Figure

[1] Carl G. Hempel, "Fundamentals of Concept Formation in Empirical Science," p. 36.
[2] See, for example, Mary Hesse, "Is There an Independent Observation Language?"

Figure 4.1   Representation of a theory as a conceptual network.

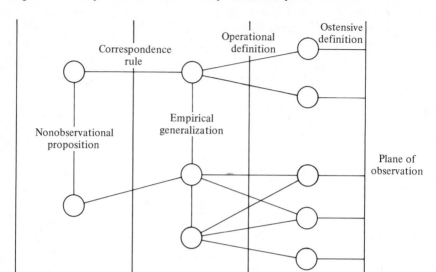

4.2). We shall need two theoretical concepts, say "response" and "reward" (or "reinforcement"). The theoretical proposition relating the two concepts is "When a response is followed by a reward (or reinforcement), the frequency or probability of its recurrence increases." The attributes of the two concepts, which are the immediate constituents of this proposition, are "the probability of recurrence" as an attribute of "response" and the existence and time-index ("following" the response) of the reward. As correspondence rules we shall have the following (two) propositions: "brand purchase is a response," "satisfaction with brand is a reward." Next, we can define "brand purchase" and "satisfaction with brand" operationally. For the first one, we may say, "entry in a purchase diary," or "a consumer putting brand X into his shopping bag at the checkout counter." "Satisfaction with brand" may be defined operationally as follows: "Check 'very satisfied' for the question 'Are you satisfied with brand X?' on a questionnaire." We have given two operational definitions of brand purchase. Consequently, we really have two correspondence rules for this concept, namely, "brand purchase 1 is response" and "brand purchase 2 is response." Some of the relatively observational concepts in our system are: "entry," "purchase diary," "consumer," "putting," "brand," "shopping bag," "check," "question," and "questionnaire."

THE DEFINITION OF A THEORY

The term "theory" has been defined in various ways; Table 4.1 gives a set of fairly representative definitions. This table illustrates the idea that it is

Figure 4.2   A response-reward theory.

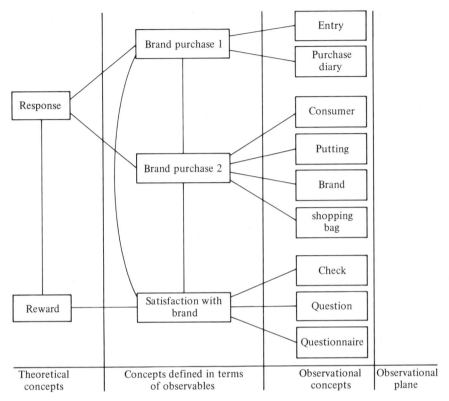

| Theoretical concepts | Concepts defined in terms of observables | Observational concepts | Observational plane |

possible to look at theories from various points of view. First, they may be seen as conceptual systems. Second, the conceptual system is represented by a linguistic structure. First, from a conceptual point of view, theories can be considered *as a set of propositions*. We recall that, in turn, propositions were previously defined as interconnected concepts. Second, looking at theories as conceptual systems raises the question of the nature of the medium. In other words, how shall the concepts be represented? Usually, one is "inclined to reserve the term 'theory' for more discursive utterances, and particularly for those which can be put into propositional or bookish form."[3]

Consequently, from a formal point of view, a theory may also be considered as *a set of sentences*.

The duality of the nature of a theory (viewed either as a set of propositions or as set of statements) explain most of the differences found in the definitions listed in Table 4.1. Some authors (Hempel and Galtung, for example) emphasize the formal aspect of theories by defining them as sets of statements and sentences, whereas others (Bunge, Achinstein, and De Groot,

---

[3] William Sackstedter, " 'Theories' and Usage," p. 310.

Table 4.1   Definitions of Theory

Achinstein:	"T is a theory, relative to the context, if and only if T is a set of propositions that (depending on the context) is (was, might have been, and so forth) not known to be true or to be false but believed to be somewhat plausible, potentially explanatory, relatively fundamental, and somewhat integrated."[a]
Brodbeck:	"A deductively connected set of laws"[b]
Hempel:	A scientific theory "may be considered as a set of sentences expressed in terms of a specific vocabulary."[c]
Bunge:	"Theory designates a system of hypotheses."[d] "A set of scientific hypotheses is a scientific theory if and only if it refers to a given factual subject matter and every member of the set is either an initial assumption (axiom, subsidiary assumption, or datum) or a logical consequence of one or more initial assumptions."[d]
Rudner:	"A theory is a systematically related set of statements, including some lawlike generalizations, that is empirically testable."[e]
Labovitz and Hagedorn:	"A scientific theory: a set of interrelated propositions that comprise a deductive system."[f]
Galtung:	"Theory, T, is a structure (H, I) where H is a set of hypotheses and I is a relation in H called 'implication' or 'deducibility' so that H is weakly connected by I."[g]
De Groot:	A theory is "a system of logically interrelated, specifically noncontradictory, statements, ideas, and concepts relating to an area of reality, formulated in such a way that testable hypotheses can be derived from them."[h]
Nagel:	"The distinction between experimental laws and theories is based on the contention that laws subsumed under the first of these labels, unlike the laws falling under the second one, formulate relations between observable (or experimentally determinable) traits of some subject matter."[i]
Caws:	A theory "is a set of universal propositions asserted by means of a corresponding set of universal sentences."[j]

[a] Peter Achinstein, *Concepts of Science: A Philosophical Analysis*, p. 129.
[b] May Brodbeck, "Models, Meaning and Theories," in May Brodbeck (ed)., *Readings in the Philosophy of the Social Sciences.*
[c] Carl G. Hempel, *Aspects of Scientific Explanation*, p. 182.
[d] Mario Bunge, *Scientific Research*, Vol. I, p. 387.
[e] Richard S. Rudner, *Philosophy of Social Science*, p. 10.
[f] Sanford Labovitz and Robert Hagedorn, *Introduction to Social Research*, p. 111.

for example) stress more their semantical aspects. In the remainder of this chapter we will try to put an equal emphasis on both aspects and consider interchangeably a theory as a set of propositions.

Let us address ourselves more explicitly to the question of what the *constitutive* characteristics of a theory are. Four criteria are generally thought to be necessary.

CRITERION 1: THERE MUST BE MORE THAN ONE PROPOSITION (SENTENCE)

The use of the term "set" in some of the definitions implies that a theory is composed of more than one proposition. The limitation of this criterion should be obvious to the reader, for it is always possible to combine propositions. Thus, the adopting of the "number of propositions"—the criterion—results in calling essentially the same conceptual system a *proposition* in one case and a theory in the other case, the only difference being the syntactical "phrasing" of the system. We must realize that syntactical manipulations can transform our "theory" into a "proposition" and vice versa. As an example, consider the following "proposition":

$$y = f(x, \ z, \ w)$$

Where Y is defined as consumer behavior, x as affective, z as cognitive predisposition, and w as behavioral intention. This "proposition" can now be easily transformed into a "theory" by simply decomposing it into

$$y = g(v)$$
$$v = h(x, \ z, \ w)$$

CRITERION 2: THE EXISTENCE OF NONOBSERVATIONAL PROPOSITIONS

If we accept the idea that theories are sets of propositions, we must specify whether we mean any type of proposition or rather certain types. These propositions are of various types. As indicated in Chapter 3, there are analytic and synthetic propositions. The analytic propositions are represented by the operational (nominal) definitions of the variables. Among the synthetic propositions, theories comprise empirical generalizations, correspondence rules, and nonobservational propositions. Which of these components are necessary in order for a system of propositions to qualify as a theory? Generally speaking, it is stated that a theory should contain nonobservational propositions. This view is however not entirely uncontested. Rudner,[4] for example, stipulates only "lawlike generalizations," which, even though he

g Johan Galtung, *Theory and Methods of Social Research*, p. 451.

h Adriaan D. de Groot, *Methodology: Foundations of Inference and Research in the Behavioral Sciences*, p. 40.

4 Ernest Nagel, *The Structure of Science: Problems in the Logic of Scientific, Explanation*, p. 81.

j Peter Caws, *The Philosophy of Science: A Systematic Account*, p. 87.

does not define them, are generally what we called "empirical generalizations" with a satisfactory degree of corroboration—that is, "laws." Nagel, on the other hand, makes a fundamental distinction between theories and what he calls "experimental laws"[4] Bunge, somewhat more tolerant than Nagel, does not make the existence of nonobservational propositions a *sine qua non* of theories.[4] Nevertheless, he suggests different names for systems that contain nonobservational propositions and for those that do not. The latter he calls black-box theories.[5] He characterizes black-box theories in the following way: "A black box theory treats its object or subject matter as if it were a system devoid of internal structure: it focuses on the system's behavior and handles the system as a single unit. A black box theory will accordingly account for overall behavior in terms of relations among global variables such as net causes (inputs) and net effects (outputs); these will be mediated by referentless intervening variables."[6] Behavioral psychology can be considered as taking a black-box approach. Its adherents believe that "a science of behavior could be built up on the level of the gross observable reactions of organisms dealt with by the everyday language of action concepts. That is, functional relations could be discovered in which these gross reactions would be the dependent variables."[7] The parameters in the equations relating observable stimulus conditions and observable responses remain, in general, uninterpreted; that is, they are treated as intervening variables rather than as hypothetical constructs.[8]

The treatment of buyer behavior in terms of Marshallian, Pavlovian, Freudian, and other models is an example of black-box models in marketing.[9] The application of Markov models to consumer behavior can also be seen as a black-box approach, for the transition probabilities are purely empirical concepts; that is, they are derived from the observations and are not hypothesized to refer to any real property for the consumers. More phenomenologically oriented approaches to consumer behavior, however, more or less posit the existence of some real referent for the parameters mediating between observable stimuli and observable responses. As an example, consider Levy's discussion of some of consumers' thoughts that mediate between a particular TV commercial and the response to it: "Women seem to feel that this commercial

---

[4] See Table 4.1.
[5] Mario Bunge, *Scientific Research*, Vol. I, pp. 506ff.
[6] Bunge, p. 509.
[7] Charles Taylor, "Psychological Behaviorism," p. 517.
[8] See K. MacCorquodale and P. E. Meehl, "On a Distinction between Hypothetical Constructs and Intervening Variables."
[9] D. L. Kanter, "The Way You Test Advertising Depends upon the Approach the Advertising Itself Takes, Says Researcher," and an unpublished 1963 item by Kanter, both cited in Francesco M. Nicosia and Barr Rosenberg, "Substantive Modeling in Consumer Attitude Research: Some Practical Uses." See also Philip Kotler, *Marketing Management*, pp. 101–112.

will convey to husband and children the rewards they are able to offer them, if they so desire. . . . Another indirect reference is derived from the emphasis respondents place on the originality of this presentation. They feel that the company wants to please and entertain them as well as sell the product. These two factors lead to good feelings toward the brand and the company."[10] There can be no doubt that in such an analysis the intervening variables are treated not as convenient calculating devices to help summarize empirical data, but that they refer to real properties and events that take place in the consumer's mind.

Bunge notes that black-box theories have the advantages of being highly general, wholistic, epistemologically simple, accurate, and safe. Their disadvantages include their low content, low testability, and low heuristic power.[11]

CRITERION 3: DEDUCIBILITY

This dimension is a syntactical property of theories and is particularly stressed by Galtung, Labovitz and Hagedorn, Brodbeck, and Bunge.[12] Note that it is not a property of a single proposition but of a set of propositions. It makes for the systematicity of the set.[13] Systematicity is usually not achieved, and may not even be desirable, during the construction stage of theories. It is being promoted, however, during the reconstruction stage. "Reconstruction" of a theory consists of the "explicit and complete symbolic (nonverbal) formulation of the theory's axioms and in the fullest possible statement, or else mention, of the theory's presupposition and rules. . . ."[14] The attempt to systematize a given field will start with establishing hypotheses that have been proposed to account for them. For example, an attempt might be made to use Howard and Sheth's theory to derive the empirical generalization reported in Engel, Kollat, and Blackwell's review of consumer behavior research. Next, it should be possible to deduce a large number of empirical generalizations that have not yet been investigated. As an example, Copley and Callom deduced that the relationship between perceived risk and information search behavior in an industrial marketing setup should follow the Berlyne function, as suggested by Howard and Sheth, and proceeded to test their deduction.[15] Similarly Bennett and Mandell tested implications of the Howard and Sheth theory for the prepurchase information-seeking behavior of new-car purchasers.[16] The deduction and confirmation of new propositions

[10] Sidney J. Levy, "Promotional Behavior," p. 402.
[11] Bunge, Scientific Research, Vol. I, pp. 512–513.
[12] See Table 4.1.
[13] Rudner, Philosophy of Social Science, pp. 10–11.
[14] Bunge, Scientific Research, Vol. I, p. 482.
[15] Thomas P. Copley and Frank L. Callom, "Industrial Search Behavior and Perceived Risk."
[16] Peter D. Bennett and Robert M. Mandell, "Prepurchase Information-Seeking Behavior of New Car Purchasers—The Learning Hypothesis."

increases the number of propositions that a theory encompasses. Thus, at any given point in time, we can distinguish between the actual and the potential set of propositions of a theory. Historically speaking, a theory is then a growing set of propositions.[17]

CRITERION 4: TESTABILITY IN PRINCIPLE

This is an epistemological characteristic of theories. A theory may be syntactically valid and it may be meaningful (that is, it is an interpreted rather than an abstract theory), but it may still lack empirical significance. In addition to the rules of interpretation that are necessary to make an abstract theory meaningful, correspondence rules are necessary to make it empirically significant—that is, provide for testability. With the addition of correspondence rules, a theory is likened to a network.[18] In such a network the knots represent the concepts and the threads connecting the latter represent, in part, definitions, empirical generalizations, correspondence rules, and hypotheses. This network floats above the realm of observation and touches it only along the edges, which correspond to the operationally defined concepts. Quine expresses this in the following way: "The totality of our so-called knowledge or beliefs, from the most casual matters of geography and history to the profoundest laws of atomic physics or even of pure mathematics and logic, is a man-made fabric which impinges on experience only along the edges."[19]

As an example of such a theoretical network, consider the partial theory shown in Figure 4.3.[20] "Purchase" and "search for information" refer to observable behavior of consumers. Between "satisfaction," "brand comprehension," and "attitude" the following relationships can be said to hold: If the purchase of a brand is followed by satisfaction, then brand comprehension will change in the direction of the new information, and consequently attitude will change. Furthermore, the more positive the attitude toward a brand, the lesser the extent to which information concerning this brand will be sought. If one wanted to test this hypothesis, observations of purchase behavior and of information-seeking behavior would be required. In addition, "satisfaction" would have to be operationally defined, and a correspondence rule linking "satisfaction" and "satisfaction'" would have to be introduced and its validation attempted. Bennett and Mandell actually attempted to test this hypothesis in two versions: (1) "As the total number of reinforced purchases of a brand increases, the amount of information seeking before purchase of *that* brand will decrease" and (2) "As the num-

---

[17] Bunge, *Scientific Research*, Vol. I, p. 410.
[18] See Carl G. Hempel, "Fundamentals of Concept Formation in Empirical Science."
[19] Willard V. O. Quine, *From a Logical Point of View*, p. 42.
[20] This example follows John A. Howard and Jagdish N. Sheth, *The Theory of Buyer Behavior*.

ber of *sequential* reinforced purchases of a brand increases, the amount of information seeking before purchase of *that* brand will decrease."[21] Judging from their presentation, however, they did not actually test these hypotheses because nowhere do they discuss how they determined whether a purchase was reinforced or not—that is, whether satisfaction was obtained after each purchase or not. Consequently, their findings lend only support to the hypothesis that as the *number of purchases* of a brand increases, the information-seeking behavior concerning this brand will decrease regardless of whether satisfaction was present or not. (Maybe their implicit assumption was that, as the number of repeat purchases of a brand increased, it is likely that the consumer is satisfied with the product, for he would not repeat his purchases otherwise.)

Figure 4.3   Example of a theoretical network.

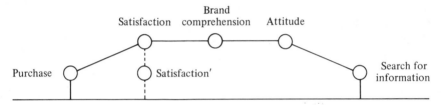

THE "COGNITIVE STATUS" OF THEORIES

The expression "cognitive status" of theories has been used by Nagel for referring to the question of whether theories have real referents or not. These questions arise primarily with respect to the theoretical concepts—that is, those concepts that are nonobservable. There are three basic positions with respect to this problem, namely reductionism, instrumentalism, and realism. These three positions are briefly described in the following.

REDUCTIONISM

This position does not make any claims as to the existence of a real referent. Moreover, since the existence of hypothetical entities and events is uncertain, it may be better not to use them at all and to rely on what supposedly is "real," namely the observational concepts that refer directly to data. Consequently, it is required that all scientific statements should be exhaustively translated into or reduced to observation statements.[22] As an example, a statement such as "if the brand proves to be more satisfactory than the buyer expected, the attractiveness of the brand will be enhanced,"[23] in order to be valid according to the reductionist doctrine, will

---

[21] Bennett and Mandell, "Prepurchase Information-Seeking Behavior of New Car Purchasers," p. 431.

[22] Mary Hesse, "Laws and Theories," p. 406.

[23] Howard and Sheth, *The Theory of Buyer Behavior*, p. 475.

have to be translated into a statement containing only operationally defined concepts such as "the verbal response to a rating scale," "differences between verbal responses to a rating scale," and so forth.

Hesse mentions two principal arguments against the reductionist position:

> First, it can be shown that in many existing theories such translation cannot in fact be carried out, and yet no reputable theorist wishes to abandon otherwise satisfactory theories on this ground alone. Second, and more fundamental, it has been demonstrated—that if explicit definitions of all theoretical terms by means of observables could be carried out, theories would be incapable of growth and therefore useless."[24]

To illustrate the second point, it would certainly be possible to develop standard operational definitions for the "hypothetical constructs" of the Howard-Sheth buyer behavior theory. The question is whether such a procedure is desirable. Lehmann, Farley, and Howard note in this respect that "until operational definitions are agreed upon, it will be very difficult to apply results of one study to another situation."[25] This request overlooks the fact that it may not be possible to use the same operational definition in each context, and that today's standard is likely to be improved upon by advances both in theory and in measurement technology. Tying in the theory thus to a particular set of operational definitions would quickly lead to its obsolescence. In addition, one must take into account the fact that any singular measure of hypothetical constructs contains not only object but also method factors: ". . . the sense data or meter readings are now understood as the result of a transaction in which both the observer (a meter) and the object of investigation contribute to the form of the data."[26] Consequently, rather than having one standard operational definition, multiple operationalizations of each theoretical concept are required.[27]

INSTRUMENTALISM

According to the instrumentalist position, theories are mere instruments, tools, or calculating devices. They constitute rules for the derivation of singular statements (explanations and predictions) from other singular statements (the initial conditions). For example, the singular statement "consumer A is more satisfied with brand X than he expected" can be "fed into" the theoretical statement that links brand satisfaction and brand

---

[24] Hesse, "Laws and Theories," pp. 406–407.
[25] Donald R. Lehmann, John U. Farley, and John A. Howard, "Testing of Buyer Behavior Models."
[26] Donald T. Campbell, "Distinguishing Differences of Perception from Failures of Communication in Cross-Cultural Studies," p. 331.
[27] See Campbell, p. 331.

attitude, as mentioned earlier. The singular statement "consumer A's attitude toward brand X has improved" results as a prediction. The theoretical concepts thus serve only to transform observation statements into different observation statements. The fact that one may use one and the same abstract theory to derive interpreted theories bearing upon widely divergent subject matters lends further plausibility to the instrumentalist position.

Hesse has advanced two arguments against the instrumentalist position.[28] First of all, the analogy between tools and theories is not quite correct in that we demand specific, well-adapted tools for different purposes. In contrast with that, we *do* look for "universal theories." Although marketing practitioners would be quite satisfied with having useful rules for predicting the sales of toothpaste, of freeze-dried coffee, color TV sets, and so forth, researchers in marketing and other areas will always look for the common theory that would integrate a number of diverse phenomena. Hesse's second argument is that theories are (or should be) subject to falsification, and that those theories that are falsified are being discarded from the scientific scene even if they continue to be used in applications—for predictive purposes, for example. Kaplan mentions a third argument— namely, that there are instances when a purely theoretical entity, due to better instruments, becomes observable.[29]

REALISM

This is the third position concerning the cognitive status of theories. Its proponents contend that "theories consist of true or false statements referring to 'real' or 'existing' entities."[30] This position has to contend with the problem of when one can say that something exists. Nagel discusses four criteria that are "commonly employed, whether explicitly or tacitly, when physical reality is either affirmed or denied of scientific objects."[31]

The first and most familiar criterion is "that the thing or event be publicly perceived when suitable conditions for its observation are realized."[31] This criterion covers concepts such as "information-seeking behavior," "a Ford Mustang," "a 30-second TV commercial" and so forth. It does not deal, however, with concepts such as "attitude," "motive," "perceived newness," and so forth.

A second criterion holds that "every nonlogical term of an assumed law (whether experimental or theoretical) designates something that is physically real, provided that the law is well supported by empirical evidence

28 Hesse, "Laws and Theories," p. 407.
29 Abraham Kaplan, *The Conduct of Inquiry: Methodology for Behavioral Science,* p. 307.
30 Hesse, "Laws and Theories," p. 407.
31 Nagel, *The Structure of Science,* p. 146.

and is generally accepted by the scientific community as likely to be true."[32]

A third criterion is that "a term designating anything physically real must enter into more than one experimental law. . . . The rationale for this requirement is to characterize as physically real only things that can be identified in ways other than, and independently of, the procedures used to define those things."[32] Campbell has dealt extensively with this criterion under the name of convergent validity.[33]

A fourth criterion notes that "the real is that which is under some stipulated set of transformations, changes, projections, or perspectives. . . . Thus some writers base denied physical reality to immediate sensory qualities, since these vary with physical, physiological and even psychological conditions."[34] It would seem that, for consumer behavior research, this is a variant of the preceding criterion of convergent validity. Observations by different researchers and/or instruments are correlated with each other and the agreement between the results supposedly represents those real properties that are invariant with respect to each observer's motives, biases, and so forth.

DEGREE OF FORMALIZATION OF THEORIES

Depending on the degree of formalization, it is possible to distinguish four main types of theoretical structures.[35]

DEDUCTIVELY COMPLETE THEORIES

These theories possess a "completely formal structure with the axioms fully specified and all steps in the deductive elaboration fully stated."[36] Within the social sciences, Hull's attempt to develop a hypothetico-deductive psychological theory can be cited as an example.

SYSTEMATIC PRESUPPOSITIONS

There are two major instances. (1) In the first instance (elliptic formulations), the theory contains formulations that presuppose a body of theory that itself is complete. For example, the use of probabilities presupposes probability theory. Every time an hypothesis is tested statistically a number of presuppositions are involved. They are not made explicit. (2) Whereas in the preceding instance the presuppositions referred to a fairly complete

---

[32] Nagel, p. 147.

[33] Donald T. Campbell and D. W. Fiske, "Convergent and Discriminant Validation by the Multitrait-Multimethod Matrix."

[34] Nagel, *The Structure of Science*, pp. 149–150.

[35] The discussion here follows the exposition of David Harvey, *Explanation in Geography*, pp. 97–99.

[36] Harvey, p. 97.

body of knowledge, in this case the area from which the presuppositions are derived is itself incomplete. This case would seem to occur extremely frequently in consumer behavior research. Every time the application of some psychological or sociological theory is proposed, the major presupposition seems to be that this theory is well adapted in the field of origin. Quite frequently, however, this is not the case. At best, the applied theory is one alternative among a set of equally plausible competing theories; at most, the theory has been disconfirmed for the particular purpose for which it is being proposed in the applied area.

QUASI-DEDUCTIVE THEORY

There are three varieties of quasi-deductive theory. First, theories containing probabilistic statements are only quasi-deductive because inductive rather than deductive logic establishes the links among the statements. Secondly, certain steps in the deduction are left out for reasons of exposition or for other reasons. Third, there are theories relying on *relative primitives*. This means that no set of terms may be designated as the basic or the ineliminable set in favor of which *all* other terms may be eliminated.

THEORETICAL ATTEMPTS

There are two kinds of theoretical attempts. The first consists of systems that can, "without any substantial modification of concept or manipulation, be rendered at least partially into formal structure."[37] Examples of such structures are Nicosia's and Howard and Sheth's models discussed in the next chapter. Both can be translated into formal structures, and the latter has already been formulated econometrically for testing purposes.[38] The second variety of theoretical statements are those verbal systems that "cannot be even partially formalized without a substantial modification of the concepts used and clarification of the deductive relationships proposed."[39] Most of the "theories" in consumer behavior research would seem to be of this kind.

CONCATENATED THEORIES

Kaplan proposes two types of theories, which also represent different degrees of formalization. The first type are *concatenated* theories. Such a theory is one "whose component laws enter into a network of relations so as to constitute an identifiable configuration or pattern. Most typically, they converge on some central point, each specifying one of the factors which

---

[37] Harvey, pp. 98–99.
[38] See John U. Farley and L. Winston Ring, "An Empirical Test of the Howard-Sheth Model of Buyer Behavior."
[39] Harvey, *Explanation in Geography*, p. 99.

play a part in the phenomenon which the theory is to explain."[40] Freudian theory is said to be of this type. For example, if one is attempting to explain a compulsive neurosis, "the theory tells us that compulsive behavior simultaneously provides substitute satisfactions for repressed desires . . . and guards against the arousal and/or satisfaction of the desire. . . . Furthermore, the theory tells us what kinds of desires are most often repressed."[41] Thus, the theory provides a pattern that suggests interpretations of particular cases. In the absence of laws specifying necessary and sufficient conditions, the theory points out plausible explanations, which can be narrowed down by the gathering of additional information. Consumer behavior, insofar as the explanation of individual behavior is concerned, would seem to be in a similar position. In order to explain a particular purchase decision there is no one set of variables nor particular law that helps us to explain it. Rather, a variety of concepts and laws that converge on this particular behavior have to be consulted. Addressing himself to those who expect to find a satisfactory explanation in terms of one set of variables (namely, personality variables), Kassarjian made the following pertinent comment: ". . . personality researchers in consumer behavior much too often ignore the many interrelated influences on the consumer decision process, ranging from price and packaging to availability, advertising, group influences, learned responses, and preferences of family members, in addition to personality. *To expect the influence of personality variables to account for a large portion of the variance is most certainly asking too much.*"[42] The theories by Nicosia and Howard and Sheth, with their comprehensive thrust, are attempts to comprise a large number of relevant concepts and relationships. They can thus be considered to be *concatenated* theories.

Concatenated theories would seem to follow primarily the *intensive* strategy for investigation. Its characteristic is that "a partial explanation of a whole region is made more and more adequate."[43] Consequently, its function is not to explain a limited subject matter, which is later on being enlarged (for example, to go from the explanation of chewing-gum brand choice to the explanation of food products and so forth), but to lay out "lines for subsequent theory and observation to follow, so as to yield a better understanding of the broad-scale phenomena which were their (the theories') primary concern."[43] Thus, Howard and Sheth make a very explicit statement of their intention to explain brand-choice behavior in general, both in consumer and industrial contexts, and not only for a particular type of product or a particular type of behavior—for example, repetitive as innovative behavior.

---

[40] Kaplan, *The Conduct of Inquiry*, p. 298.
[41] William P. Alston, "Logical Status of Psychoanalytic Theories," p. 514.
[42] Harold H. Kassarjian, "Personality and Consumer Behavior: A Review," p. 416.
[43] Kaplan, *The Conduct of Inquiry*, p. 305.

HIERARCHICAL THEORIES

Kaplan's second category encompasses *hierarchical* theories, in which the "component laws are presented as deductions from a small set of basic principles."[44] This type corresponds to what we have previously called deductively complete theories. For example, it is conceivable that Howard and Sheth's theory is deducible from some "master" psychological theory such as Hull's. This would mean that every relationship as proposed by Howard and Sheth can be shown to be a logical consequence of the basic principles. As a matter of fact, at the origin of this attempt lies such a derivation as can be seen from previous presentations by Howard.[45]

MODEL

DEFINITION OF THE TERM "MODEL"

The term "model," similarly to the term "theory," shows a "melancholic lack of uniformity in the vocabulary of scientists and others who talk about science."[46] It seems that there is only one common characteristic of the various usages. According to Kaplan, "we may say that any system A is a model of system B if the study of A is useful for the understanding of B without regard to any direct or indirect causal connection between A and B."[47] Hence, in most general terms, when there are at least two systems, one may function as a model of the other. The nature of either system does not matter; that is, it may be a physical, symbolic, conceptual, or real system. Consequently, the term "model" is not a one-place but a two-or-more-place predicate. In other words, it is meaningless to talk about a model without specifying to what other system(s) the model is to be related, just as it is meaningless to talk about leadership as a property of an individual.

Two notions are important with respect to models, namely *isomorphism* and *analogy*. Both terms designate relational properties between two or more systems. Analogy is the more general concept. It consists of formal and material analogy. *Formal analogy* is "analogy of structure or isomorphism between model and system, deriving from the fact that the same formal axiomatic and deductive relations connect individuals and predicates of both the system and its model."[48] In more general terms, Kaplan says that for two systems to be isomorphs means that "whenever a relation holds between two elements of one system a corresponding relation holds between the corresponding elements of the other system."[49] *Material or substantive analogy* refers to similarity between the individuals and predicates of the

44 Kaplan, p. 298.
45 John A. Howard, *Marketing Theory.*
46 Rudner, *Philosophy of Social Science*, p. 23.
47 Kaplan, *The Conduct of Inquiry*, p. 263.
48 Mary Hesse, "Models and Analogy in Science," p. 355.
49 Kaplan, *The Conduct of Inquiry*, p. 263.

two systems.[50] Systems may have formal but no material analogy, or they may have both types of analogy. Material without formal analogy is unlikely. "It does not seem possible to conceive of a material analogy without some formal analogy; if there is material analogy, there is presumably some consequent structural similarity that could—at least in principle—be formalized."[50] Material analogy is often used as the basis for inductions: "A simple generalization relating *A* and *B* is extended to cover cases of another kind, say *C* and *D*, because C is like *A* and *D* is like *B*."[51] Experiments on rats are often called analog experiments. Because of material analogies between rats and humans certain stimulus-response patterns observed with rats are generalized to cover humans too.

MODELS AND THEORIES

The distinction between these two concepts is not very clear. Rudner, for example, complains that "sometimes the two are employed simply as synonyms, sometimes 'model' is used to refer to any theoretical formulation other than a theory."[52] Simon is one of the authors to consider the two as synonymous: "In contemporary usage the term 'model' is, I think, simply a synonym for 'theory.' "[53] Lachman, for example, argues that "it will be useful to distinguish the formal theory from the *separate system* which is the model. . . . The model, consisting of a separate system, brings to bear an external organization of ideas, laws, or relationships upon the hypothetical propositions of a theory or the phenomena it encompasses."[54]

In order to delineate the relationship between models and theories we should recall that the immediate components of theories are linguistic entities—that is, verbal or mathematical signs and their combinations. This would seem to rule out the existence of material or substantive analogy between a theory and any other system. Harré explains why this is the case: "Whatever may have been the source of the symbol, no likeness or unlikeness it may bear to its subject matter counts as a reason why it is a symbol for, or of. Any sign would do as well, provided a symbol convention had been agreed for it."[55] Hence, if a theory stated in symbolic form were ever to serve as a model, it could only be in virtue of its structural analogy—that is, isomorphism—with some other system.

What are some of the systems to which a theory might stand in the relation of isomorphism? Before answering this question, we should make the distinction between abstract and interpreted theories.[56]

---

[50] Hesse, "Models and Analogy in Science," p. 355.
[51] Kaplan, *The Conduct of Inquiry*, p. 106.
[52] Rudner, *Philosophy of Social Science*, p. 23.
[53] H. A. Simon and A. Newell, "The Uses and Limitations of Models."
[54] Roy Lachman, "The Model in Theory Construction."
[55] R. Harré, *The Principles of Scientific Thinking*.
[56] See Bunge, *Scientific Research*, Vol. I, pp. 413ff.

A theory, if considered as a set of sentences, can be called *semantically abstract* if and only if none of its terms are interpreted or meaningful; *semiabstract* if some but not all of the symbols are interpreted, and *interpreted* if they are all interpreted.[57] One important characteristic of an abstract theory is that it "contains in seed an unlimited number of interpreted theories or models: abstract theories are *generic* by being uncommitted. In other words, a single abstract theory may underlie a number of specific (interpreted) theories; and once this is discovered formal derivations can be made once and for all for the entire set of interpreted theories having the same skeleton."[58] Kaplan calls this abstracted system a "formal model, a model *of* a theory which presents the theory purely as a structure of uninterpreted models."[59] On the other hand, consider that we start with an abstract theory. This is the case that has been extensively investigated by logicians: "Any set of entities that constitutes an interpretation of all the axioms and theorems of a system and in which those axioms and theorems hold true is called a model (in the logician's sense) of that system."[60] Consequently, an interpreted theory (that is, an empirical theory) can be regarded as a model of an abstract theory. Kaplan calls this an "interpretive model, providing an interpretation *for* a formal theory."[61] Remember also that "a simple abstract theory may underlie a number of specific (interpreted) theories.[62] Consequently, there may be a multitude of interpretive models for a formal theory, and all of the interpretations are structurally analogous. Hence, one interpreted theory may be a model for another interpreted theory, and vice versa. Rudner expresses this as follows: "One of such a pair of isomorphic theories may be regarded as being a model of, or furnishing a model for, the other. Which is regarded as the model, and which the theory of primary concern, will not depend on any structural feature of the two theories, but merely on which subject matter we are primarily interested in."[63] So far, we have looked at the isomorphism between a theory and some other linguistic system. A theory may however also be isomorphic to some nonlinguistic system. Kaplan describes this view: "The model is conceived as a structure of symbols interpreted in certain ways, and what it is a model of is the subject matter specified by the interpretation. Relations among the symbols are presumed to exhibit corresponding relations among the elements of the subject matter."[64] In addition to the subject matter, a theory may also stand in a relation of analogy to some other physical system.

[57] See Chapter 2 for the concept of interpretation.
[58] Bunge, *Scientific Research*, Vol. I, p. 414.
[59] Kaplan, *The Conduct of Inquiry*, p. 268.
[60] Hesse, "Models and Analogy in Science," p. 354.
[61] Kaplan, *The Conduct of Inquiry*, p. 268.
[62] Bunge, *Scientific Research*, Vol. I, p. 414.
[63] Rudner, *Philosophy of Social Science*, p. 25.
[64] Kaplan, *The Conduct of Inquiry*, p. 264.

Such systems have been called physical models or analogies. Kaplan gives the following examples: ". . . computer simulation of personality, or physical systems that model the economy or some part of it. . . . Psychodrama (role playing) and operational gaming may also be regarded as the use of physical models whose components are acts and events as well as objects."[65] Simon further illustrates the use of analogies in economies: "The idea that the flow of goods and money in an economy are somehow analogical to liquid flows is an old one. There now exists a hydraulic mechanism, the Moniac . . . one part of which is so arranged that when the level of the colored water in one tube is made to rise, the level in a second tube rises (*ceteris paribus*), but less than proportionately. I cannot 'state' this thing here, since its statements is not in words but in water. All I can give is a verbal (or mathematical) theory of the Moniac, which is, in turn, a hydraulic theory of the economy."[66] Later on, he asserts that the "content of the theory embodied in the Moniac is identical with the content of the theory embodied in the corresponding set of Keynesian equations or the corresponding set of verbal statements."[67] Figure 4.4 depicts the various systems with which a particular theory may enter into a model relationship. The tentative conclusion from the discussion of the theory vs. model problem is that the two concepts are quite compatible. A given system can be both a theory and a model at the same time, for it is a theory on the basis of its possession of certain characteristics (that is, testability, systemicity, and the presence of theoretical concepts), while it may be a model because of its relationship to other, similar systems.

Figure 4.4   Systems with which a particular theory may enter into a model relationship.

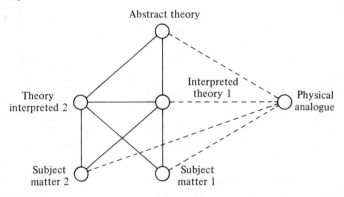

[65] Kaplan, p. 273.
[66] Simon and Newell, "The Uses and Limitations of Models," p. 93.
[67] Simon and Newell, p. 97.

CHAPTER 5

EVALUATING THEORIES

INTRODUCTION

The knowledge of the properties of any theory (and more generally of any symbolic system) is essential to building it and to using it. For example, if a researcher sets out to create *the* theory of consumer behavior he must know, in advance, some of the properties that his final theory must have. On the other side, he must have adequate knowledge of the limitations of existing theories.

Table 5.1   Criteria of "Good" Theories as Induced from the Literature

Accuracy	Generality	Promise
Applicability	Growth	Quantitativeness
Brevity	Importance	Reliability
Brilliance	Inclusiveness	Rigour
Clarity	Ingenuity	Simplicity
Closure	Insight	Stability
Coherence	Instrumentality	Standardization
Comprehensiveness	Interrelatedness	Symmetry
Consistency	Integration	Systematicness
Constancy	Invariance	Timeliness
Control	Logicalness	Time-binding
Correlatedness	Measurability	Understandibility
Correspondence	Objectivity	Unity
Definiteness	Observability	Ubiquity
Efficiency	Operationally	Universality
Elegance	Order	Univocality
Exactness	Organization	Utility
Experimentability	Parsimony	Validity
Explanatory power	Permanence	Value for—
Familiarity	Plausibility	Verifiability
Flexibility	Practicality	Versatility
Frequency of use	Precision	Wide acceptance
Fruitfulness	Predictivity	
Functionality	Probability	

Source: S. C. Dodd, "Introducing 'Systemmetrics' for Evaluating Symbolic Systems: 24 Criteria for the Excellence of Scientific Theories," *Systematics*, 1968, 6(1), p. 31.

The researcher in marketing, when trying to evaluate a theory,[1] is unavoidably confronted with two problems: (1) The literature concerning the evaluation of theories is pregnant with evaluation criteria. One author assembled a list of 70 criteria, which, by his estimation, was a conservative number. These criteria are shown in Table 5.1. Since it is not practical nor is it even desirable to pursue all 70 or more criteria, the researcher is confronted with a problem of selection. What properties are commonly suggested by scientists? To contribute to answering such questions is one aim of this chapter. (2) Having reduced the number of criteria to those that he, somewhat subjectively, considers most relevant, the researcher is still faced with the problem of ordering them. The selection and hierarchy suggested by Dodd will be found in Table 5.2.

---

[1] For an example of evaluation of a marketing theory, see Shelby D. Hunt, "The Morphology of Theory and the General Theory of Marketing"; see also the critique of this attempt by Christian R. A. Pinson, Reinhard Angelmar, and Eduardo Roberto, "An Evaluation of the General Theory of Marketing."

Table 5.2   Dodd's Hierarchy of Evaluative Criteria

1. Verifiability	9. Multipliability	17. Recurrency
2. Predictivity	10. Univocability	18. Translatability
3. Consistency	11. Controllability	19. Durativity
4. Reliability	12. Standardizability	20. Durability
5. Accuracy	13. Synergy	21. Acquaintancy
6. Generality	14. Parsimony	22. Popularity
7. Utility	15. Simplicity	23. Efficacy
8. Importancy	16. Stability	24. Density

Source: S. C. Dodd, "Introducing 'Systemmetrics' for Evaluating Symbolic Systems: 24 Criteria for the Excellence of Scientific Theories," *Systematics*, 1968, 6(1), p. 49.

At this point the reader must be sensitive to the fact that, depending upon his background and objectives, the researcher will emphasize different aspects of the theory. A philosopher of science will certainly put the emphasis on such properties as logicalness, consistency, rigor, validity; a mathematician, on axiomatization, generality, quantitativeness, precision; a statistician, on predictivity, representativeness, standardization; a social scientist, on insight, explanatory power, experimentability, predictivity, objectivity; a practitioner, on applicability, familiarity, flexibility, fruitfulness, practicality, utility; and so forth. Consequently, it is our contention that there is no "absolute" and "perfect" hierarchy of evaluation criteria. Therefore the reader should not expect to find in this chapter *the* scientific way of assessing theories. All hierarchies should be understood as being tentative and highly dependent upon the context. Our observation can be understood as a corollary of the belief held by most philosophers of science and social scientists that there is a myth of *the* scientific method.

As a result of these two observations we will merely "suggest" in the first part of this chapter a set of criteria that *we* found relevant and that we hope to be of some help to our readers. In the second part of this chapter we will apply our set of evaluation criteria to three major models of consumer behavior.

The discussion borrows part of its comprehensive schema from Bunge.[2] We distinguish among four kinds of criteria, namely, formal, semantical, epistemological, and methodological. These criteria are discussed in detail on the following pages.

FORMAL CRITERIA

"WELL-FORMEDNESS"

The theoretical statements should be well formed. "Well-formedness" is the term used by Bunge[3] to convey the idea that the propositions contained

[2] Mario Bunge, *Scientific Research*, Vols. I and II; see especially Vol. II, pp. 352–355.
[3] Bunge, Vol. I, p. 52.

in the theory and the ways they are interconnected should conform to (1) some rules of "composition" or formation (we have already stressed in Chapter 3 that some combinations of linguistic signs are not permitted) and (2) some rules of "transformation" that correspond to what is required by elementary logic or more complex syntax. Such a criterion is generally left aside by most philosophers because of its triviality and consequently should be considered as a *sine qua non* condition for any theory that purports to be communicated to others.

INTERNAL CONSISTENCY

A theory is internally consistent if and only if no logical contradictions are contained therein. This is an absolute requirement that is stressed by all scientists. It goes beyond the requirement of "well-formedness" in the sense that a theory can be "well formed" and can nevertheless contain contradictions. As an example, consider the perception of innovators in Rogers' theory:[4] From his generalizations[5] one can derive the proposition that "opinion leaders are perceived and perceive themselves as deviants." This, however, is in direct contradiction with another of his generalizations: "Opinion leaders conform more closely to social system norms than the average member."[5]

One particular problem in consumer behavior or any behavioral theory that manifests contradiction is determining whether or not the contradiction is only "apparently" contradictory due to the absence of any explanatory statement which, if present, would eliminate the perceived contradiction. The basic theory simply might not be complete enough to handle the contradiction. For example, dissonance theory predicts that, in the face of conflicting information leading to discrepant attitudes, one of the attitudes will be changed in saliency or valuation. However, there exists evidence that individuals can and do maintain sharply discrepant attitudes. This does not mean that dissonance theory or balance theory is wrong in this case. What needs to be added is simply an additional psychological mechanism, namely, compartmentalization or disassociation of conflicting attitudes.

INDEPENDENCE

"Independence" in Bunge's sense[6] is mainly a property of "axiomatic theories" and may have limited applicability to consumer behavior.[7] Theories have sets of "primitive" or undefined concepts that nevertheless infuse meanings into other components of the theory. As such, they are included

[4] Everett M. Rogers, *Diffusion of Innovations.*
[5] Rogers, pp. 313–314.
[6] Bunge, *Scientific Research*, Vol. I, p. 441.
[7] The reader is referred to the discussion of the degree of formalization of theories (Chapter 4).

among the building blocks of theories. A usable theory has at least one so-called *primitive concept* and at least one *primitive assumption* (or axiom). It is important that primitive concepts be mutually independent; that is, should we decide to assign definitions to each, the definition given one is unaffected by the definition given the other. It is also important that the theory have axiom independence: "An axiom set is independent if and only if its members are not interdeducible, i.e., if none of them is derivable from the others (even though it may turn out to be a theorem in a different theory."[8] For example, in social exchange theories the concept of utility or satisfaction is independent of the assumption of rationality and purposive behavior. The primitive concept and the assumption are certainly consistent with each other and would remain consistent through various formulations. In effect, the marketing man should ask whether the underlying assumptions and stated concepts are mutually independent.

STRENGTH

The property of "strength" is also designated in the literature by the terms of "formal comprehensiveness" or "generality." Of two rival hypotheses both consistent with the same set of data, the stronger one will be the more general of the two. This formal property can be viewed as associated with a semantical property of "representativeness" (see below) in the sense that the more general hypothesis is more likely to correspond to a broader semantical domain; in other words, a theory containing a higher number of variables and sentences is more likely to cover a broader range of referents. Dodd also speaks of this. "The more comprehensive or general a [theory] is, the more the [theorist] gains power over symbols of lesser coverage or generality."[9]

SEMANTIC CRITERIA

LINGUISTIC EXACTNESS

As discussed previously, every concept has an "intension" or connotation and virtually always has at least one "extension" or denotation. The intension of a concept consists of those properties subsumed and synthesized by the concept. The intension of the variable concept "social class" consists of the cluster of variables—for example, education, occupation, and so on—we have in mind when we use the term "social class." The extension of a concept is the applicable domain or set of objects to which the concept can apply. A theory is linguistically inexact when its concepts and/or the relationships among the concepts are vague.[10] *Intensional vagueness* is due to the partial

[8] Bunge, *Scientific Research*, Vol. I, p. 441.
[9] Dodd, "Systemmetrics for Evaluating Symbolic Systems," p. 42.
[10] See Bunge, *Scientific Research*, Vol. I, pp. 97ff.

indefiniteness of the intension whereas *extensional vagueness* is due to a partial indetermination of the extension of a concept.[11] If a concept is intensionally vague it may still be extensionally definite, whereas if a concept is extensionally vague then it is necessarily intensionally vague. The dimension of linguistic exactness is suggestive of Dodd's criterion of *accuracy*.[12] The exactness or precision of a theory in describing, explaining, and predicting is very important, particularly where intervention is an important factor or goal. The more accurate a marketer is in anticipating some event (for example, the percentage of persons of a particular nature purchasing a given product brand over a specified range of time), the more successful he will be in formulating and implementing his marketing strategy.

CONCEPTUAL UNITY

Conceptual unity is especially important when taking an interdisciplinary approach or evaluating interdisciplinary hypotheses and theories. There are several requisite conditions to the achievement of conceptual unity.[13] The principle of these conditions will be discussed here. In evaluating a particular learning theory, role theory, or any other theory, the marketing researcher should ask whether the components of the theory refer to the same set of behavioral phenomena. This is an especially important consideration in marketing because of the laudable, but precarious, tendencies of marketing researchers to take interdisciplinary approaches to marketing problems. When combining sociological propositions and economic propositions (for instance, to develop a theory explaining reactions to a real or expected change in income), care should be taken that the respective social and economic concepts refer to the same set of phenomena—that they have intensional and extensional compatibility with one another and that they are rooted in identical or at least compatible assumptions. The interdisciplinary approach so common in consumer behavior research increases the opportunity for mismatching along these lines. Care must be exercised in assuring compatibility between the nonmarketing context in which a concept or theory has been empirically tested and the marketing context in which it is to be applied.[14] The more disparate the contexts are, the greater the likelihood that different theories are involved.

EMPIRICAL INTERPRETABILITY

Empirical interpretability is what is referred to elsewhere in this book as "testability in principle." There appears to be, in Blalock's words, "an inherent gap between the languages of theory and research which can

---

[11] Bunge, p. 98.

[12] Dodd, "Systemmetrics for Evaluating Symbolic Systems," p. 39.

[13] See Bunge, *Scientific Research*, Vol. I, pp. 391ff.

[14] See T. S. Robinson and S. Ward, "Consumer Behavior Research: Promise and Prospects."

never be bridged in a completely satisfactory way."[15] The distinction between the theoretical concept and its referent on the one hand and the operational definition used in an empirical test on the other hand is a crucial one to make in marketing.[16]

Dodd believes this criterion to be the chief criterion of a good theory. It concerns the closeness of correspondence between the symbol and its referent. Closely related is another concept of Dodd's, univocability.[17] This involves a one-to-one correspondence of symbols to referents. It is the name of the ideal semantic relation of "one symbol, one referent." The fewer the number of different referents a given symbol within a theory brings within its scope the better that aspect of the theory is.

REPRESENTATIVENESS

The criterion of "representativeness" here refers to the scope of the black box. A good illustration is given by Lazarsfeld's distinction between the distributive and the morphological approaches.[18] The distributive approach used a "big" black box with variables—such as price, distribution, and others—as inputs and purchase decisions as outputs. The morphological or "decision-process" approach goes inside the black box and splits it up into several small related ones.

Representativeness is very similar to the criterion of depth.[19] Depth refers to the basicness of the mechanisms involved in a theory. It is usually said, for instance, that Skinnerian psychology is deeper than Pavlovian psychology and Darwin's theory of evolution is deeper than pre-Darwinian evolution theories. There are many dimensions and special conditions attached to this evaluative criterion. It must suffice here to say that the higher the level of abstraction, the more the basic units are mechanistically related; and the more the theory subsumes other theories, the better it is.

METHODOLOGICAL CRITERIA

FALSIFIABILITY

Falsifiability is a means of evaluating the truth of a theory and/or theoretical statements. The empirical test does not obtain or create truth, it merely increases or diminishes the credence we give to an existing theory or statement. The more empirically testable (that is, open or sensitive to experience) an hypothesis is, the more falsifiable it is. The optimal condition

---

[15] Hubert M. Blalock, Jr., *Causal Inferences in Nonexperimental Research*, p. 5.

[16] See Gerald Zaltman, "Marketing Inference in the Behavioral Sciences." A good treatment of this problem is to be found in John A. Howard and Jagdish N. Sheth, *The Theory of Buyer Behavior.*

[17] Dodd, "Systemmetrics for Evaluating Symbolic Systems," p. 45.

[18] See James Engel, David Kollat, and Roger Blackwell, *Consumer Behavior*, 1968, pp. 183–184.

[19] See Bunge, *Scientific Research*, Vol. I, pp. 506ff.

of falsifiability occurs when a theory has the possibility of being both confirmed and refuted by the results. This is to say, both favorable and unfavorable evidence can be conceived. The falsifiability of a theory is obviously highly dependent upon other attributes, such as interpretability, linguistic exactness, and representativeness.

On this same point Galtung notes that generally as one cuts closer and closer to the core of a theory it becomes increasingly difficult to test the core hypotheses and assumptions because of their higher order of abstraction.[20] The more readily this problem is overcome the better the theory. However, it must be pointed out that the inability to test higher-order hypotheses may be a function of the investigators' imagination and not necessarily a "fault" of the theory itself.

METHODOLOGICAL SIMPLICITY

Tests of a theory should not be so complicated or expensive as to make refutation impossible. This is related to Pinson and Roberto's treatment of *pragmatical simplicity* as simplicity of *understanding and simplicity of application*.[21] Simplicity of understanding is dependent upon what is sometimes conceptualized as syntactical simplicity.[21] One theory may be syntactically simpler than another. For example, it may involve fewer concepts and propositions. Simplicity of understanding is also dependent upon what is occasionally called ontological simplicity. Thus Wallace adds: "If one theory deals with a *more complex explanandum* than another theory, we should naturally expect the former to be more complex than the latter. But the requirement that even the former theory should nevertheless be 'parsimonious' means that it should be free of redundancy; that is, it should be simple, relative to other possible theories accounting for the same explanandum. If the theory, in short, could do as well or better without a given element of form or content, that element is an unnecessary complexity and, according to the rule of simpler theories are somehow better theories than more complex theories: parsimony, should be discarded."[22] It is difficult to accept the argument that "The progress of science is not always in the direction of the simpler theory."[23] Only when the simpler theory provides the same power of explanation as a more complex theory or more complex formulation of the same theory is it to be preferred. Kaplan summarizes our position quite well in quoting Whitehead: "Seek simplicity and distrust it."[23]

[20] Johan Galtung, *Theory and Methods of Social Research*, pp. 324–328.
[21] The reader will find a presentation of three kinds of simplicity (syntactical, semantical, and pragmatical simplicities) with the corresponding available measures in: Christian Pinson and Eduardo Roberto, "Simplicity, Parsimony, and Model Building."
[22] Walter W. Wallace, *The Logic of Science in Sociology*, pp. 112–113. Italics added.
[23] Abraham Kaplan, *The Conduct of Inquiry: Methodology for Behavioral Science*, p. 318.

EPISTEMOLOGICAL CRITERIA

CONFIRMATION

A theory is generally said to be true when it has been *confirmed* or *corroborated*. The degree of corroboration concerns "measuring the closeness of [the] correspondence of a theory to the facts which it is meant to describe, explain, and predict. . . ."[24] Statistically it is represented by the coefficient of determination.

The reader should be sensitive to two important points offered by Galtung relating to theory evaluation. First is the principle of independent confirmation: "The only way to obtain complete confirmation of [a theory] is to confirm independently all hypotheses in [the theory]."[25] Second, the principle of coexistence: "One does not have to choose between two or more noncontradictory theories from which the same set of hypotheses can be deduced."[26]

At this juncture we should note the *correspondence theory of truth*. According to this theory, to say that a theory is true or false is "to say that it coheres or fails to cohere with a system of other statements; that it is a member of a system whose elements are related to each other by ties of logical implication as the elements in a system of pure mathematics are related."[27] Quine describes the consequences of this coherence law for the case when a proposition derived from a theory conflicts with observation. Using the network analogy, he argues that:

Total science is like a field of force whose boundary conditions are experience. A conflict with experience at the periphery occasions readjustments in the interior of the field. Truth values have to be redistributed over some of our statements. Reevaluation of some statements entails reevaluation of others, because of their logical interconnection—the logical laws being in turn simply certain further statements of the system, certain further elements of the field. Having reevaluated one statement, we must reevaluate some others, which may be statements logically connected with the first or may be the statements of logical connections themselves. But the total field is so underdetermined by its boundary conditions, experience, that there is much latitude of choice as to what statements to reevaluate in the light of any simple contrary experience. No particular experiences are linked with any particular statements in the interior of the field, except indirectly through considerations of equilibrium affecting the field as a whole.[28]

Cronbach and Meehl discuss the choices of an investigator whose data do not bear out his prediction. He has three possible interpretations.[29] First,

[24] Dodd, "Systemmetrics for Evaluating Symbolic Systems," p. 43.
[25] Galtung, *Theory and Methods of Social Research*, p. 455.
[26] Galtung, p. 456.
[27] Alan R. White, "Coherence Theory of Truth," p. 130.
[28] W. V. O. Quine, *From a Logical Point of View*, pp. 42–43.
[29] L. J. Cronbach and P. E. Meehl, "Construct Validity in Psychological Tests," p. 295.

the operational definitions do not properly reflect the concepts under investigation. For example, if Bennett and Mandell's data had not been in conformance with the hypotheses, they still would not have been invalidated for they did not actually measure the construct under investigation—that is, reinforced purchases—but rather purchases only.[30]

A second possibility is that the theory that generated the prediction is incorrect. Bennett and Mandell tested a third hypothesis in their study, which said that "the buying experience itself is instructive, whether or not the choice is positively reinforced. As this experience increases, evidenced by the total purchases in the individual's history, the amount of effort expended on information search will decrease."[31] The result obtained did not confirm the prediction and thus "tends to deny the notion in the Howard-Sheth theory that all experience is instructive and reduces the need for information seeking."[32] The authors did not discuss the consequences of this negative result for the theory. One would have to find out what the position of the generating hypothesis in the theoretical network is and what the consequences of this negative finding for the rest of the network are. If the generating hypothesis were at the boundary of the network, it could be eliminated without much effect on the remainder. If it came from the core of the theory, an effort at adjustment would probably take place. For example, the network could be modified by splitting a concept into two or more portions, or additional conditions modifying the original relationships could be added.[33] Consider, for instance, the notion of congruity. Hughes and Guerrero propose to resolve difficulties with the congruity model in brand-purchase behavior by distinguishing between social-congruity and self-congruity.[34] In addition, they indicate conditions under which each concept may be more relevant: "Perhaps social-congruity models should be considered for products consumed in public and self-congruity models for products consumed privately."[35] Thus they do not reject the notion of congruity and the underlying theoretical network. Instead, they modify and elaborate it. A similar approach was taken by Copley and Callom, who tested the function in an industrial marketing setting.[36] In order to account for their data they proposed three types of risk and search behaviors, namely the "search simplifiers," the "search norms," and "the searchers: mirror-image groups." Whenever such a modification of

[30] Peter D. Bennett and Robert M. Mandell, "Prepurchase Information-Seeking Behavior of New Car Purchasers—The Learning Hypothesis."
[31] Bennett and Mandell, p. 431.
[32] Bennett and Mandell, p. 432.
[33] See Cronbach and Meehl, "Construct Validity in Psychological Tests," p. 295.
[34] David G. Hughes and Jose L. Guerrero, "Automobile Self-Congruity Models Reexamined."
[35] Hughes and Guerrero, p. 125.
[36] Thomas P. Copley and Frank L. Callom, "Industrial Search Behavior and Perceived Risk."

the theoretical network is proposed, according to Cronbach and Meehl, the investigator is now "required to *gather a fresh body of data* to test the altered hypotheses. If the new data are consistent with the modified network he is free from fear that his nomologicals were gerrymandered to fit the peculiarities of his first sample. He can now trust his test to some extent because his test results behave as predicted."[37]

Another possibility for dealing with disconfirmed predictions is to claim that the experimental design did not test the hypothesis properly. Maybe the manipulation of dissonance was not strong enough, maybe there were disturbing background factors, and so on. Raymond Bauer gives an example of this strategy in discussing a study undertaken "to see if one could differentiate 'problem solving' and 'psycho-social' situations and if the two different patterns of relationship (between self-confidence and persuasibility) would be found under the two conditions. The support for the main proposition was weak, but in my opinion the reason was a technical one: we were not sufficiently ingenious to create the proper differentiation between the two situations."[38]

ORIGINALITY

Theories that force one to be creative in formulating problems and constructing empirical tests may yield a richness in new predictions and new syntheses not possible with mundane theories. Thus another major aim of theory construction is "to *increase knowledge* by deriving new propositions (e.g. predictions) from premises in conjunction with relevant information."[39] The opportunities for the use of original theories in a marketing context seem especially great. A considerable competitive advantage may accrue to the marketer who successfully exploits original theories.

EXTERNAL CONSISTENCY

A theory should be compatible with a sizable segment of existing tested knowledge in other fields as well as its own.[40] Theories of consumer behavior should be compatible with such theories as learning theory or role theory, for example, as they are developed in marketing and nonmarketing contexts. However, caution is important here. External inconsistency is not a sufficient and immediate reason for rejecting a theory. It may well be the case that the other previously established theories need correction or modification. For example, one methodologically sound study attempted to replicate, in part, the classic two-step flow of communication notion and related ideas

[37] Cronbach and Meehl, "Construct Validity in Psychological Tests," pp. 295–296.
[38] Raymond A. Bauer, "Self-Confidence and Persuasibility: One More Time," p. 257.
[39] Bunge, *Scientific Research*, Vol. I, p. 383.
[40] See Thomas S. Kuhn, *The Structure of Scientific Revolutions*.

put forth by Katz and Lazarsfeld.[41] The study results not only failed to confirm the validity of the work of Katz and Lazarsfeld but contradicted it. Because of the basic scientific merit of the study one cannot reject it as the result of poor methodology and because of the consistent contradiction of the Katz and Lazarsfeld work throughout this study it cannot be conveniently dismissed as simply a random occurrence. The lack of external consistency in this case suggests modification of the previously established related theories.

Kaplan has called external consistency the norm of coherence.[42] This norm involves how well a theory fits in with other theories and with known facts—that is, how well integrated it is with other knowledge. Kaplan points out that there is a very real danger of overemphasizing this norm: "Coherence is a conservative principle. . . . The unyielding insistence that every new theory must fit those theories already established is characteristic of closed systems of thought, not of science."[42] Nevertheless, the validation of theories does involve considering it in relation to other theories. A theory of a phenomena consistent with another related, well-established theory has greater validity than a theory inconsistent with the other established, related theory, other things being equal. The other related theory, in effect, "lends" validity.

UNIFYING POWER

The criterion of *unifying power* refers to the ability of a theory to extend to areas previously unrelated.[43] Utility theory, for example, originating in economics has been fruitfully extended to political science, sociology, and psychology. A theory that brings together a wide range of previously unconnected and confirmed propositions concerning a variety of phenomena can be considered a "good" theory. As Kaplan puts it: "What counts is the range of facts that the theory takes into account and especially their heterogeneity."[44] Thus one of the major aims of scientific theorizing should be to *"systematize knowledge* by establishing logical relations among previously disconnected items."[45]

HEURISTIC POWER

A good theory should have a high potential for suggesting and directing new research. It should help structure new learning opportunities for the researcher, "either (a) by posing or reformulating fruitful problems, or

[41] ATV House, *Opinion Leaders, A Study in Communication.*
[42] Kaplan, *The Conduct of Inquiry*, pp. 314ff.
[43] See Bunge, *Scientific Research*, Vol. I, p. 353.
[44] Kaplan, *The Conduct of Inquiry*, p. 313.
[45] Bunge, *Scientific Research*, Vol. I, p. 383.

(b) by suggesting the gathering of new data which would be unthinkable without the theory, or (c) by suggesting entire new lines of investigation."[46] This is a very pragmatic dimension, which concerns the number and nature of questions a theory raises. Does a theory raise new important questions? If so, to what extent?

Dodd speaks of this as *multipliability*, which concerns the fruitfulness of a theory in leading to further theory—that is, its ability to multiply itself and increase. Does it result in any efforts to build new theories in areas where none existed before? Does it suggest more plausible theories for those situations already covered by one or more theories? For measurement, "a weighted score based on the number of further theories developed from a theory at issue or modified by it as cited in a relevant set of journals and textbooks in a period...."[47]

STABILITY

A theory should not be rigid or inelastic in the face of evidence it did not predict.[48] It should have a degree of flexibility that makes it possible to amend the theory to encompass the new evidence so long as the evidence is not in contradiction to the main body of the theory. The theory must be dynamic, not static.

Table 5.3 summarizes and conveniently represents the preceding discussion of the 16 criteria for theory evaluation.

AN EVALUATION OF THREE MAJOR CONSUMER BEHAVIOR MODELS

In the following section we shall evaluate three models or theories of buyer behavior, which have come to dominate the consumer behavior area, at least in terms of popularity or citation frequency. The evaluation of each model is in terms of the 16 criteria previously suggested. In all instances the discussion assumes that the reader is familiar with the model under consideration.

One observation must be made. The evaluative criteria are, for the most part, stringent. There does not exist in the behavioral sciences a meaningful theory of at least modest comprehensiveness that fully satisfies even most of the important theory evaluation criteria. Moreover, as we soon learned, different individuals may evaluate differently the degree of success with which a given theory satisfies a particular evaluation criterion. Accordingly, it requires no substantial effort to find things "wrong" with a theory or model. Critique is always easier than development.

---

[46] See Bunge, p. 353.
[47] Dodd, "Systemmetrics for Evaluating Symbolic Systems," p. 46.
[48] Bunge, *Scientific Research*, Vol. I, p. 353.

Table 5.3   16 Criteria for Theory Evaluation[a]

Formal Criteria	
1. Well-formedness	The theory obeys the rules of "formation" and "transformation" (elementary logic).
2. Internal consistency	The theory contains no logical contradictions.
3. Independence	The theory has primitive-concepts independence and axioms independence.
4. Strength	The theory entails other theories.
Semantical Criteria	
5. Linguistic exactness	The theory exhibits minimum intensional and extensional vagueness.
6. Conceptual unity	The components of the theory refer to the same set of behavioral phenomena.
7. Empirical interpretability (or testability in principle)	The theory is operationalizable (interpretable in empirical terms).
8. Representativeness	The theory deals with deep mechanisms.
Methodological Criteria	
9. Falsifiability	The theory is falsifiable—that is, confrontable with reality (facts).
10. Methodological simplicity	The theory is easy to build and test.
Epistemological Criteria	
11. Confirmation	The theory coheres with facts.
12. Originality	The theory increases knowledge by deriving new propositions.
13. External consistency	The theory is consistent with existing knowledge.
14. Unifying power	The theory connects previously unconnected items.
15. Heuristic power	The theory suggests new directions for research.
16. Stability	The theory is able to accommodate new evidence.

[a] This table is based largely on Bunge, *Scientific Research*, Vols. I and II.

THE NICOSIA MODEL OF CONSUMER DECISION PROCESSES[49]

The Nicosia model is represented in Figure 5.1.

Formal properties

Well-formedness   Such a criterion is irrelevant in this context since any published model must be at least syntactically correct.

[49] Francesco M. Nicosia, *Consumer Decision Processes: Marketing and Advertising Implications*.

Internal Consistency   Internal formal consistency is an absolute logical condition for every scientific model. Indeed Nicosia's model meets this requirement.

Independence   It has been previously said that such a criterion is not very relevant in the context of consumer behavior models. Nicosia's model as well as the two other models cannot claim to be axiomatic. However, we recall that a theory is said to be formalized if "it contains an explicit and exhaustive enumeration of its primitives and its rules (both syntactical and semantical)."[50] With respect to this point it must be said that Nicosia is remarkable.[51] Throughout the book there is a constant concern for defining the primitive terms,[52] the basic assumptions of each approach to consumer behavior,[53] and finally the postulates underlying the "comprehensive scheme"[54] and the different "illustrative" models of consumer behavior process.[55]

Strength   The coverage of the model is very broad. However, Nicosia's model cannot be said to be able to entail other existing models. They are too different in their selection and treatment of dependent, independent, and mediating variables even if they purport to deal with an apparently similar phenomenon. In order to determine whether each of the three theories can be *formally* derived from one or both of the others it should be necessary to formalize them using a uniform terminology.

Semantical properties

Linguistic Exactness   With respect to this point Nicosia's model exhibits minimal ambiguity and vagueness; most of the variables and relationships are *clearly* defined.

Conceptual Unity   Because of the central role played by the concept of the decision-making process in the building of the model there is, through-

---

[50] Bunge, *Scientific Research*, Vol. I, p. 443.
[51] Nicosia has attempted a formalization of his model through the use of derived models. This would allow the researcher to take account of a new property, namely, that of "syntactical simplicity." It must be mentioned that a measure of syntactical simplicity is available not for the "comprehensive model" but for one of the derived models expressed by the following equation (Nicosia, *Consumer Decision Processes*, p. 126):

$$\frac{d^2B(t)}{dt^2} + (a_a + bB)\frac{dB(t)}{dt} + (dB - m)abB = mbc\overline{C}$$

This model yields by Harré's index a syntactical simplicity coefficient of 4. (This example is treated in Pinson and Roberto, "Simplicity, Parsimony, and Model Building.")
[52] Nicosia, *Consumer Decision Processes*, p. 20.
[53] Nicosia, pp. 75ff; pp. 57ff.
[54] Nicosia, pp. 153ff.
[55] Nicosia, pp. 197–198, 208–221.

Figure 5.1 The Nicosia model of consumer decision processes.

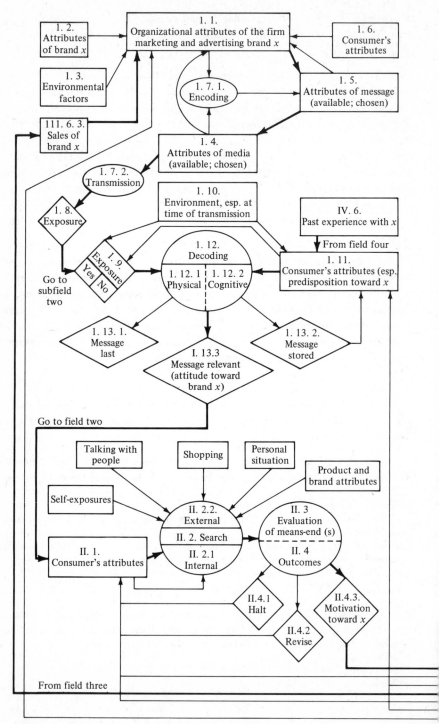

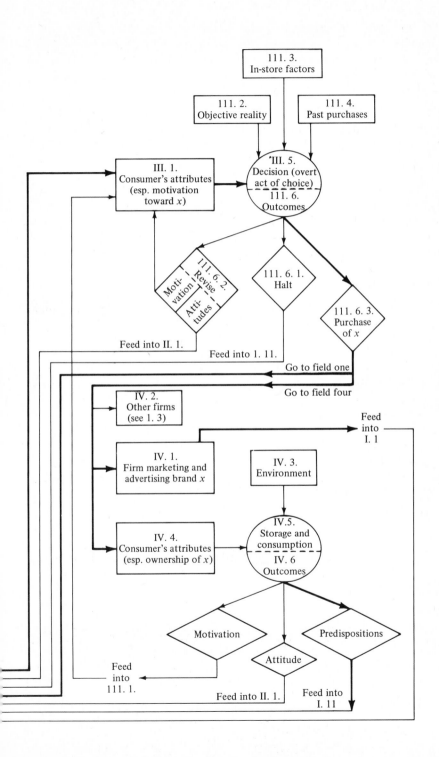

out the book, a constant reference to the *same universe of discourse*. It should be also of interest to note that all the variables that were introduced seem to fulfill a necessary need; by necessary need we mean that they are not introduced opportunistically after the theory has already been formulated. (Some researchers have the bad habit of introducing new variables whose only function is to "protect" the previously introduced ones.)

Empirical Interpretability   Because of its low level of abstraction, Nicosia's model raises fewer problems of interpretability than its competitors do; most of the variables included in his model are observables.

Representativeness   Nicosia's model aims at developing "explanations of why the consumer behaves the way he does."[56] One major advantage of this model over, for example, the ones of Howard and Sheth and of Engel, Kollat, and Blackwell is that it includes more marketing variables and treats them more in detail. Another favorable point is that, in spite of what was thought by some authors,[57] Nicosia postulates a marketing setting which is more realistic, in the sense that his model primarily stresses the *interactions* between the firm and the consumer instead of focusing on the consumer alone. However it remains true that the model gives integrated and thus idealized views of marketing and advertising problems rather than entailing facts. This is not surprising since Nicosia's aim was not to derive a theory (model) from data but to present an *a priori* model that could be later validated by data.

Methodological properties

Falsifiability   An aim of scientific theory construction is "to *enhance the testability* of the hypotheses, by subjecting each of them to the control hypothesis of the system."[58] Testability was certainly not absent in Nicosia's preoccupations and there is a true effort of operationalizations throughout the book and quite explicitly in Chapter 7. However the attempted "illustrative" applications expressed in a mathematical form either pose new problems of their own or rely too heavily on unrealistic assumptions; for example, the stimulus (message) is postulated to be applied uniformly through time. In conclusion, it may be said that with respect to this criterion the model performs poorly. One can even fear that no test of the model will be possible

---

[56] Nicosia, p. 18.

[57] Engel, Kollat. and Blackwell claim that "finally, and most important, only one extremely limited situation is encompassed, that of exposure to an advertisement and formation of an attitude where none existed before . . . It is anything but clear how this conceptual approach is applicable to the common kinds of problems that are daily faced by a marketing manager." James F. Engel, David T. Kollat, and Roger D. Blackwell, *Consumer Behavior*, 1968, p. 40.

[58] Bunge, *Scientific Research*, Vol. I, p. 383.

without a significant alteration of its very nature. As noted by Nicosia, "simulation of the scheme requires much more 'fine grain' data than those usually generated by current marketing, advertising, and consumer research."[59]

Methodological Simplicity   Indeed, Nicosia's model does not "seem" to be methodologically simple. This is due to three other properties of the model: (1) its large "representativeness," (2) its "syntactical complexity," and (3) its low level of "testability." On the other side it must be said that the model's methodological simplicity is improved by its satisfactory level of "formalization," "empirical interpretability," and "linguistic exactness."

Epistemological critiera

Confirmation   To our knowledge Nicosia's model has never been tested.

Originality   Another aim of scientific theory construction is "to *increase* knowledge by deriving new propositions (for example, predictions) from premises in conjunction with relevant information."[60]

Nicosia's work represents a real contribution to marketing knowledge in the sense that it is an admirable analysis of almost every position taken by theorists on the problem of consumer decision making. Nicosia was original —at least at the time the book was first published—in his stressing the fact that consumer behavior should be viewed and investigated as a decision-making process. He does not, however, introduce new theoretical constructs that could significantly modify our "scattered" knowledge on consumer processes. Nicosia himself makes this point very clear: "Neither 'discoveries' nor 'scientific laws' will be revealed. We shall only build upon the efforts of others and present some new ways of thinking about consumer behavior and its dynamics. . . ."[61] Nor does Nicosia's model make a significant contribution at the level of "normative marketing" because, as it is admitted, it is not "concerned with rules for making 'good' decisions."[62]

External Consistency   On the whole, Nicosia's model is certainly consistent with the bulk of most approaches to consumer behavior. Nicosia is definitively working within the "paradigm" held in common by the marketing community.

Unifying Power   A theory (model) should "*systematize knowledge* by establishing logical relations among previously disconnected items."[63]

This aim was certainly among Nicosia's most constant concerns: His

[59] Nicosia, *Consumer Decision Processes*, p. 239.
[60] Bunge, *Scientific Research*, Vol. I, p. 383.
[61] Nicosia, *Consumer Decision Processes*, p. 18.
[62] Nicosia, p. 19.
[63] Bunge, *Scientific Research*, Vol. I, p. 383.

model "attempts to order what are now fragmentary findings and institutional practices."[64] With respect to that goal Nicosia's model provides not only one of the most extensive reviews of the plethora of approaches to consumer behavior in the fields of marketing, behavior sciences, and economics, but also an integration of the analysis and results into a comprehensive framework.

However it is crucial to understand that Nicosia's attempt suffered from what should be considered as the major weakness of most integrative attempts: The ideal procedure would consist in *first* reviewing the literature and *then* integrating it. Actually, what happens is that one starts with a more or less well-documented intuition about the "right," "best" way in which consumer behavior should be portrayed and then goes into a "selective" analysis of the literature in order to build his model. For example, Nicosia states: "As we examined existent theories and empirical findings in the literature, we did in fact distill a view common to a good deal of research: the behavior of the consumer (usually defined as the act of choice) is the result of a decision process. It appeared that this view explained many facets of consumer action, the observable variety of individual and societal patterns of life. *Further* we saw that it could be extended to yield a broader integration of knowledge and generate findings important to marketing and advertising. We *then* decided to adopt this view *as our initial premise*, i.e., that consumer behavior is the outcome of decision processes. In the first part of this study we shall review the literature *in the light of this premise* attempting at the same time to change and improve it."[65]

Such an approach—should we say hardly unavoidable—may result in a distorted view of the literature in the sense that a reviewer, at least theoretically, should strive for letting the facts (the literature) speak for themselves instead of selecting and organizing them according to a set of more or less *a priori* propositions. In any event, one should be as clear as possible not only about his premises—Nicosia stated them in a very explicit way—but also about the reasons that led him to select them. An integrative model should not be said to be "useful" or "valid" simply because it provides "a reasonably consistent frame of reference" but because its premises are found to be adequately justified. With respect to that point Nicosia seems to be faulty: In his introductory chapter he does explain at length that his model will not be built "by first collecting empirical data and then determining the relevant variables and perhaps their forms of interaction by means of statistical manipulations" mainly because "findings produced by statistical virtuosity would be difficult to interpret and apply."[66] The approach taken by

[64] Nicosia, *Consumer Decision Processes*, p. 17.
[65] Nicosia, pp. 8–9. Italics added.
[66] Nicosia, p. 18.

Nicosia is clearly defined as one that "is based upon propositions identified in our review" because "it is also necessary to formulate theory *a priori* and collect data accordingly."[66] It seems to us that Nicosia's statement would be superficial if he did imply that it is more difficult to interpret and integrate data than theories. He certainly meant that it is easier to postulate an integrative framework. In conclusion, Nicosia's model should be considered as being of a postulative nature; that is, his own theoretical premises are clearly stated but not justified.

Heuristic Power   Another aim of scientific theory construction is "*to guide research* either (a) by posing on reformulating fruitful problems, or (b) by suggesting the gathering of new data which would be unthinkable without the theory, or (c) by suggesting entire new lines of investigation."[67] It is certainly one of Nicosia's major achievements to have documented the need for future research on (1) the impact on buying of changes in the intensity and mode of applications through time of marketing variables and (2) on the basic mechanisms intervening between a stimulus and a response, but it could hardly be said that his model has historically directly inspired new directions of research. This is certainly one of the most severe failures of Nicosia's endeavor, since his claimed primary goal was wholly pragmatic: Nicosia cites twice Tolman's statement according to which "a model can be defended only insofar as it proves helpful in explaining and making understandable already observed behavior *and insofar as it also suggests new behaviors to be looked for. . . .*"[68] Although such a failure is certainly due to the very nature of Nicosia's contribution, it is also attributable to a lack of creativity and imagination from his various readers.

Stability   Nicosia claims that his model was intended to meet Tolman's requirement that "any such model must, of course, be ready to undergo variations and modifications to make it correspond better with new empirical findings."[69] In our view such a property is hardly met at the level at least of the core structure of the model. What Nicosia's model basically postulates is that there is a chain of interrelated causal linkages between six elements: choice of a certain message—exposure to the message—formation of an attitude—formation of a motivation—decision to buy—purchasing behavior. It does not seem that such a process could be changed without, by doing so, altering the basic nature of the model. It is true, nevertheless, that within each of the four fields there exists a high flexibility and also that the structure of the scheme would not be affected by the choice of different starting points.[70]

---

[67] Bunge, *Scientific Research*, Vol. I, p. 383.
[68] Tolman, cited in Nicosia, *Consumer Decision Processes*, pp. 20, 241. Italics added.
[69] Tolman, cited in Nicosia, pp. 20, 242.
[70] Nicosia is quite explicit on this possibility (Nicosia, pp. 156–157).

THE HOWARD-SHETH MODEL OF BUYER BEHAVIOR[71]

The Howard-Sheth model of buyer behavior was put forth in 1969 "to describe, apply, and assess those elements of the theory of human behavior that we believe to be essential for understanding the range of activities that we call 'buying'."[72] To aid recall, both a simplified description of the model and a complete description are provided in Figures 5.2 and 5.3, respectively. In both instances it can be seen that two sets of hypothetical constructs (constructs not immediately based on observable reality)—perceptual and learning constructs—are linked to form a single network, which is influenced by various measurable external stimuli and has as an output measurable behavior patterns.

The model has been both lauded and criticized by Maloney.[73] He commends the model in going beyond the simplistic approach to theory building that is characteristic of most of the literature in marketing and advertising and views the model as a necessary step toward a broader understanding of social-change behavior. At the same time, he notes that the model involves some unduly simplistic assumptions—for example, "that virtually all purchase decisions are made on the basis of a brand or product preference and that if a clear-cut preference is lacking, the buyer actively seeks information that will lead to a preference."[73] Another criticism is that the model is particularly weak in its treatment of timing effects and stimulus-decay effects.[73]

Engel, Kollat, and Blackwell have praised the theory because of the multiplicity of variables it links in a precise way.[74] They criticize the model for introducing variables that cannot be measured at present (although one may wonder how progress would be made without introducing challenges of that sort). They also indicate that the model suffers from recursiveness, substantial measurement error, and that some variables are either difficult to define operationally or difficult to measure. We shall now review this theory in terms of the evaluative criteria discussed earlier.

Formal properties

Well-formedness   Indeed, the theoretical structure follows the patterns of elementary logic.

Internal Consistency   To the extent that the danger of multiple interpretation does not manifest itself, at least in the form of incompatible interpretations of hypothetical constructs by the same scientist, then the theory appears to score well on the criterion of internal consistency. As Howard and

[71] John A. Howard and Jagdish N. Sheth, *The Theory of Buyer Behavior*.
[72] Howard M. Sheth, p. 30.
[73] John Maloney, "Separate Parts Bin For a New Social Psychology."
[74] James F. Engel, David T. Kollat, and Roger D. Blackwell, *Consumer Behavior*, 2d ed., in press.

Figure 5.2 Simplified description of the theory of buyer behavior. (Solid lines indicate flow of information; dashed lines, feedback effects.)

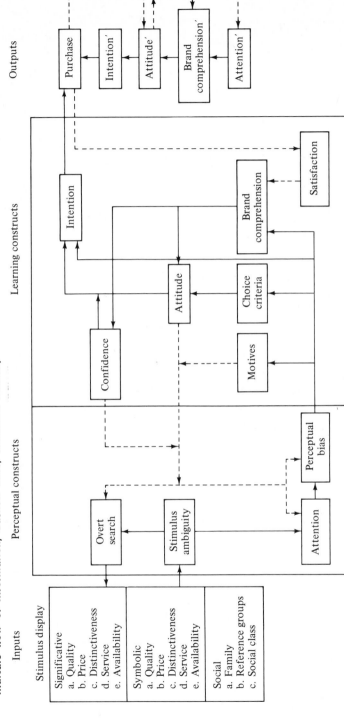

Inputs   Perceptual constructs   Learning constructs   Outputs

Source: John Howard and Jagdish Sheth, *The Theory of Buyer Behavior,* p. 30, © 1969 by John Wiley & Sons, Inc. Reprinted by permission of John Wiley & Sons, Inc.

Figure 5.3 Theory of buyer behavior.

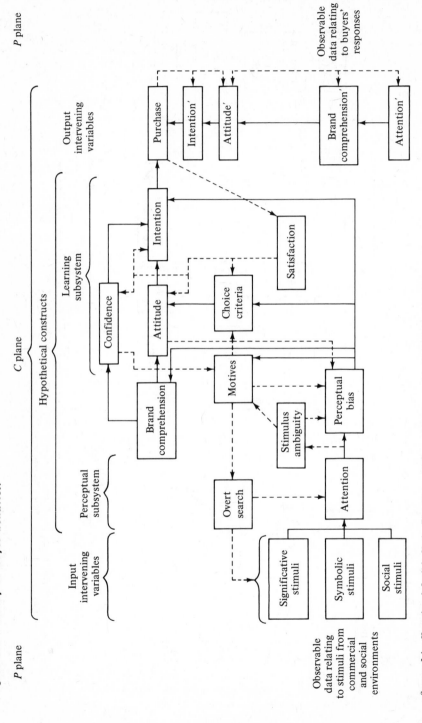

Source: John Howard and Jagdish Sheth, *The Theory of Buyer Behavior,* p. 54, © 1969 by John Wiley & Sons, Inc. Reprinted by permission of John Wiley & Sons, Inc.

Sheth present their model it is internally consistent, which is a singular achievement in itself given the relative complexity of the model.

Independence   In many ways the hypothetical constructs in this model are primitive concepts in that their definition is not explicit, although they clearly account for most of the general character or flavor of the theory. The major primitive assumption of the theory concerns the selection of learning theory (particularly Hull's) as the proper theoretical basis for studying buyer behavior. The primitive assumptions of the theory and its primitive concepts seem to be mutually independent, but the theory is not sufficiently axiomatized to enable one to a less subjective evaluation.

Strength   The theory is indeed a very general one in intent since it purports to cover both consumer and industrial buyer behavior and to apply to innovations as well as noninnovations. However, the model seems primarily restricted to frequently purchased items and does not cover collective decision making. As we already mentioned in the review of the Nicosia model, it is not possible to conduct a more rigorous analysis of that property.

Semantical properties

Linguistic Exactness   The intension of each of the concept-variables of the theory, at least at the input and output phases, are quite clear. The intension of the hypothetical constructs, however, are not as exact as those of the input variable, for example. As indicated, with regard to strength the claimed extension or denotation is quite broad.

Conceptual Unity   One problem in the Howard-Sheth theory is that the individual hypothetical constructs within the perceptual and learning subsystem exist or at least are treated at different levels of abstraction, and this is not acknowledged adequately in the theory. It is true, however, that the components of the theory are oriented toward the same behavioral phenomena. Given the lack of an explicit statement of assumptions in the theory, it is not easily determined whether the propositions implied by the theory stem from the same set of assumptions. Also, the contexts in which Hull's learning theory has been developed are not particularly comparable to marketing situations. This constitutes a weakness in the conceptual foundations of the theory.

Empirical Interpretability   Throughout their model, Howard and Sheth show great sensitivity to the problems involved in establishing correspondence rules relating theoretical concepts to real-world phenomena. This is one of the strengths of the model and one of the first treatments of the problem in a marketing context. The output variables are suggested as the result of the functioning of the hypothetical constructs. The output variables are established through correspondence rules, and herein lies a problem. The output of a set of independent variables should be some qualitatively distinct dependent variable and not merely some more operationalized or lower level of abstraction of the independent variables.

Representativeness   As indicated earlier, this theory involves very fundamental mechanisms in perception and learning. This is not uniformly true throughout the entire model, however. The relationship between perceptual bias and stimulus ambiguity is more fundamental (that is, "deep") than the relationship between brand comprehension and confidence. The latter mechanism can be reduced still further, whereas the former cannot. The brand comprehension-confidence relationship is at least not at the same core level as the perceptual bias-stimulus ambiguity relationship.

Methodological properties

Falsifiability   One of the most crucial requirements a theory must meet is falsifiability. The model under discussion here is the first comprehensive model to be subjected to empirical test.[75] The results of these efforts have been mixed. In general, indications are that in the foreseeable future any one test should be restricted to a particular segment of the model rather than apply to the model in its entirety. At the present state of its development— or, alternatively, given the methodological technology used to test the entire model—too much "noise" enters the test and therefore it becomes difficult to assess the whole model at once. Lehmann, Farley, and Howard have recently pointed to areas of empirical investigation that would be relevant to the model:[76] (1) different operational definitions should be used; (2) use of nonlinear forms of the model should be allowed for; and (3) lagged forms of analysis should be employed.

Methodological Simplicity   For the above reasons the model does not seem to be methodologically simple.

Epistemological criteria

Confirmation   In general, the model has received modest support.

Originality   The theory is not original in terms of the constructs it presents, and indeed could not fairly be expected to be original in this manner. The nature of the relationships between and among constructs or variables are relatively original, for example, the relationship postulated between confidence and satisfaction and the three-step relationship between satisfaction and stimulus ambiguity.

---

[75] John U. Farley and L. Winston Ring, "An Empirical Test of the Howard-Sheth Model of Buyer Behavior"; also John U. Farley, John A. Howard, and Donald R. Lehmann, "After Test Marketing, What?"
[76] Farley, Howard, and Lehmann.

External Consistency   The theory is very deeply rooted in one particular learning theory developed outside of marketing,[77] in Osgood's cognitive theory, [78] and in Berlyne's theory of exploratory behavior.[79] Thus in an important way the Howard-Sheth model benefits from the strong points of these theories and suffers from their limitations. Hull's theory of learning is perhaps the weakest of the theoretical foundations and is also one of the most heavily relied upon nonmarketing works in the Howard-Sheth model. Also, some elements of the model—perceptual bias, for example—are treated in very general ways without adequate tie-ins within some of the recent experimental research. However, for the most part the various elements of the model are linked very well with the existing empirical research data in marketing.

Unifying Power   The Howard-Sheth model does bring together relatively confirmed hypotheses from learning theory, cognitive theory, and exploratory behavior theory. These are, of course, highly related areas and students of each area have on occasion assumed the others to be a subpart of their own area. The model also brings together ideas from conflict theory and information processing theory. Also, for example, the construct of "confidence" brings together processes involving the selection of information inputs and the cognitive and behavioral consequences affecting future and current purchases, respectively. The Howard-Sheth model, however, would have had greater unifying power had it attempted to better integrate the input intervening variables with other aspects of the model, although Howard and Sheth acknowledge this limitation and claim that to have done so would have made the model unwieldy.

Heuristic Power   One of the strongest features of this model is its heuristic power. It is particularly fruitful in structuring new learning opportunities by raising new and important questions concerning such things as the nature of the loyalty-disloyalty cycle and the information-purchase equilibrium. Another new important topic the authors of the model point out concerns the concept of motivational equilibrium within the purchase-information equilibrium.

Stability   The model would seem to be highly stable as far as the component parts are concerned. Changes in the particular relationships between these parts, however, have to be expected.

---

[77] Clark L. Hull, *Principles of Behavior*; also Clark L. Hull, *A Behavior System*.

[78] Charles E. Osgood, "A Behavioristic Analysis of Perception and Language as Cognitive Phenomena;" also Charles E. Osgood, "Motivational Dynamics of Language Behavior."

[79] D. E. Berlyne, "Motivational Problems Raised by Exploratory and Epistemic Behavior"; also D. E. Berlyne, "Curiosity and Exploration."

THE ENGEL-KOLLAT-BLACKWELL "MULTIMEDIATION MODEL OF CONSUMER BEHAVIOR"

In the second edition of their book on consumer behavior, Engel, Kollat, and Blackwell present a revised version of their model of consumer behavior.[80] Their model consists of both static components, such as attitudes and personality, and of dynamic components, such as consumer processes. Figure 5.4 shows the complete model we shall be evaluating in terms of the criteria discussed earlier.

Formal properties

Well-formedness   The statement of the theory is well formed.

Internal Consistency   The internal consistency of the present model is difficult to evaluate, since the propositions that it encompasses are not very precise. For example, a proposition such as "The outcome also *can* change circumstances and thus trigger additional action"[81] can hardly be subject to contradiction. Otherwise the presentation of the model is quite logical.

Independence   Like the two other models, this model is not sufficiently axiomatized to enable one to assess the independence of its basic assumptions and primitive concepts.[82]

Strength   The model aims at broad coverage, encompassing extended problem solving as well as limited—and habitual decision—process behavior. Its *actual* strength, as compared with its *intended* strength, will have to be assessed by putting it through a series of tests in a number of contexts.

Semantical Criteria

Linguistic Exactness   Some of the concepts are quite clearly defined, such as exposure, attention, comprehension, and retention. Others, such as the concepts comprised by the central control unit, are less clearly defined. For example, consider the definition of personality: "Each individual has certain ways of thinking, behaving, and responding that make him unique. The sum total of these factors is referred to here as personality."[83] The intrusion of personality thus defined is very broad and its delimitation to other concepts such as attitude would appear to be difficult. Most difficult to define, finally, are the processes. How does one determine whether a particular behavior is external search or not, for example? Finally, the functional relationships are left relatively unspecified, so the possibilities of mathematical representation are limited.

---

[80] Engel, Kollat, and Blackwell, *Consumer Behavior*, 2d ed., 1973.
[81] Engel, Kollat, and Blackwell, 2d ed., p. 25. Italics added.
[82] Engel, Kollat, and Blackwell, unlike Nicosia, do not *explicitly* state their assumptions. They can be found, however, in their section entitled "Some Provisional Generalizations About Consumer Behavior;" see Engel, Kollat, and Blackwell, 2d ed., Chapter 27.
[83] Engel, Kollat and Blackwell, 2d ed., p. 11.

Figure 5.4   A complete model of consumer behavior, showing purchasing processes and outcomes.

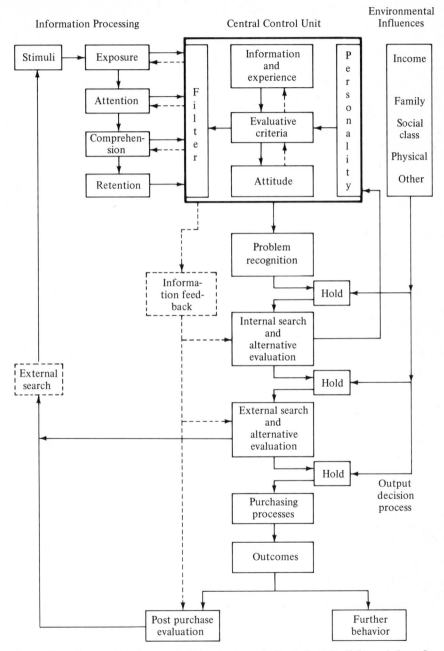

Conceptual Unity   There is one violation of conceptual unity. Despite the general sociopsychological conception of the model, a whole set of variables, namely the "environmental influences," is directly input into the decision process from the outside. Conceptual unity would require that these variables either pass through the information-processing state (that is, exposure, attention, and so on) or be contained in the central control unit.

Empirical Interpretability   Difficulties with respect to empirical interpretability will arise for precisely those concepts whose linguistic exactness is not well established. This is the case for all of the processes, namely problem recognition, internal search, and so forth. Most of the other more traditional concepts can be interpreted in the usual fashion—for example, attitude questionnaires and personality inventories.

Representativeness   The model certainly represents an advance over the traditional "distributive" approach.

Methodological properties

Falsifiability   According to the authors, "a complex model of behavior never can be proven or validated in any final sense."[84] The basic structure of the model is not really testable. Although it can be superseded by models that prove of greater utility for particular purposes, it cannot really prove to be true or false.

Methodological Simplicity   As a result of the comprehensiveness of the model it should lead to greater possibility of control in the testing of hypotheses. Much of the research done in consumer behavior is correlational in nature, and a list of potentially operative variables could go a long way toward controlling for rival hypotheses.

Epistemological properties

Confirmation   To our knowledge, this model has never been tested.

Originality   The model is not very original, either in its component parts or in the relationships indicated. This is not surprising in view of the integrating objective: Since the principal objective seems to be to provide a comprehensive framework for inserting existing research it cannot go much beyond the assembly of existing partial schemes.

External Consistency   The foregoing comment implies that the model is quite consistent with the prevailing views on consumer behavior research.

Unifying Power   The model has merit in providing a fairly inclusive view of consumer behavior. The quest for inclusiveness explains also the somewhat

[84] Engel, Kollat, and Blackwell, 2d ed., p. 7.

lower level of accuracy. It is difficult to cover everything and to be very specific about it too.

Heuristic Power   The model's relative emphasis on the processes of consumer behavior suggests closer scrutiny of prevailing stage schemes. What stages, if any, should be distinguished? What sequences of stages can occur, and what determines a particular sequencing?[85]

Stability   The lack of specificity makes the model stable with respect to any developments that do not transcend the basic conceptual framework. Only entirely new ways of looking at consumer behavior could become a threat to this model.

CONCLUSION

It is difficult to compare the different models with one another. For one thing, they make different assumptions. Nicosia assumes a decision-making orientation covering a large range of consumer behavior. Howard and Sheth, on the other hand, assume a learning-theory framework and develop their model with particular reference to frequently purchased products and services. Are these assumptions mutually exclusive? That is, does the adoption of a decision-making foundation rule out a learning theory foundation and vice versa? Probably not. If the two assumptions or foundations are simultaneously valid, does one subsume the other? If so, does the domain of the Howard-Sheth model fall within the Nicosia model? Totally? In part? These questions are raised here without answers. Many other questions could be presented. Before answers are forthcoming, systematic empirical testing of all three theories is required; virtually none has been attempted thus far. Very few efforts have attempted to evaluate the Howard-Sheth model, but for the most part these efforts have not done justice to the model. The study of theory in a consumer behavior context is still very much in its infancy, and until the various models are tested in whole or in part we cannot draw firm conclusions about their inherent worth or relative power. It should be added, however, that these models are not pure abstractions without any empirical support. All three models, but particularly the Nicosia and Howard-Sheth models, derive some support as well as their inspiration from empirical studies conducted prior to their construction. Basically, these models bring us to cell 2 in Figure 1.4 or the upper left cell of Figure 1.5. Table 5.4 represents a convenient summary of our evaluation of the three models. The only major difference is that one model (Howard-Sheth's) has received some beginnings of testing and application. Two things may equally account for our failure to discriminate in a significant way among the three models.

[85] Engel, Kollat, and Blackwell, 2d ed., 26–29.

Table 5.4 An Evaluation of Three Major Models of Consumer Behavior

Criteria	Nicosia	Howard-Sheth	Engel-Kollat Blackwell
Formal Criteria			
1. Well-formedness	very good	very good	good
2. Internal consistency	good–very good	good–very good	good
3. Independence	*	*	*
4. Strength	good	good	good
Semantical Criteria			
5. Linguistic exactness	good	fair–good	fair
6. Conceptual unity	good	fair	fair
7. Empirical interpretability	good	good	fair
8. Representativeness	fair–good	good	fair–good
Methodological Criteria			
9. Falsifiability	poor–fair	fair	poor
10. Methodological simplicity	poor–fair	poor–fair	poor
Epistemological Criteria			
11. Confirmation	(untested)	fair	(untested)
12. Originality	good	good	fair
13. External consistency	fair–good	fair–good	fair–good
14. Unifying power	good–very good	good–very good	good
15. Heuristic power	good	good–very good	fair–good
16. Stability	fair	fair	fair

* The criterion does not apply.

First, it may be the case that our criteria are insufficient; that is, they do not take account of the distinctive qualities of the models. It is true that most criteria are in fact very subjective—badly or not at all operationalized. In our defense, it must be said that we found in the specialized literature no satisfactory measures for any of these.

Second, it is also certainly true that the three models are much alike, not in their assumptions but in their resulting properties. They all seem to belong to the same tradition of verbal models, built around an intuition of the "right" theoretical framework.

CHAPTER 6

THE NATURE OF EXPLANATION

INTRODUCTION

This chapter is concerned with the first purpose of information, the explanation of phenomena. The discussion will focus initially on the nature of science and explanation and will then treat the concept of causality in explanation. Following this there will be a discussion of various types of explanation and further discussion of different levels of understanding in explanation. The major criteria by which explanations are to be evaluated are then presented, followed by an illustration of how explanation can serve marketing strategy.

WHAT IS AN EXPLANATION?

Little disagreement exists concerning the goal of science: It is the extension of certified knowledge.[1] Explanation plays a crucial role in the process of extending certified knowledge. Nagel is quite specific about this point: "It is the organization and classification of knowledge on the basis of explanatory principles that is the distinctive goal of the sciences."[2] Given the importance of explanation, the first question which must be asked is "What is an explanation?"

An explanation is an answer to a why question of the form "why p?" where p designates a statement that supposedly is true and refers to some fact, event, or state of affairs.[3] Examples of such "why" questions are: "Why do consumers buy more of brand X than of brand Y?" "Why do certain consumers adopt new products earlier than other consumers?" and "Why is the correlation between attitude scores and actual purchase behavior so low?" Explanation—that is, the answering of "why" questions—is one of the three major purposes of science (the other two are prediction and control, although some scholars do not distinguish between explanation and prediction).

Scientific explanations must meet two requirements. These have been labeled the *requirement of explanatory relevance* and the *requirement of testability*. Explanatory relevance means that the account of some phenomenon provided by an explanation would constitute good grounds for expecting that the phenomenon would appear under the specified circumstances. Explanatory relevance is achieved when "the explanatory information adduced affords good grounds for believing that the phenomenon to be explained did, or does, indeed occur. This condition must be met if we are to be entitled to say: 'That explains it—the phenomenon in question was indeed expected under the circumstances.' "[4] Most briefly, the "facts" adduced by the explanation must be relevant to the point at issue—that is, the phenomenon.

An explanation having no test implications is devoid of empirical content. No empirical findings could support it or disconfirm it and consequently it provides little or no ground for expecting a particular phenomenon; it lacks what Hempel calls "objective explanatory power." Thus the requirement of

[1] Robert Merton, *Social Theory and Social Structure.*
[2] Ernest Nagel, *The Structure of Science*, p. 4. Italics added.
[3] Carl G. Hempel, *Aspects of Scientific Explanation*, pp. 334–394; also Mario Bunge, *Scientific Research*, Vol. II, p. 3.
[4] Carl G. Hempel, *Philosophy of Natural Science*, p. 48.

testability is that scientific explanations must be capable of empirical test. An explanation that meets the first requirement (empirical relevance) also meets the requirement of testability, whereas the converse does not hold.[5]

CAUSALITY AND THE CONCEPT OF CRUCIAL TEST IN EXPLANATION

The definition of an explanation employed in this chapter relies heavily on the concept of causation, and a very brief exploration of the meaning of the term "cause" will be helpful at this point. The usual lexical definition holds that cause is something that occasions or effects a result. For the researcher, the objective of explanation should be to provide, with as high a degree of certainty as possible, information about what variables influence or produce other variables. Thus, "cause, in one way or another, is central to the goal of establishing scientific laws. In general terms, causation refers to the factors that make designated phenomena happen or change."[6]

It is necessary to determine in a given context what the marketing decision variables (causes) are so that procedures can be established for manipulating them. It is also necessary to know what causal forces cannot be manipulated; however, even in this situation behavioral statements in causal form should be provided. When one is told that two variables are related, it is essential to ask how they are related. *There should be a clear statement of the nature of the mechanism whereby one variable affects another.* Only when hypothesis or theoretical statements are presented in this way can they be of greatest utility in deriving marketing implications. One of the most important factors inhibiting fuller exploitation of behavioral research in marketing is that the marketer is generally presented only with associational statements. Presumably, the relationships between variables within a statement are not believed to be spurious or they would not be presented. If the association is a direct (or even indirect) one, causality is implicit and should be made explicit. It is an excellent exercise for the researcher to make explicit what the causal mechanisms are that he is assuming. This will clarify his own conceptual scheme and help identify intervening variables not otherwise readily apparent.

A causal statement, then, is a statement or proposition in a theory that states that there exist environments in which a change in the value of one variable can produce a change in another variable without the necessity of changes in still other variables in the environment. An important element in the preceding statement is the idea that one variable, X, *produces* a change in another variable, Y.

Before noting any further characteristics of causal statements, it will be useful to formulate a statement in a marketing context and use this state-

5 Hempel, *Philosophy of Natural Science*, p. 5.
6 Sanford Labovitz and Robert Hagedorn, *Introduction to Social Research*, p. 3.

ment to illustrate the properties of causal statements. Such a statement might be: *Norms of reciprocity among customers affect the outcome of personal selling situations*. Stinchcombe describes this level of generality as one in which a particular of the variables within a broad class of phenomena explains another particular variable in another class of phenomena. The two variables are norms or feelings of reciprocity and the outcome of a selling effort. The connecting mechanism at the individual level might be that feelings of obligation (in turn explained by social-exchange theory; develop within a consumer as he comes to perceive the salesman as investing in the selling situation resources valuable to the salesman. Because of an apparent opportunity cost incurred by the salesman (as perceived by the prospect) in his relationship with the consumer, the consumer will reciprocate by rewarding the salesman with a purchase. A number of things in the causal sentence that are properties of causal statements should be noted:

1. The statement assumes, for example, that high levels of reciprocity among consumers are found in successful personal selling situations; this statement would probably be better stated as a probabilistic explanation, a type to be discussed later.
2. Changes in the level of reciprocity produce changes in the frequency of successful personal selling.
3. Successful selling efforts by salesmen do not produce feelings of reciprocity among consumers. (This may at first glance seem contradictory but salesmen may only activate or stimulate this variable, not create it. The question of reciprocal causation will not be considered here.)
4. For a change in reciprocity to produce a change in sales there do not have to be changes in other variables.
5. The variables involved in a given causal statement may be of different measurement classes; for example, one variable may be dichotomous and the other continuous.
6. There can be contexts where the causal statement does not apply. Presumably, it would not apply to "creative" personal selling situations.
7. Other variables such as changes in level of disposable income or advertising could cause a change in sales without invalidating the causal statement, although ideally these other variables should be incorporated in the statement.
8. Most important, we do not know that a given change in sales is in fact caused by a change in reciprocity (either among a given group or by exposure of other groups to the sales effort). Even if we hold constant the effect of advertising, income change, and other imaginable variables and still find variations in reciprocity to be associated with variations in sales, we cannot conclude with absolute certainty that the causal statement is true. There is always the chance that a variable or set of variables

(including measuring errors and problems in the research design) that we have overlooked has produced the change in sales. This problem, according to Stinchcombe,[7] can be minimized by the *crucial experiment*— that is, selecting as tests of a theory those hypotheses whose confirmation automatically eliminates competing theoretical explanations. Somewhat differently, we should look for those consequences of our theory whose negation is implied by alternative theories.[8]

Many scientists dispute the utility of the crucial experiment as the means of eliminating rival hypotheses, and a brief excursus on this topic is in order here.[9] There are two ways in which we can interpret the rule "one should eliminate rival hypotheses." The first one is illustrated by the use of control groups. Before one experiment is being performed there are two *empirically equivalent* hypotheses available; that is, two hypotheses yield much the same testable predictions. For example: (1) "Pretesting leads to higher scores on the same test when performed later" and (2) "Exposure to information that is favorable to product X leads to positive attitude changes toward X among the exposed individuals." Now, if we want to test hypothesis (2) experimentally and perform pretest and post-test attitude measurement, we cannot be sure whether the positive change in attitudes, if any, is a result of (2) or of (1). Hence, we have to use a control group in order to eliminate the plausible hypothesis (1). Note that the use of the control group *presupposes* the truth of hypothesis (1) for, if (1) were not plausible, it could not invalidate (2). Elimination of (1), thus, does not mean that we invalidate (1) or control for its effect but it means that we are less convinced of its validity.

Crucial hypotheses represent the second way in which one can talk about the elimination of plausible rival hypotheses. In contrast with the above sense, here we have two hypotheses that yield *empirically conflicting* predictions. Under these circumstances, an experiment serves to falsify (that is, to invalidate) one of the two or more hypotheses, subject to the logical difficulties involved. Copi, a critic of the crucial experiment device (in contrast to Stinchcombe) acknowledges that an experiment can be crucial in showing the untenability of a group of hypotheses that make up the rival theory. However, no individual hypothesis can ever be subjected to a crucial experiment (except in one special situation). There may always be hidden assumptions that need to be made explicit and open to evaluation. In the process of "dragging hidden assumptions" out into the open, one may discover the falsity of a previously supposed hypothesis and the credibility of a

---

[7] Arthur L. Stinchcombe, *Constructing Social Theories.*
[8] Donald T. Campbell, "Prospective: Artifact and Control."
[9] See, for example, Hempel, *Philosophy of Natural Science*, 1966, and Irving M. Copi, "On Crucial Experiments," pp. 29–33.

previously rejected hypothesis. The special situation referred to above is as follows: When a single hypothesis is *added to the framework* of an accepted theory, the hypothesis can be subjected to a crucial experiment. If a prediction involving the questionable hypothesis, together with accepted parts of a theory, fails, then the experiment is crucial and the hypothesis is rejected.

Because of the impossibilities, except in some few situations, of being able to say that a causal statement is unshakably true, many researchers do not make causal statements but merely those of association. Association, of course, is a necessary but not sufficient condition for establishing causal relations. It is particularly important to consider both the magnitude and consistency of associations between two variables.[10] The greater the magnitude of association and the greater the consistency of occurrence of the association, the more plausible the argument of causal relations between two variables. Many scientific theories do involve observable temporal sequence; in the social sciences, however, causes precede their effects in such a way that the temporal sequence may be hardly noticeable. There is a quasi-simultaneity of cause and effect. Moreover, in almost all behavioral situations the variables in the dynamic system are directly interdependent, so the value of each variable at a given time depends significantly on the values of almost all other variables at a slightly earlier time. In those cases causal relationships are almost impossible to locate and measure. As Labovitz and Hagedorn and others[11] point out, many factors influence the ease with which time priority can be established. The logic of the situation is one factor, observational technique another, and the state of theory and data analysis still another factor affecting the establishment of time priority. It will suffice here to say that a better understanding of the innate and learned processes in the perception of causality should shed light on the problem of how social scientists develop causal interpretations—that is, finding the psychological determinants of the perception of causality underlying the conscious rational selection of indicators of causal relationships.

There is implicit in associational or covariation-type statements and in the assumptions of nonspuriousness the further assumption that the two or more variables are, in fact, causally related. Stronger theories—better explanations—would be built and more effective marketing programs would be developed if the inherent character of causality were made explicit. To give a practical example of how knowledge of "working relationships" between variables can be of practical assistance, consider the following illustration. If it is known that cosmopolitness and innovativeness have a positive association then the working relationship might be that cosmopoliteness, because

[10] Labovitz and Hagedorn, *Introduction to Social Research.*
[11] See, for example, Adriaan de Groot, *Methodology: Foundations of Inference and Research in the Behavioral Sciences*, pp. 331–332.

of the more flexible and broader frame of mind it produces, enables an individual to incorporate new elements (innovations) in his cognitive structure. The national planner could put this information to use by structuring the infrastructure of the formal communications system, thus eventually broadening the outlook of the population, which in turn facilitates acceptance of innovations necessary for national development.

LEVELS OF UNDERSTANDING IN EXPLANATION

There are at least four levels of understanding in explanation in the behavioral sciences.[12] The first level is simply establishing the fact that some phenomenon *exists*. Next is the establishment of *what* the phenomenon is. Specifying *how* the phenomenon functions is the task of the third level of explantion. The fourth level of explanation is concerned with *why* the phenomenon exerts its influence. These are shown in Table 6.1. In reference to this table, level one is the empirical determination that a phenomenon exists. Level two involves defining it—conceptualizing it explicitly—as being of a certain nature, Q, and explaining it in terms of the facts and conditions, producing the phenomenon. The third level is concerned with how factors X_1 and so on interact to produce Q. The fourth level is concerned with the reasons why (W_1 and so on) the factors isolated produce the effects they do. Level three tends to involve empirical generalizations and level four involves higher-order hypotheses and premises.

Table 6.1   Levels of Understanding in Explanation

Level of Understanding in Explanation	Explanation
One	A certain phenomenon has an empirical existence.
Two	The phenomenon is of the nature Q and is produced by factors $x_1, x_2, \ldots, x_n$.
Three	Factors $x_1, x_2, \ldots, x_n$ are interactive or have interacted in manner $y_1, y_2, \ldots, y_n$ to produce in some past or present time a phenomenon of the nature Q.
Four	Factors $x_1, x_2, \ldots, x_n$ interact in a manner $y_1, y_2, \ldots, y_n$ for reasons $w_1, w_2, \ldots, w_n$, thus producing a phenomenon of the nature Q.

A good illustration of these four levels of explanation involving behavioral phenomena of relevance to marketing is presented by H. G. Barnett's *Theory of Innovation* as a basis for cultural change.[13] Only elements of this theory,

---

[12] See, for example, John T. Doby, "Logic and Levels of Scientific Explanation."
[13] Homer G. Barnett, *Innovation: The Basis of Cultural Change.*

his notion of basic wants as necessary conditions for innovation, will be treated. At level one a phenomenon, an act of innovation (that is, adoption) is *observed*; it is known (not just assumed) *to have occurred or to be in the process of taking place.* The phenomenon is observed to be of a certain nature, Q—in this instance, the purchase of an ultramodern architectural blueprint for a permanent home or possibly the actual purchase of such a home. Thus the nature of the event, Q, consists of a purchase (a particular behavior) of an object perceived as new with "new" being defined in terms of qualitative distinction rather than in terms of time. Q then is composed of three factors: (1) purchase behavior, (2) perceptual processes, and (3) an object having qualitative distinction from other objects in the same general class of objects. Q may have been produced by or be a result of central subliminal wants (a type of self-want) and creative wants (a type of want that we relabel as autotelic wants). These two wants represent x_1 and x_2 in Table 6.1. Central subliminal wants are those that relate to the individual's need for self-preservation and self-definition. They influence how we structure and organize our environment. Creative wants emphasize accomplishment, with the process or act of being creative being at least and probably more important than the resultant innovation or objects. In general, wants of this nature result from dissatisfaction with the accepted way of doing things.

Level three is concerned with explaining how central subliminal wants x_1 and creative wants x_2 interact in manner y_1 to produce the adoption of the innovation in question. Explanation in this case takes the form of describing what y_1 is. In our example, creative wants interact with central subliminal wants. The need to define oneself as unique, avant-gardish, and the like, together with dissatisfaction of existing modes of architecture as means of achieving this self-definition, leads to the adoption of radical architectural style. But in level three the emphasis is upon the *manner* of interaction. It could be explained that creative wants stimulate (the manner of interaction) central subliminal wants and that for reasons of congruence or cognitive consistency the central subliminal wants are expressed in creative ways; that is, the individual establishes a self-definition of being an innovator. Being interested in doing innovative things and being dissatisfied with existing conditions bring about the idea that he is an innovator—an idea that becomes expressed in such behavior as the acquisition of a radically or at least significantly different home. The manner of interaction has a mathematical side and we would state further that the factors are additive or multiplicative.

At level four, explanation goes beyond the relationship of the x_i's to each other and attempts to account for reasons (w_1, w_2, . . .) factors x_1 interact in manner y_1. An explanation at this level has already been given. It was stated previously that for reasons of cognitive consistency, the x_2's (creative wants) cause the x_1's (central subliminal wants) to express themselves in innovative (that is, creative) ways. The notion of cognitive consistency in this illustration constitutes the reason, w_1.

TYPES OF SCIENTIFIC EXPLANATION

There are basically four types of models of scientific explanation: the deductive-nomological, the probabilistic model, the functional or teleological model, and the genetic model.[14] Each of these is discussed below.

DEDUCTIVE-NOMOLOGICAL EXPLANATIONS

In deductive-nomological explanations the explanans assert universal deterministic relationships. The universal statements in this case are of the form: "In all cases when conditions of kind F are realized, conditions of kind G are realized as well."[15] Examples of such statements are: "High perceived risk ($=$ condition F) will always result in high-information-seeking behavior ($=$ condition G)" or "Extreme brand name ambiguity ($=$ condition F) will always result in a negative attitude toward the brand ($=$ condition G)."[16] Given that the explanans contain deterministic universal statements and the corresponding initial conditions, the explanandum follows with logical certainty from the explanans. The classic example of this logical argument is:

C : Socrates is a man
L : All men are mortal
―――――――――――――――
E : Socrates is mortal

The complete explanation of the examples given above would be as follows:

C : Consumer A perceives high risk
L : High perceived risk results in high information-seeking
―――――――――――――――
E : Consumer A shows high information-seeking behavior

C : Brand name X is extremely ambiguous
L : Extreme brand ambiguity results in a negative attitude
        toward the brand
―――――――――――――――
E : The attitude toward the brand is negative

14 See Nagel, *The Structure of Science*, pp. 20–25; Hempel, *Philosophy of Natural Science*, pp. 46–69; and Carl G. Hempel and P. Oppenheim, "Studies in the Logic of Explanation."
15 Hempel, *Philosophy of Natural Science*, p. 55.
16 Stephen J. Miller, Michael B. Mazis, and Peter L. Wright, "The Influence of Brand Ambiguity on Brand Attitude Development."

PROBABILISTIC EXPLANATIONS

Probabilistic explanation can be contrasted with deductive explanation: "With a deductive explanation, the explanatory premises would, if true, provide *conclusive* evidence for the conclusion, constituting a *totally sufficient* guarantee of the explanatory conclusion. With a probabilistic explanation, the explanatory premises do not provide a guarantee of the conclusion, but merely render it relatively likely. . . ."[17] Examples of such sentences are: "When a product is not subject to testability, it is highly probable that personal influence will be operative"[18] or "When a product is highly conspicuous, the probability of reference-group influence is high."

Social scientists usually encounter probabilistic explanations when the explanatory premises (for example, reinforcement theory) contain a statistical assumption about some class of elements (for example, consumers exposed to random reinforcement as opposed to routine reinforcement) and the explanandum (brand loyalty) refers to a given consumer in that class of consumers. Thus if we want to explain why a given consumer is brand loyal (assumed to be a dichotomous variable for purposes of illustration) we would point out that a known percentage of consumers exposed to random reinforcement will be brand loyal. Notice that this is not deducible. To use another context, we cannot say with certainty that because a man is black he will consume prestigious brands of scotch whisky. However, we can say that if a man is black there is some ascertainable likelihood (established through research) that he will be a consumer of prestige scotch whisky.

It is generally accepted that probabilistic statements, as interpreted in the social sciences, cannot be finally confirmed or even disconfirmed by observational evidence. It is also accepted that we cannot deduce from any statistical generalization a statement to the effect that any *particular* event must occur: The explanans of a probabilistic explanation does not logically imply the explanandum; the former gives only a more or less high degree of inductive support or confirmation to the latter. Thus the truth of the explanans is compatible with the falsehood of the explanandum.

The basic form of the probabilistic model is as follows:

$$\frac{\begin{array}{l} b \text{ is an } F \\ p(G, F) = r \end{array}}{b \text{ is a } G} \quad \text{(the explanans)}$$

(the explanandum)

In this case, the universal statement (the law) is $p(G, R) = r$; that is, "whenever an event of type F is the case, the probability of the occurrence of an event of type G is r." The singular statement is "b is an F," where b refers to a particular event. The conclusion, "b is a G," in this case, is not

---

[17] N. Rescher, *Scientific Explanation*, p. 37.
[18] Thomas S. Robertson, *Innovative Behavior and Communication*, p. 191.

implied logically but has only a more₁or less high degree of inductive confirmation. For example, a certain individual (b) is a successful salesman
(F). The probability that high achievers (G personality types) are successful salesmen (F) is very high. Thus, individual b is a high achiever. Again,
the conclusion that the individual salesman is a high achiever is not logically
implied but only has a high degree of inductive support.

The orthodox view of explanation corresponds to the "nomological-
deductive model" and the "probabilistic model." The two models are called
"the covering-law models of explanation"; the thesis that explanations in
science are analyzable in terms of these two models is called *the covering-
law theory of explanation.*[19]

The explanatory connection effected by a probabilistic explanation may be
said to be weaker than that effected by a deductive explanation. This fact
has led some philosophers to deny the explanatory efficacy of probabilistic
explanations; it has led others to claim that probabilistic explanations,
although acceptable as temporary stopgap measures, are eventually to be
replaced by fully deductive ones as our knowledge of relevant causal factors
grows.

It may seem that deterministic explanatory premises lead to a pattern
of explanation that is of the deductive type, whereas probabilistic premises
imply inductive subsumability. The former assumption is correct; the latter
is not. It is possible to have an explanation of the deductive-nomological
type with probabilistic explanatory premises. This will be the case when the
explanandum is an empirical generalization involving probabilities. As an
example, consider the following model of brand-purchase behavior. We need
two hypotheses as explanans. First, the probability of a consumer's purchasing brand X is 0.5. Second, the outcomes of different purchase trials are
statistically independent of each other. These two hypotheses imply deductively that the probability of purchasing brand X is 0.5 even after a long
sequence of nonbrand X purchases. Explanations of this kind are called
deductive-statistical explanations.[20]

In the case where one has to explain individual events, the use of probabilistic explanatory premises does lead to inductive subsumability.

GENETIC EXPLANATIONS

Genetic explanations are those that account for a particular state or
condition of some unit in terms of some prior state or, more frequently, in
terms of a sequence of some prior states. Stinchcombe refers to this as
historicist explanation; that is, "One in which an *effect* created by causes at
some previous period *becomes a cause of that same effect* in succeeding

---

[19] Nagel, *The Structure of Science.*
[20] See Hempel, *Aspects of Scientific Explanation.*

periods."[21] It is the task of genetic explanations to determine the sequence of events through which an earlier system has been transformed into some subsequent one.[22]

Gentic explanations are used quite frequently in the explanation of consumer behavior. Actually, most of the explanations involving principles of learning can be regarded as genetic. In Kuehn's learning model of brand-choice behavior,[23] the probability of purchasing a brand A is a function of past brand purchases, and it is revised after each purchase. It is easy to see that this model conforms to the covering-law approach. The explanandum is a particular brand choice. The explanans consist of general principles and initial conditions. The initial conditions describe the past purchase behavior of the consumer and, in particular, the purchase probability that was applicable to the particular brand choice one wants to explain. The rule according to which this probability is to be computed then is given by the general principle in the explanans. Explanations of product-life-cycle change are essentially genetic in nature. To the extent that life-style behavior is self-reinforcing, it too is genetic in nature.

FUNCTIONAL OR TELEOLOGICAL EXPLANATIONS

"This type of explanation is that in which the 'why' question about a particular event or activity is answered by specifying a goal or end towards the attainment of which the event of activity is a means."[24] Explanations involving the symbolic attributes of products are illustrative of this type of explanation.

There is an attempt to reduce all teleological explanations to causal explanations. The way it is done "is to emphasize the similarity between teleological explanations of the type with which we are not concerned and the teleological explanations of intentional actions in which the future reference can be explained away, and to argue by analogy that in all cases the teleological explanation is reducible to one in which an intention, or something analogous to an intention, in the agent is the 'efficient' cause, so that goal directed activity is always a sort of goal-intended activity."[25]

To repeat, functional or teleological explanations are those that indicate one or more purposes that a unit serves in maintaining or achieving a certain situation, state, or goal. Alternatively, it is one "in which the *consequences* or some behavior or social arrangement are essential elements of the

[21] Stinchcombe, *Constructing Social Theories*, p. 103.

[22] Nagel, *The Structure of Science*, pp. 25, 568.

[23] For a brief description of Kuehn's model see, James F. Engel, David T. Kollat, and Roger D. Blackwell, *Consumer Behavior*, pp. 599ff.

[24] R. B. Braithwaite, *Scientific Explanation*, p. 322.

[25] Braithwaite, pp. 325–326.

causes of that behavior."[26] In other words, in this type of explanation "the 'why' question about a particular event or activity is answered by specifying a goal or end towards the attainment of which the event or activity is a means."[27] Such explanations are abundant in marketing. Thus the purchase of a particular product can be explained in terms of the psychosocial needs it satisfies. Blacks supposedly drink scotch whisky proportionately more than any other demographic group because it serves as a symbol of achievement. Product categories—for example, convenience goods, luxury items, and so on—are defined on the basis of the functions served by members of the product groups; the functions served explain the reason for the purchase decision.

Just as there are types of explanans and thus explanations so are there types of explananda. The latter fall into two basic categories: individual events and empirical generalizations. These are discussed below.

INDIVIDUAL EVENTS

Explanations that have individual events as their explananda are low-level explanations because the explanatory premises invoked for the explanation of individual events are usually empirical generalizations containing only observational concepts—that is, concepts that are operationally defined. Examples of such explanatory premises are: "Education is positively related to income" and "moderate fear appeals are positively related to accident prevention." These explanatory premises can be used to explain individual events such as the results of an analysis of panel data or the results of a survey.

Notice that we talked about the explanation of the "results" of studies, and not about the events directly. Scientific explananda are *descriptions of events* rather than the *events* themselves. Therefore, instead of pointing to examples of consumer behavior, we describe it verbally with sentences such as: "Consumer *A* purchased one giant size of detergent" or "Consumer *A* reported the purchase of five six-packs of beer during the month of May, four of which consisted of brand *X* and one consisted of brand *Y*." Such descriptions of events constitute the data language of consumer behavior research, and the sentences involved can be called protocol sentences or observation statements. Incidentally, the covering-law model presupposes such a description of events, for we would be hard pressed to apply logical derivations to objects. Accordingly, in order to "explain" the preceding two observation statements, we may establish the following explanatory argument: "Consumers who are highly dogmatic have a high brand loyalty,"

---

[26] Stinchcombe, *Constructing Social Theories*, p. 103.
[27] Braithwaite, *Scientific Explanation*, pp. 325–326.

"Consumer A is brand loyal to detergent X," and "The higher the brand loyalty to X, the higher the purchase probability for X."

One important implication of the fact that scientific explananda are descriptions of events rather than the events themselves is that one never gives explanations of events in their totality, but only of certain selected aspects of them.[28] "For a concrete event has infinitely many different aspects and thus cannot ever be completely described, let alone completely explained."[29] For example, when describing consumer behavior, one is usually not interested in whether consumers seize the products with their left or right hand, what kind of glasses they wear on their shopping trips, and so forth.

The fact that our explananda consist of descriptions of selected aspects of the referent events raises the question of how these aspects are being selected. What, for example, makes it unlikely that the facts described above will be collected by a researcher interested in consumer behavior? The answer is that the potential explanations one has in mind dictate the choice of observations. Thus one might say that the *explanans determines the explanandum*. A side effect of this dependency of the explanandum on the explanans is that the set of possible explanations is being limited. For example, the collection of behavior data of brand-purchase behavior alone forces the researcher to rely primarily on learning hypotheses. Before one is able to apply cognitive explanations, for example, additional explananda will have to be supplied.

The foregoing argument hopefully has shown that no hard and fast line can be drawn between explanation and description where the description provides the explanandum.[30] The gap between explanation and description is even smaller when we consider the explanation of individual events by means of theoretical principles. In consumer behavior, this means that, instead of subsuming the individual event under some empirical generalization, the components of explananda are regarded as indicators of certain underlying variables, in terms of which they are then explained. Hence, the function of explanation, in this sense, consists of stating "what the explanandum really is and, *hence*, relating it to other systems which are then seen to be essentially similar to it."[31] As an example, reconsider the illustration of brand loyalty and brand satisfaction given previously. There, we linked "brand loyalty" to "response probability" and "brand satisfaction" to "reinforcement." By doing so, we have related the brand-choice behavior to the entire field of learning theory. This has beneficial effects both for the learning theory and for researchers in the field of consumer behavior. To the learning

[28] S. Morgenbesser, "Scientific Explanation," p. 121.

[29] Hempel, *Aspects of Scientific Explanation*, 1965, p. 422.

[30] Rescher, *Scientific Explanation*, p. 3.

[31] Mary Hesse, "Is There an Independent Observation Language?" p. 72.

theorists, the benefit consists of a new context in which their theory can be tested and further developed. To marketing researchers, the benefit consists of a host of explanations and predictions that can be generated on the basis of learning theories and that otherwise would not have been conceived.

EMPIRICAL GENERALIZATIONS AS EXPLANANDA

At the next higher level of explanation the explananda consist not of individual events but of empirical generalizations that subsume and inductively generalize these findings. Examples of empirical generalizations as explanada are "innovators are more cosmopolitan than noninnovators," "brand loyalty is negatively related to deal proneness," and "the higher the brand satisfactions, the higher the brand loyalty." These empirical generalizations are now treated as explananda; that is, one is looking for universal statement that inductively or deductively subsume such statements expressing empirical regularities. Since this type of explanation usually involves theories, it is also called theoretical explanation.

At this point it seems appropriate to give a short characterization of theories before proceeding with the presentation of theoretical explanation. Theories consist of concepts that are connected by propositions. Some of their concepts refer to events that are directly observable, whereas other concepts have no directly observable counterpart in the real world. Theories have been likened to networks, where the concepts are represented by the knots, and the threads connecting the latter correspond, in part, to definitions, empirical generalizations, correspondence rules, and nonobservational propositions. This network is entirely conceptual and impinges on experience only along the edges.[32] These edges correspond to the operationally defined concepts. Those concepts which are in the interior of the network—that is, somewhat removed from the realm of observation—are linked to the latter either directly by means of correspondence rules or indirectly through propositions connecting them with other concepts which, in turn, do have correspondence rules.

On the basis of this view of theories, theoretical explanation means that the operationally defined concepts of which empirical generalizations consist have somehow to be attached to a network consisting of theoretical (that is, relatively nonobservational) concepts. As an example, consider the Howard and Sheth theory of buyer behavior. It consists of a system of theoretical concepts—including attention, motives, attitude, and intention—some of which are linked to the realm of observation by correspondence rules. These correspondence rules (recall the discussion in Chapters 3 and 4) stipulate that certain operationally defined concepts—for example, the numerated response to a set of bipolar scales reflecting salient purchase criteria—are indicators of theoretical concepts (for example, of attitude). Consequently,

---

32 W. V. O. Quine, *From a Logical Point of View*, p. 42.

empirically found regularities between operational measures of attention and attitude, for example, may be explained using hypotheses that connect the theoretical concepts of intention and attitude with other theoretical concepts, such as motives and choice criteria, providing the connecting links.

One important factor about theoretical explanations and explanations in general is that a given explanation automatically generates the need for a new explanation. This is the case with empirical generalizations. Once an empirical relationship has been established, the question "why p?" arises and has to be theoretically explained. Suppose one manages to find an adequate theoretical explanation. Immediately, the question "why p?" arises again, and so forth. As an example, consider Singer's discussion of Osgood and Tannenbaum's congruity theory, which they have developed in order to explain the direction and magnitude of attitude change: "It predicts that if a person's cognitive system contains related attitudes that are inconsistent, the person will restructure toward a consistent attitude complex. They provide a detailed and objective method for stating the changes and final attitude values; algebraic rules based on some of their assumptions are provided. Once again, however, no rationale is given for why the particular changes they predict should occur."[33] Osgood and Tannenbaum's explanans becomes Singer's explanandum. He proposes a motivational approach to explaining why inconsistency should result in particular attitude changes. It is clear that a motivational explanation, once found, would again be subjected to the "why?" question. To answer it, it might be necessary to have recourse to physiological concepts and hypotheses. These explanations might then in turn be explained by physiochemical concepts. Such regress in explanation raises the problem of theoretical reduction. Is consumer behavior reducible to psychology? Is psychology in turn reducible to physiology, and so forth? In general, the problem of reduction cannot be decided by *a priori* arguments. It depends on whether suitable, connecting propositions can be found which link the phenomena and concepts of one theoretical domain with another one. Until such connecting propositions are found, the reductionist proposition should be construed "as a heuristic maxim, as a principle for the guidance of research."[34]

EVALUATING EXPLANATIONS

Suppose an explanation has been offered to account for an explanandum. We can now ask the question: "How good is this explanation?" Or, in cases when we have more than one explanation, we ask ourselves, "Which explanation is the best?" What are some of the criteria that help to make these decisions?

---

[33] Jerome Singer, "Motivation for Consistency," p. 53.
[34] Hempel, *Philosophy of Natural Science*, p. 106.

EVIDENTIAL STRENGTH

One group of such criteria looks at the *evidential strength* of an explanation—that is, the strength with which the explanatory premises imply the explanandum. The evidential strength of an explanation plays only a role for inductive explanations. Deductive explanations imply the explanandum with certainty, and there can be no difference in the strength with which the explanans implies the explanandum. Such differences exist, however, for inductive-statistical explanations. The explanatory premises may imply the explanandum with greater or smaller probability. It appears desirable to have a high rather than a low probability for the occurrence of the explanandum. Consequently, the first criterion of evidential strength is a criterion of explanatory power. The explanatory power of an explanation can be defined as "the extent to which it renders the occurrence to be explained *more likely than other alternative occurrences.*"[35] This is to say that as an explanation becomes better, the greater the probability of the occurrence of the explanandum.

Several points are particularly helpful in assessing the *usefulness* of an explanation. Of course, these are not unrelated to the criteria for evaluating theories. The first point is whether an explanation holds for a given class of phenomena. Can the explanandum be logically deduced from the explanaiton? Since this has already been discussed at length we shall not dwell on it beyond saying it is the crucial test of any explanation. The remaining evaluation points are simplicity, scope, precision, power, and accuracy.[36]

SIMPLICITY

Situations may arise in which one has several alternative explanations of approximately equal evidential strength. One possible choice criterion is to choose the simplest explanation. This criterion has great intuitive appeal, and as mentioned by Hempel, "Many great scientists have expressed the conviction that the basic laws of nature are simple."[37] Alas, the criterion of simplicity is difficult to apply, for "it is not easy to state clear criteria of simplicity in the relevant sense and to justify the preference given to simpler hypotheses and theories."[38] To illustrate, it would seem preferable to have an explanatory operation involving three variables as compared to one with 15 variables, provided that both of them account equally well for the explanandum. However, the equation involving 15 variables can easily be made as simple as the one involving three variables by the simple device of redefinition. If one regards each five of the original variables as indicators of three "underlying"

---

[35] Rescher, *Scientific Explanation*, p. 66.
[36] For a treatment of most of these see E. J. Meehan, *Explanation in Social Science: A System Paradigm.*
[37] Hempel, *Philosophy of Natural Science*, p. 42.
[38] Hempel, p. 41.

variables, one obtains an equation with only three variables. Consequently, the criterion of simplicity has to be refined in order to take into account the complexity of the variables. This, however, as one may suspect, opens up a host of new problems.

SCOPE

Scope refers to the range of events to which an explanation can be applied. It is difficult in the social sciences to achieve wider scope without introducing ambiguity. "Social power" for example is a concept of wide scope, having considerable vagueness and differing interpretations. In fact the meaning of the term "power" is frequently defined by the context in which it is used, thus resulting in numerous definitions inductively derived. Such use of concepts not only limits their scope and thwarts the goal of achieving standardized meanings of concepts but involves poor scientific reasoning. The concept of rationality in the context of consumer behavior (and other contexts of behavior) is illustrative of another term with (potentially) wide scope but considerable ambiguity. Part of the ambiguity involved stems from different assumptions made by market researchers on the relative importance of conscious and unconscious motivations, and beyond this, the way in which they function in the consumer arena. Indeed, the concepts of conscious and unconscious motivations themselves are ambiguous. This is due in part to the fact that a given consumer event may be logically derived from and explained by very different and sometimes mutually exclusive psychoanalytic concepts. Determining which of the competing concepts is "correct," or most plausible, is exceedingly difficult because of measurement problems and the wide range and depth of collateral information required on an individual basis.

A number of hypotheses and theories relevant to marketing and having broad scope can be cited briefly. The two-step flow hypothesis mentioned earlier is a good example of an explanation of marketing-relevant communication behavior. Exchange theory as articulated by George Homans[39] and Peter Blau[40] is a theory of wide scope. Parsons' general theory of action has wide scope but, unlike exchange theory (or at least compared with exchange theory), it is difficult to put to empirical test. The theories and working concepts in the decision sciences are currently receiving wide application. E. T. Hall's theory of culture as communication is another explanans with extremely broad scope although, like Parsons' theory, it is difficult to test empirically.[41]

[39] George E. Homans, *Social Behavior: Its Elementary Forms.*
[40] Peter M. Blau, *Exchange and Power in Social Life.*
[41] Edward T. Hall, *The Silent Language.* For a marketing discussion of this work see Gerald Zaltman, *Marketing: Contributions from the Behavioral Sciences.*

PRECISION

"The precision of an explanation refers to the degree of specification of the variables involved and of the relationships between those variables."[42] Note that there are two areas of precision referred to in this quotation. The first concerns the specification of the variables. The second concerns precision in the statements concerning the relationship among variables.

There are, of course, excesses in precision that may cause theoretical and conceptual problems. For example, the use of relative time of adoption in diffusion theory as an operational measure of innovativeness is quite precise and widely practiced. However, it is very misleading and not a variable that is always conceptually distinct from the independent variables in adoption and diffusion equations. The chief objection in this case rests in part on the argument that time is simply a proxy variable masking several other variables, some of which are themselves used to predict time of adoption and adopter categories. There are other techniques that are being developed and refined to provide good empirical measures of innovativeness—that is, measures having relatively good isomorphism with the theoretical notion of innovativeness.

Measurement is a key factor influencing precision. In the first case, it affects the accuracy of the operationalized concept: The smaller the measurement error the more isomorphic the relationship between theoretical concepts and their empirical indicators. In the second place, measurement affects the detection of such things as interaction effects, which influence the interpretation of relationships among explanatory variables.

POWER

Power refers to the degree of control over the environment an explanation provides. Power depends upon the precision of the description and explanation and upon the completeness of the variables. An explanation encompassing all or many relevant variables and providing linking statements as discussed in the preceding section on precision is considered more powerful than an explanation or explanans that involves a few variables inarticulately expressed and relies heavily on the clause, "other things being equal." The *ceteris paribus* clause may be invoked because not all relevant variables have been identified or because their functioning is not understood.

ACCURACY

Accuracy refers to the frequency with which factors not included in the explanation interrupt the situation the explanation concerns. With regard to accuracy in the first case there is always an unavoidable gap, a lack of accuracy, between a concept and its empirical operationalization. This involves what some writers call validity. "In a very real sense no theoretically defined

---

[42] For a different definition see Meehan, *Explanation in Social Science*, p. 117.

concepts can be directly translated into operations nor can theoretical propositions be tested empirically."[43] In an article largely devoted to this problem of accuracy, Zaltman concludes: "Perhaps one of the greatest obstacles inhibiting the effective application of the behavioral sciences to marketing problems is that this very important quality of isomorphism (between theoretical and operational systems) can only be determined intuitively."[44] This is shown graphically in Figure 6.1.

Figure 6.1   Levels of abstraction and epistemic relationships in applying concepts to marketing.

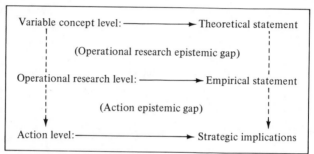

The second aspect of accuracy concerns accuracy in the stated relationships between variables. Blalock argues vigorously for specifying relationships in the form of direct causal links stated in terms of covariations and temporal sequences for reasons of explication, measurement, and testing. Consider two concepts: sales productivity (number of sales made, for example) and reference group. French found that productivity among salesmen was associated with social level of their reference group as well as effort expended.[45] The important question that should always be asked after being given a statement of hypothesis such as this is *how* does the reference-group phenomenon influence or affect productivity? (The apparent relationship between the two concepts is that identification with high-status reference groups stimulates levels of aspiration, which then motivate the salesman to greater effort even at the risk of violating the norms of the immediate group of colleague salesman.) It would be unusual of course to have complete accuracy in marketing and the behavioral sciences in general. Accuracy must be considered as a relative quality and not in absolute terms. In some ways it is related to degree of precision. We can say that a certain behavior is accounted for—or explained by—the life style of the actor. This statement is rather accurate

[43] Blalock, "The Measurement Problem: A Gap Between the Languages of Theory and Research."

[44] Gerald Zaltman, "Marketing Inference in the Behavioral Sciences."

[45] Cecil L. French, "Correlates of Success in Retail Selling."

given its vague all inclusiveness but not very precise; certainly not as precise as breaking life style down into principal component parts and explaining behavior in terms of these parts. Accuracy is also related to control. The more control one has over a system of variables the more accurate an explanation will be.

THE ROLE OF EXPLANATION IN DEVELOPING MARKETING STRATEGY

Ultimately, the value of studying the process of scientific explanation in a consumer context is that it enables marketers to improve the efficacy of their actions. The explanations obtained must somehow highlight or provide clues and insights resulting in more effective marketing strategies. An illustration is presented below.

ILLUSTRATION

One common marketing situation concerns the behavioral aspects of the dyadic interaction between customers and salesmen in creative selling situations. The problem can be translated into an exchange theory issue. The empirical marketing observation may be simply that consumers appear to be more attracted to salesmen whose psychosocial traits are perceived similar to their own. This is the explanandum. We then proceed to translate this marketing fact or phenomenon into a theoretical issue, the explanans. This process of utilizing explanations in marketing is treated below as a series of steps.[46]

Step One   First it is necessary to state the explanandum: Consumers are more attracted to salesmen whose psychosocial traits are perceived as similar to their own.

Step Two   Consider now a possible explanans: "An individual may be attracted to others because associating with them is intrinsically gratifying or because the association furnished extrinsic benefits for him."[47]

Intrinsic rewards received from others include social approval by one's peers, or the feeling of security brought about by being with people whose opinions or values are like one's own. Intrinsic rewards are highly subjective; extrinsic rewards are more objective. Alternative sources of extrinsic rewards are easier to compare than in the case of intrinsic rewards. Advice and material assistance are examples of extrinsic rewards other people provide. The individual receiving either or both of these rewards may, in turn, provide the other person with intrinsic and/or extrinsic gratification. In this case an

[46] The discussion is adapted from Zaltman, "Marketing Inference in the Behavioral Sciences." Reprinted from *Journal of Marketing*, published by the American Marketing Association.

[47] Blau, *Exchange and Power in Social Life*, p. 58.

exchange relationship comes into existence. For convenience in this example, this relationship will be viewed through the eyes of just one party. An assumption is made that a sale is a function of attraction.

The theoretical statement above identifies three variables: intrinsic gratification, extrinsic gratification, and attractiveness. The statement indicates that attractiveness is a result of, or is dependent upon, one or both of the other two variables.

Step Three   The third step is to derive an empirical statement describing the functioning of the theoretical proposition in a marketing context. The empirical statement might be as follows: A consumer may be attracted to a salesman because the salesman is perceived to be supportive of the consumer's value system (the intrinsic reward) or because the salesman provides needed material assistance (the extrinsic reward).

Step Four   The implications of the empirical statement are shown in Figure 6.2, which depicts four selling situations. The ideal situation exists when the consumer receives both high intrinsic rewards (he believes the salesman holds views similar to his own on important matters) and high extrinsic rewards (the product is perceived to be of good quality). The likelihood of a sale is high when the consumer finds the salesman personally attractive and the product or service the salesman represents appealing. By reverse analogy, the situation in cell 4 is bleak; neither the salesman nor his product provides the consumer with any satisfaction.

Cells 2 and 3 represent rather interesting states. Consumers in these two cells might be in a state of cognitive inconsistency or imbalance. The resulting cognitive strain toward consistency could cause consumers to move toward either cell 1 or cell 4 depending on the relative magnitude of the intrinsic and extrinsic rewards.

It is the task of promotional efforts to shift consumers in cells 2 and 3 to cell 1. Because of their possible cognitive imbalance and consequent strain toward consistency, consumers in these cells would probably respond to promotional efforts; they are already disposed toward change. Consumers in cell 4 may display the greatest sales resistance.

Step Five   At this point it becomes necessary to outline the appropriate strategy or strategies.

Assume that a sales manager with limited resources has obtained data describing the relative importance consumers place on intrinsic and extrinsic rewards. Because of his limited resources, the manager may do only one of two things: (1) He may attempt to increase the intrinsic appeal of the selling situation for the consumer. This could be accomplished by identifying consumer groups on the basis of sociopsychological variables, and by recruiting or reassigning salesmen so that there is a greater matching between salesman

Figure 6.2   Reward conditions and market implications.

		Extrinsic rewards	
		High	Low
Intrinsic rewards	High	1 *Conditions:* 1. Consumer receives social support 2. Consumer perceives product or service favorably *Implications:* 3. Full attraction 4. Sale very likely	2 *Conditions:* 1. Consumer receives social support 2. Consumer perceives product or service unfavorably *Implications:* 3. Partial attraction 4. Moderate likelihood of a sale
	Low	3 *Conditions:* 1. Consumer receives little social support 2. Consumer perceives the product or service favorably *Implications:* 3. Partial attraction 4. Moderate likelihood of a sale	4 *Conditions:* 1. Consumer receives little social support 2. Consumer perceives product or service unfavorably *Implications:* 3. No attraction 4. Sale very unlikely

Source: Zaltman, "Marketing Inference in the Behavioral Sciences," July, 1970, p. 31. Reprinted from *Journal of Marketing*, published by the American Marketing Association.

and consumer on those variables. (2) He may use his resources to increase the extrinsic appeal of the selling situation through an advertising campaign stressing the advantages of the particular product, or by a training program giving salesmen more knowledge about customer needs and uses for the product.

In analyzing the data, the manager will be concerned with (1) the frequency with which consumers fall into each of the four cells in Figure 6.2; (2) which of the two situations, cells 2 or 3, has the largest number of consumers; and (3) the frequency of sales among consumers in each cell.

Step Six   The final step is to implement the appropriate strategy. Before doing this on a large scale, however, it may be very desirable to test the implications of both steps four and five through test marketing, survey research, controlled laboratory experiments, simulation, or other suitable techniques.

CHAPTER 7

THE NATURE OF
PREDICTION

INTRODUCTION

There is probably no intellectual problem as pervasive as that of drawing inferences from what we know to something we would also like to know. In the previous chapter we saw that such inferences usually take the form of trying (1) to elaborate from accumulated data general principles that govern these data, and (2) stating the future consequences of these general principles as they continue to operate on existing or comparable new data. This is

146

basically what prediction is about. In the social sciences generally, prediction refers to a stated expectation about a particular aspect of behavior or some particular set of circumstances that may be verified by subsequent observations. For example, it might be predicted that individuals with high levels of psychological detachment will display low levels of brand loyalty to convenience goods.[1] This expected behavior with regard to branded convenience goods could be verified relatively easily.

The problem of prediction in marketing is of great importance.[2] Predicting buyer response to new products, predicting competitors' behavior, predicting what levels of fear appeal will be optimal in a promotional campaign, and predicting channel effectiveness are just a few areas where prediction is important. In all instances marketers respond by predicting—that is, by estimating some property of a phenomenon, *prior* to actual knowledge about that property. If the marketer is fortunate enough to be dealing with phenomena governed by precise, known laws, prediction can be easily reduced to a problem of deductive logic. If a monopolistic situation holds and the shape of the demand curve is known, then revenues produced by different prices can be predicted fairly accurately. Unfortunately, most of the predictions marketers are faced with in practical affairs are not so clear-cut. Uncertainty usually surrounds the competitive environment and the shape of the demand curve. For example, there is the problem of knowing what the general principles are that operate in the market. This involves the problem of explanation and understanding. For example, consider the problem of new product introductions. Two general principles that apply to this situation are the following: (1) The higher the perceived risk, the higher the word-of-mouth activity among consumers. (2) The nature of word-of-mouth messages—that is, positive or negative comments about the product—influences the diffusion of the product.[3] Given that a marketer is aware of these general principles he can predict that they will be operative among targeted consumers, although before being able to adjust his marketing strategy he still has to determine the actual state of the two crucial variables: (1) Is the product perceived as involving high risk? (2) What is the nature of the word-of-mouth messages?

The problem of understanding general principles that can be expected to operate in the future under some set of expected conditions suggests that the better our understanding and our explanations the better our predictions. It is true of course that there are instances when accurate prediction can be obtained without our being able to explain the phenomena involved. These situations are not very common in the world of marketing, particularly con-

[1] Joel B. Cohen, "An Interpersonal Orientation to the Study of Consumer Behavior."
[2] See, for example, David Aaker, "Using Buyer Behavior Models To Improve Marketing Decisions," and David B. Montgomery and Glen Urban, *Management Science in Marketing.*
[3] Donald F. Cox, ed., *Risk-Taking and Information Handling in Consumer Behavior.*

sumer behavior. Consequently, the initial discussion in this chapter concerns the relationship between explanation and prediction. Different levels of understanding in prediction are then treated and followed by an excursus on various methods for predicting consumer behavior. The concluding section is concerned with evaluating prediction. Since the purpose of this chapter is to convey an understanding of the nature of prediction with maximal clarity and a minimum of distraction by tangential issues, we shall minimize discussion of technical complications caused by measurement problems.

THE NATURE OF PREDICTION

The term "prediction" is generally used in two ways. First, it is often used "for making deductions from known to unknown events within a conceptually static system"[4] An example is the use of regression analysis to estimate one variable from one or more other variables. This is a frequent practice in using personality variables to "predict" buyer behavior[5] or to use discriminant function analysis to predict adopter categories on the basis of psychosocial and demographic variables.[6]

Using the term "prediction" on the basis of discriminant function analysis is criticized by some on linguistic grounds: They argue that since to predict is literally to say in advance, the term "prediction" should be limited to forecasting the future and the term "retrodiction" should refer to what might be called "aftercast" or assertions about the past or present.[7] An example of retrodiction is any quality control test wherein the quality of a shipment is established from the quality of a presumably representative sample. Similarly, in inferential statistics, characteristics of a population are inferred from the characteristics of a representative sample. Philosophers such as Margenau point out that prediction does not necessarily mean forecast: "Pre" implies "prior to complete knowledge" and does not contrast with "post."[8]

A second use of the term involves making assertions about future outcomes on the basis of recurring sequences of events. Sometimes, such statements are timebound, as in predicting for a given period. This is a form of prediction frequently labeled "forecasting." Another form of prediction common to marketing is test marketing, which assumes that processes occurring in the test market will be "reoccurring" not only in the test market but in

---

[4] R. Schuessler, "Prediction," p. 418.
[5] Franklin B. Evans, "Psychological and Objective Factors in the Prediction of Brand Choice."
[6] Thomas S. Robertson and James N. Kennedy, "Prediction of Consumer Innovators: Application of Multiple Discriminant Analysis."
[7] For a detailed treatment of retrodiction see Mario Bunge, *Scientific Research*, Vol. II, pp. 665–674, and N. Rescher, *Scientific Explanation*, pp. 34–35.
[8] H. Margenau, *The Nature of Physical Reality*, p. 105.

comparable other areas, so that the recurring sequence of events in the test market adequately predict an outcome in the relative future in other contexts.

In the remainder of this chapter the term "prediction" will be largely restricted to the following meaning: prediction refers to statements (1) about future outcomes and (2) generally—but not always—based on the observation of regularities among events of the past.

SCIENTIFIC VERSUS NONSCIENTIFIC PREDICTION

Scientific prediction may be contrasted with other forms of prediction sometimes used by marketers. Bunge, for example, distinguishes scientific prediction from the following nonscientific types, which are listed in Table 7.1.[9] *Expectation* is an automatic attitude of anticipation acquired through prior learning experiences. Consumers expect that a brand of product customarily stocked by their food store will be available to them on the shopping trip there or consumers expect through prior experience to find particular kinds of goods in particular stores. In fact, retailers often stock low-profit products simply because consumers expect to find these products in their retail outlets.

Table 7.1 Major Types of Prediction

Type of Prediction	Main Characteristic (as opposed to those of preceding type)
Expectation	*Automatic adjustment* to environment through learning processes
Guess	*Conscious* operation
Prophecy	Conscious operation made on *a larger scale*
Prognosis	*Rational* operation guided by common-sense rules
Scientific prediction	Rational operation guided by *scientific* rules

Source: Adapted from Mario Bunge, *Scientific Research*, Vol. II, p. 66. Berlin: Springer-Verlag, 1967. Reprinted with permission of Springer-Verlag, New York.

Guessing is a conscious, but nonrational (that is, unfounded), effort to determine what a situation was, is, or will be. This would be characteristic of a consumer choosing a product from a selection of brands with which he is totally unfamiliar. The process of predicting a good brand is based on a process of random choice. *Prophecy* is large-scale guessing on the alleged ground of revelation. *Prognosis* is an informed guess or common-sense prediction; it is forecast with the help of more or less tacit empirical generalizations. For example, the quality of a new product might be predicted on the basis

[9] Bunge, *Scientific Research*, Vol. II, p. 66.

of prior experience with other products sold by the same producer. Vicarious modeling or the use of someone else's experience with a product as a basis for decision making is another example of consumer prognosis.

All types of prediction shown in Table 7.1 differ in their formulation and approximation to scientific prediction. They are all alike, however, in their broad social purpose, which is "to secure a measure of control over what would otherwise be a less manageable circumstance."[10]

THE STRUCTURE OF SCIENTIFIC PREDICTION

Scientific prediction is prediction with the help of scientific or technological theories and data. It is a statement or set of statements (1) whose premises are true, (2) that contain data statements that are true but refer to times no later than the present, and (3) that relate to the relative future. All scientific prediction involves some theory from which deductions are possible. Also required is some factual evidence relevant to the proposition of the theory.

Most philosophers of science feel scientific prediction to be a special form of explanation (future-oriented explanation) with slight modification.

Hempel and Oppenheim view the logical structure of scientific explanation as follows:[11]

> *Requirement 1.* The explanandum must be a logical consequence of the explanans.
>
> *Requirement 2.* The explanans must contain general laws required for the derivation of the explanandum.
>
> *Requirement 3.* The explanans must have empirical content.
>
> *Requirement 4.* The sentences constituting the explanans must be true.

It is this pattern that is said to be identical with that of scientific prediction. As Hempel and Oppenheim put it, ". . . the same formal analysis, including the four necessary conditions, applies to scientific prediction as well as to explanation."[12] The pragmatic difference as they formulate it in agreement with most other authors, lies in the fact that explanation "is directed toward past occurrences," whereas prediction is directed "toward future ones." Figure 7.1 is a paradigm of the position taken by Hempel and Oppenheim.

This implies that every scientific explanation, if stated prior to the event

---

[10] R. Schuessler, "Prediction," p. 418.
[11] Carl G. Hempel and P. Oppenheim, "Studies in the Logic of Explanation," pp. 137–138.
[12] Hempel and Oppenheim, p. 138.

Figure 7.1   Scientific explanation and prediction viewed in time.

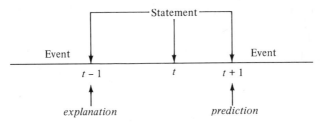

described by its explanandum will be predictive, whereas every scientific prediction stated after the event in question will be explanatory.

"The test then is . . . to use the deductive technique of explanation on a future event; that is, to take the risk of being proved wrong by making a prediction. The argument involved in making a prediction is a slight modification of that involved in an explanation. In a prediction the conditions—some antecedent event or events—are the starting point, working through a law to the predicted event, whereas, in an explanation, the explanandum is the starting point, and only such conditions are involved as to make its following from the law plausible."[13] In other words, one assumes that the event has predictive power *if the initial conditions of the explanation are ascertained before t and the laws or principles used in the explanation are also known before t.* The explanation of the event at time *t* could have functioned prior to *t* as a prediction of the event occurring at time *t.* For example, if we know that norms of reciprocity are operating in a particular sales context (these are the initial conditions), the we can use the general principle that norms of reciprocity render personal selling particularly effective to predict that the actual use of personal selling will be very successful in this context. Using additional principles such as those involving heterophilous and homophilous phenomena, which are also explanatory principles, we can make still more accurate predictions of outcomes of particular salesman-prospect interactions. Thus the more refined our explanations are involving states of the context of concern prior to *t*, the more accurate and more complete will be our predictions. As another example, we may have as a starting point the purchase of a product or service (for which there are many comparable alternatives) involving a major commitment of resources by the consumer. In this case the principle of cognitive dissonance can be used to predict with a relatively high degree of accuracy that the buyer will experience dissonance and seek information supportive of his particular action. This is in contrast to observing postpurchase information-seeking behavior and explaining it in terms of the need to reduce the dissonance that arises when a major decision is made in the face of alternatives having highly attractive features.

---

[13] Peter Caws, *The Philosophy of Science: A Systematic Account*, p. 94.

In recent years some methodologists and philosophers of science have vigorously criticized the principle of structural identity of prediction and explanation.[14] According to them, the most basic difference between explanation and prediction is with respect to the grounds they each offer for their claims.

It seems to us that the above controversy is groundless, since when Hempel and Oppenheim speak of prediction they obviously mean "scientific prediction" (according to Bunge's terminology) whereas their opponents deal rather with a meaning of prediction closer to that of prognosis.

Despite the parallel between explanation and prediction it is possible to perform one of the functions and not the other. Kaplan notes, for example, that "if we look at the explanations which actually occur in science as well as in everyday life, and not only at what an ideal explanation would be or at what all explanations are 'in principle,' it appears that we often have explanations without being able to predict, that is without being in a position where we could have predicted if only we had had the explanation in time."[15] For example, explanations of the occurrence of earthquakes and evolutionary explanations of the emergence of a new biological species are lacking in predictive power. Similarly, we may have rich explanations of consumer response to an innovation in terms of how they perceive the innovation—that is, what they perceive the relevant attributes to be. Yet the very nature of the innovation phenomenon makes the accurate anticipation of future consumer response very difficult. Other philosophers have also pointed out the paradox of being able to predict without explaining.[16] This paradox is again due to semantic intricacies, for "predictive," in this context, refers to scientific explanations. Another author to fall into the semantic trap is Dubin. He notes that:

> High precision in prediction may be independent of any understanding of the process producing the forecasted outcome. [Moreover] powerful understanding of the process of interaction [of explanatory variables] does not, by itself, guarantee precision in prediction.[17]

This leads to what Dubin calls the precision paradox (the ability to predict an outcome of some human phenomenon without being able to explain it)

[14] See M. S. Scriven, "Definitions, Explanations, and Theories," and I. Scheffler, *The Anatomy of Inquiry.*

[15] Abraham Kaplan, *The Conduct of Inquiry: Methodology for Behavioral Sciences,* p. 347.

[16] John G. Kemeny, *A Philosopher Looks at Science,* p. 165; Rescher, *Scientific Explanation,* pp. 30–36; and Hempel and Oppenheim, "Studies in the Logic of Explanation," p. 138.

[17] Robert Dubin, *Theory Building,* p. 25.

and the power paradox (the ability to provide profound insight into some phenomena without being able to predict tc any precise degree future states of those phenomena). Dubin's paradoxes are based on a confusion of the two types of scientific explanation (and prediction), namely low-level explanation, which is based on empirical generalizations, and theoretical explanations. When Dubin talks about "understanding" and "profound insight" he presumably refers not even to theoretical explanation but to psychological correlates of them.

We can, however, make fairly precise predictions that consumers who have low degrees of self-confidence and low self-esteem and who buy a durable good recently placed in the market and involving some risk of social disapproval will experience some considerable degree of cognitive dissonance. Moreover, we can predict with a high probability of being correct that the consumer under these circumstances will actively seek information supporting his decision. These predictions may be made simply on the basis of past surveys or experiments that demonstrated statistical association among the variables mentioned. There is no need or requirement that we understand how low self-confidence is related to cognitive dissonance or how such dissonance is converted into actual behavior in order to make those rather accurate predictions. Note too that the information-gathering process enabling us to make those predictions also enables us to say rather precisely what the probability is that the predicted situation will come about. In fact, behavioral scientists think of prediction as one aspect of probability, since predictions are never certain as to their ultimate accuracy.[18] Similarly, the extrapolation of time-series data permit good prediction without needing theoretical explanations of why the variables used behave as they do.

It is also the case, however, that lack of explanation or understanding of the variables in some system state may lead to poor prediction. For example, market researchers and others have long been concerned with discrepancies between attitudes and behaviors. There is a consensus that despite the strong logical appeal of the argument that people should act in ways consistent with their thoughts and feelings, attitudes are a poor predictor of behavior. Perhaps Deutscher has expressed this as well as anyone: "No matter what one's [a researcher's] theoretical orientation may be, he has no reason to expect to find congruence between attitudes and actions and every reason to expect to find discrepancies between them."[19]

Attitude research in marketing has a long tradition and currently a strong popularity despite serious problems. Undoubtedly, as research continues in and out of marketing on the basic nature and dimension of attitudes and attitude measurement devices, attitude-behavior relationships will become

[18] Joseph F. Rychlak, *A Philosophy of Science for Personality Theory*, p. 151.
[19] I. Deutscher, "Words and Deeds: Social Science and Social Policy," p. 247.

better understood. This in turn will improve our ability to predict behavior from attitudes in those situations where attitudes imply behavior.[20]

LEVELS OF UNDERSTANDING IN PREDICTION

Given the structural parallel between explanation and prediction and, in some instances, the subsumption of prediction by explanation, we can specify four possible levels of understanding in prediction. This is presented in Table 7.2 which is an adaptation of Doby's discussion of explanation.[21] Corresponding marketing illustrations will be presented. Note, however, that nothing is said about the values of the different variables or the nature of their attributes. The statements in Table 7.2 are purely verbal statements corresponding to different levels of *knowledge or understanding* in prediction. Moreover, they do not state the direction of events.

Table 7.2   Levels of Understanding in Prediction

Understanding in Level of Prediction	Prediction[a]
Level 1	A certain phenomenon will be in existence in the relative future.
Level 2	The phenomenon will be of the nature Q as a result of (produced by) factors $X_1, X_2, \ldots, X_n$.
Level 3	Factors $X_1, X_2, \ldots, X_n$ have interacted in the past, and are now interacting or will interact in the future in manner $Y_1, Y_2, \ldots, Y_n$ to produce in the relative future a phenomenon of the nature Q.
Level 4	Factors $X_1, X_2, \ldots, X_n$ will interact in manner $Y_1, Y_2, \ldots, Y_n$ for reasons $W_1, W_2, \ldots, W_n$, thus producing a phenomenon of the nature Q in the relative future.

[a] Y_1, Y_2, and so forth, in levels 3 and 4 represent forms of interaction between factors; for example, "the more X, the more X_2" or "X_1 causes X_2."

Consider now an example of different levels of understanding in prediction derived from theoretical models relevant to international marketing discussed by Rogers[22] and others concerning innovation in developing societies. The basic theory involves four interrelated concepts: literacy, cosmopoliteness, empathy, and innovativeness. Table 7.3 and Figure 7.2 present concept definitions and theoretical statements and relationships.

At level 1 in Table 7.2, the simple statement is that in the relative future more innovative social units (society, group, individual) will exist. The social unit is the phenomenon of concern.

[20] See, for example, Martin Fishbein, "Attitude and the Prediction of Behavior"; Milton Rokeach, "Attitude Change and Behavior Change"; and George Day, "Theories of Attitude Structure and Change."

[21] John T. Doby, "Logic and Levels of Scientific Explanation," pp. 147–152.

[22] Everett M. Rogers, *Modernization among Peasants: The Impact of Communication.*

Table 7.3 Hypotheses and Concept Definitions[a]

Hypotheses

Literacy is positively associated with (produces) empathy
Literacy is positively associated with (produces) cosmopoliteness
Literacy is positively associated with (produces) innovativeness
Cosmopoliteness is positively associated with (produces) empathy
Cosmopoliteness is positively associated with (produces) innovativeness
Empathy is positively associated with (produces) innovativeness

Concept Definitions[a]

Literacy: the degree of mastery over symbols in written form
Cosmopoliteness: the degree of orientation to events outside the immediate social system
Empathy: the ability to project oneself into the role or situation of another who is different
Innovativeness: the degree to which one is earlier than others to adopt new practices or ideas

[a] Definitions adapted from Rogers, *Modernization among Peasants*.

Figure 7.2 Causally related variables. (Plus sign indicates positive causal impact.)

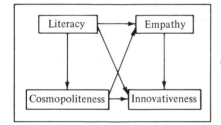

Indep. Var.	Dependent Variables		
	Cos.	Emp.	Innov.
Lit.	+	+	+
Cos.		+	+
Emp.			+

The second level of prediction is that more innovative social units, Q, will exist as a result of increases in literacy, cosmopoliteness, and empathy. These three variables are the factors X_1, X_2, and so forth, referred to in Table 7.2. Q is the nature of the phenomenon.

At the third level of prediction we say that the three factors have interacted in the past, and/or are now interacting and/or will interact in the future in such a manner as to produce a change in innovativeness.[23] The "in such a manner" is the focus of prediction at this level. For example, we might predict the following manner or type of interaction between literacy and empathy: Higher degrees of mastery over symbols in written form (liter-

[23] By "interaction" we mean the interplay that occurs between concepts—that is, the occurrence of the impact each concept has on the other.

acy), widen experiences through meaningful encounters with the print media, and unlock mental abilities, allowing the social unit to encompass these new experiences. This, in turn, increases the ability to project oneself into the role or situation of another. Such identification is a direct antecedent of being innovative.[24]

At level 4, emphasis is on the reasons why (W_1) literacy and empathy (and the other factor combinations, such as, literacy-cosmopoliteness, and others) interact in the manner (Y_1) just described and why empathy and the other variables may produce innovativeness directly independent of the impact of interaction effects. The reason why empathy affects innovativeness may be found in the concept of vicarious modeling. The reason for the literacy-empathy relationship may be found in contemporary theories of creativity. Thus, the prediction that Q is of a specified nature ultimately rests on the prediction that vicarious modeling, certain creative processes, and other reasons have been or will be in operation. The reasons just cited are themselves subject to analytical analysis at each of the four levels of explanation and prediction.

Let us consider a second example of different levels of understanding in prediction in a communications context. The marketing problem is to predict the probable impact of a communication on a preselected market segment. At level 1 we can only say, optimistically, that in the future, after exposure to the communication, consumers will be better informed about our product. The phenomenon Q in this case is a better-informed consumer. The second level states that better-informed consumers will exist as a result of the particular appeals (factors X_1, X_2, and so forth) used in the communication. More specifically, the factors may consist of a fear appeal, the use of unbiased information, and a testimonial. At a still higher level of understanding, resulting in a more accurate prediction, we know that the fear appeal, testimonial, and unbiased information when coupled in a single communication will interact in manner Y_1, Y_2, and so forth, to produce or result in a more informed consumer group.

The manner of interaction may be as follows: The use of a fear appeal sensitizes the audience to a problem about which information is required to permit action to reduce the fear. The testimonial is used in two ways: (1) to "verify" or confirm for the potential consumer that the fear is well founded and (2) to provide legitimately for the recommended means (some product or service) of reducing the fear. The use of unbiased information adds to the credibility of the person used in the testimony and lends realism to the basis of the fear. Thus the fear appeal widens a person's information-seeking behavior to encompass data relevant to the fear. Through this widening, the indi-

---

[24] Homer G. Barnett, *Innovation: The Basis of Cultural Change*, and Max Bruck, *Empathy and Ideology: Aspects of Administrative Innovation.*

vidual is more likely to be exposed and attentive to information provided by presumably unbiased sources presenting unbiased information. The unbiased source lends strength to the fear appeal and the seemingly unbiased information makes the testimonial more effective and credible. What is happening here is the interaction of two persuasive tactics of change, the use of fear and testimonials, with an educational tactic, the use of unbiased information. Thus, having knowledge of the factors and the way they interact—in this case, favorably—enables one to predict with greater confidence that consumers will be more informed after exposure to the communication.

A still higher level stresses the reasons why fear appeals, testimonials, and unbiased information will interact favorably to produce more informed consumers. Understanding the *why* dimension, however, does not add to the accuracy of the prediction. Level 3 provides a better basis for making predictions than do the lower levels; but level 3 is no less powerful in prediction than level 4, it is only lower in terms of understanding. Thus, although better understanding will generally produce better predictions, this is not always the case.

To complete the illustration, however, the reasons why the factors mentioned interact as they do may be found in the psychological process of information decoding. The consumer has a need to interpret or decode the fear message in a way that is meaningful and permits fear reduction. The testimonial using unbiased information and recommending a course of action enables the consumer to decode the fear in a meaningful way and offers him a channel for reduction of the fear. The decoding process brings the various elements in the communication together in an interactive way.

PREDICTION TECHNIQUES

There are several techniques for predicting in the social sciences.[25] Among these techniques one can distinguish two basic types depending on the nature of the independent variable(s). *Extrapolation* techniques predict a variable from itself. *Associative techniques*, on the other hand, predict a variable from one or more other variables. A combination of both is also possible. For example: Brand loyalty$_{T+1}$ = f(advertising$_{T+1}$, brand loyalty$_T$). Let us give two examples of each type of technique.

EXTRAPOLATION TECHNIQUES

Social physics is a prominent example of extrapolation techniques. It is based on the assumption that there are basic regularities in human behavior that are independent of the will of any individual or, in the long run, independent of the actions of any group of individuals. Accordingly, because these

---

[25] See Schuessler, "Prediction," pp. 418–423, and I. D. J. Bross, *Design for Decision*, pp. 33–35.

regularities have occurred in the past and are largely unalterable, they will occur in the future. The assumption of the classic S-shaped diffusion curve as describing the rate of the adoption of innovations is an example. Another example is provided by the product-life-cycle concept.[26]

Consumption patterns varying with the life cycle is yet another illustration. Demand forecasting for many products and services is based on an estimate of the size of a given age category at different points of time. The assumption here is that there are regularities in product purchases associated with age such that people in retirement during time period 2 will display consumption practices very similar to people in retirement at period 1.

Another form of prediction, *trends and forecasts*, involves some form of extrapolation from time-series data on the use of statistical demand analysis. Trends and forecasts are frequently used in economics, demography, and marketing and need not be elaborated further here. From these two techniques is the expectation of regularities, which is well founded in many instances. One more illustration of an extrapolation technique in a marketing context, however, shows that there are exceptions to the regularity assumption. Most researchers have argued that dynamics of brand loyalty is a first-order Markov process. They feel that purchase probability as a measure of brand loyalty, at time t is dependent only on the immediate past purchase at $t - 1$ and *any earlier history is irrelevant for prediction*. It is assumed that the first-order conditions represent the stable forces. It is noticeable also that under some certain circumstances, looking at past regularities is a very poor way of marshaling evidence. Consider the trivial but illustrative case of consumer C, who has been buying his corn flakes weekly for two years for a price of 55 cents. One day he is required to pay 70 cents. C may wonder if next week he can expect to pay 55 cents again. On the basis of the great preponderance of 55-cent corn flakes in his sample, C should answer "yes," which is highly unlikely to happen since C knows that food prices cannot change twice in such a short period of time.

ASSOCIATIVE TECHNIQUES

As mentioned before, associative techniques predict a variable from one or more variables. The two examples of such techniques that we shall pose differ in the type of independent variables. The first one, structural certainties, uses structural variables of a given system in order to predict a particular system behavior. The other one, the operational code, uses behavioral norms in order to predict behavior.

An example of structural certainties would be legally prescribed and/or traditionally reinforced behaviors—that is, behaviors based on custom and law. Thus, one could have predicted with a high degree of certainty, assuming adequate knowledge about social customers, that do-it-yourself type products

---

[26] Philip Kotler, *Marketing Management*, pp. 429–438.

would not succeed in the middle and upper classes of Venezuela for reasons related to the relationship between manual labor and social status. Similarly, knowing the communication network in a group makes it possible to predict, with some degree of reliability, the diffusion pattern of information among members of that group. That is, given the hypothesis that some individuals compared to others have relatively substantial communication contact with other group members (structural characteristics) and given the empirical knowledge that information on some product has or has not been given this person as opposed to a less well-integrated member of the same group, we could predict whether the information dissemination will be relatively fast or slow. Similarly, one could also predict the flow of influence within a social system, knowing the structural properties of that system and knowing where the first attempt to exert influence originated or where the information first made its entry into the system. Through simulation techniques it is possible to predict how different structural properties affect communication flows.[27]

The operational code refers to the dos and don'ts of conduct—that is, norms and expected role behavior. To some extent, this is a refinement of the structural certainties techniques. This form of prediction is based on the assumption that people will behave in a manner consistent with the pre-scribed rules governing action in a particular role. Thus, to an increasing degree, as marketing research has become more behaviorally oriented, we find creative use in advertising and other forms of sales promotion based on what research has led us to expect of innovators, gatekeepers, and opinion leaders in prescribed contexts. When introducing a new product or service it is neces-sary to adapt both the product and the strategy for its introduction to existing norms and the attitudes and values that support those norms. In particular, care should be taken to identify the product or service with a highly valued activity or attitude object and to minimize the likelihood of its conflicting with the sacrosanct.

Not quite at the same level as the two preceding examples but still belonging to associative techniques are *analogue predictions*.[28] They are dis-tinguishable not because of the kinds of variables they use but because of the methodology involved. Such predictions set up a correspondence between two sets of events. This is one of the most frequently used forms of predic-tion in marketing, for it includes both laboratory and field (test marketing) experimentation of promotional techniques and new products. This usually involves substantive analogues as opposed to structural analogues, where some concept—say, epidemiology—is taken from medicine and used as a basis for predicting a social phenomenon, such as the diffusion of an innovation. Analogue prediction is apparently what Greer refers to as *guided metaphor*,

[27] Barbara Koehler, Mary Beth Beres, and Gerald Zaltman, "A Simulation of Invisible Colleges."

[28] Bross, *Design for Decision*, p. 37.

in which forms or models "useful in other contexts are applied to the problem at hand." In this type of prediction "we must be certain to include all the elements necessary for the explanatory predictive power the original had. . . ."[29]

EVALUATING PREDICTIONS

Earlier discussion in this chapter asserted that for a prediction to be considered scientific, it had to satisfy a number of requirements. Here we shall discuss some additional properties that can be used to evaluate scientific predictions.

CONFIRMABILITY

The confirmability of a prediction refers to whether it is possible to assign a truth value to it. A predictive statement cannot have any practical value if it is true only by virtue of its form. There are two possibilities: Predictions may be confirmable only or they may be both confirmable and refutable.[30] The latter are the more desirable.

One reason predictions are refutable only is the insufficient development of theory or sometimes, in addition, the lack of imagination in devising test situations. Consider the application of social facilitation theory to personal selling. The current state of the art on this matter only permits a purely refutable or falsifiable statement such as the following: "The presence of a salesman, while a potential customer is reaching a decision, will affect the potential customer's decision-making process." It is obvious that a prediction based on this statement can be refuted only because it includes all possible outcomes. What is needed is a statement of the conditions under which the salesman's presence will have a positive and/or negative impact and a statement in a form which is confirmable. It might even be argued that a necessary condition for a prediction is that it will be confirmable.

An example of a prediction that is both confirmable and refutable is the following: "Consumers with moderate generalized self-confidence are more persuasible than consumers with either low or high generalized self-confidence."[31] This prediction can be confirmed and refuted by factual evidence.

As knowledge about phenomena increases, some statements capable of being refutable lose that character at least until additional knowledge is generated. One of the most widely accepted principles of mass communication and social psychology is that people seek out information that supports or reinforces their beliefs, and avoid information that challenges their opinions. This principle is central to cognitive dissonance theory and much of the literature on communication behavior. Cohen *et al.*, for example, formulated

---

[29] Scott Greer, *The Logic of Social Inquiry*, p. 143.
[30] Bunge, *Scientific Research*, Vol. I, p. 266.
[31] Raymond A. Bauer, "Self-Confidence and Persuasibility: One More Time."

a purely refutable prediction that "a person experiencing dissonance will avoid further inconsistent information and seek out consistent information in order to reduce his dissonance."[32] Further research, however, has since challenged this. For example, it has been demonstrated that some people deliberately seek out discrepant facts in order to refute them and thereby reduce dissonance. Other people apparently seek useful information, regardless of its context. Consequently, the only possible statement is that: "Some people seek out consistent information and some people seek out inconsistent information." This leads to predictions that can be confirmed but not refuted. Thus, empirical research in this instance has led to the replacement of a refutable by a nonrefutable hypothesis. Whereas the original hypothesis could serve as the basis for useful but false predictions, the new one yields true but uselsss predictions.

SCOPE

The scope of a prediction refers to the range of events that it covers. The range of events may be viewed both longitudinally and latitudinally. First, if there is a long chain of events which must take place before a given phenomenon will occur, and there are no other causal events capable of producing that phenomenon, then a prediction of that phenomenon must encompass or include accurate prediction of the state of events in the chain. This involves subpredictions for each event in the chain. It is possible, of course, that the distorting effect of one incorrect subprediction could be counterbalanced by the distortion produced by a second or more incorrect subprediction. The simple case of longitudinal prediction is shown below:

The X's represent causally related subevents which must be predicted accurately in order to predict Q accurately. In the simplest case there may only be one X.

For example, a prediction of a decision-making process outcome may be based on the simple relationship shown below:

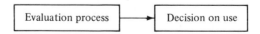

Knowing the state of the evaluation process at a given time provides a basis for estimating when a decision will be made and what that decision will be. However, knowing the nature of stages prior to evaluation provides an even

---

[32] A. R. Cohen, J. W. Brehm, and B. Latané, "Choice of Strategy and Voluntary Exposure to Information under Public and Private Conditions."

stronger basis for predicting the outcome. This becomes particularly relevant in the instance of predicting responses to products perceived by consumers as significantly different from other products and new. Thus the following situation, which is longitudinally broad in scope, would permit a more accurate prediction of the decision outcome (for purposes of simplicity, feedback loops and the possibility of skipped stages are not shown):

Knowledge about each stage provides a more accurate prediction of its effects on the subsequent stage and hence provides more insight into the functioning of that stage, which in turn permits a better (more accurate and complete) insight into the functioning of the following stage. Thus there contain "residuals," which accumulate as each decision stage is entered and experienced. These residuals enhance the ability to predict the decision outcome from the workings of the evaluation stage. Knowing how the innovation or product was initially perceived, the nature of attitudes formed, and so forth eventually help the researcher to understand evaluation processes, the stage most immediately preceding the final decision in the above paradigm. There may also be an independent—that is, noncausally related—subprediction such as this:

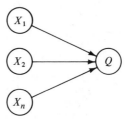

An example might involve the past experience of the potential customer, knowledge of the availability of the good or service, the physical and social environment, and the effect of special incentives provided by the producer:

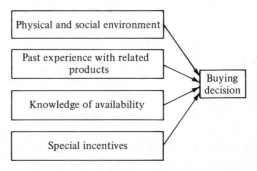

It could be argued, of course, as is always the case, that there is some relationship among the variables shown. However, they are not likely to be
strong in all instances where these factors might be found.

There are variations of course: Each independent variable could also have
a set of predictors that must be known; each X may be a necessary and
sufficient cause of Q so that knowledge of one X alone is sufficient to predict Q; or each X might be a necessary but not sufficient condition to
predict Q, requiring the addition of one or more X's.

Scope of prediction may also be viewed laterally—that is, in terms of the
number of final events, Q_n, the prediction covers. Thus we have the following situation:

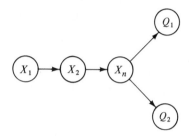

where knowledge of one or more causally related subevents X_1, and so on,
can predict two phenomena. It is necessary to distinguish between two situations. First, Q_1 and Q_2 can be two events occurring more or less at the same
time or at least coexisting. For example, the outcome of the decision-making
sequence described above may be the commitment to a radically new product
or service, Q_1. Q_2 might be the new state of cognitive equilibrium necessary
to support that commitment.

In the second situation, Q_1 and Q_2 are both potential but mutually
exclusive outcomes at any one time. If we assume the buying situation is
discrete, then the outcome of the decision-making process at any one time is
either adoption (Q_1) or rejection (Q_2). There may conceivably be still a
third possibility, Q_3, resolution, subsequent to Q_1 or Q_2. Thus, although
the Q_1 or Q_2 would remain as the independent variable, the figure in this
case should be

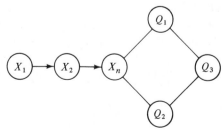

Following our earlier pattern we may also have the following situation with the same conditions concerning the necessity and sufficiency of the causal events, X_1. Each X in the paradigm immediately above could have prior causal events whose prediction must be made.

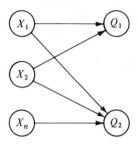

Another likely situation is where independent variables coexist and relate with multiple potential outcomes. One variant of this is shown paradigmatically as

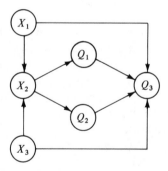

In this case, X_1 may represent psychological sources of resistance acting upon the decision-making process X_2, and X_3 represents facilitating factors also influencing the decision-making process Q_1 and Q_2, respectively, refer to an adoption or rejection decision and Q_3 refers to a resolution process affected directly by X_1 and X_3.

A more detailed illustration will be helpful here and will provide an opportunity to indicate that the more that is known about the dynamics of each X the stronger the foundation for prediction. Accordingly, in the example to follow we shall elaborate briefly upon the internal dynamics of the decision-making process described earlier. Also, we shall focus only on the following aspects of the paradigm above. That aspect of the system involving X_3 is omitted for simplicity purposes.

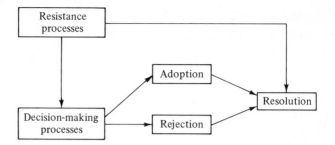

Notice that in the above example, considerable longitude is achieved (although the specific components of the decision processes are not repeated nor the resistance processes detailed) and presented in a causal chain such that the nature of one state can help predict the nature of the next state. Notice also that variables and processes operating more or less at the same time are taken into account, as are their relationships to one another, and that they are interpreted in terms of their ultimate effect on the future state of the dependent variable.

Thus when evaluating the scope of a prediction or in developing a prediction with good scope it is necessary to consider the following questions:

1. *Do the variables involved constitute sufficient longitude? (That is, is the causal chain sufficiently inclusive?)*
2. *Have variables that function more or less at the same time been taken into account?*
3. *Is there a relationship between the variables in (2) above?*
4. *Are there unrelated independent variables that begin functioning at different points in time?*
5. *Are there independent variables that are related only at certain times and not at others?*
6. *What is the "necessity" and "sufficiency" state of the variables?*
7. *Is there more than one dependent variable—that is, more than one resultant phenomenon?*
8. *If more than one, are they mutually exclusive or can they coexist?*
9. *Are there latent consequences of a set of independent variables that could negate their normal consequences?*
10. *Under what conditions are countervailing or dysfunctional latent consequences likely to become manifest? What is the likelihood of their manifestation?*

PRECISION

The precision of a prediction refers to the degree of specification of the events or variables involved and the relationships between those events or variables. For example, a statement such as "sales volume will change next

year" is imprecise. Here, prediction involves only one aspect of the concept
"sales," namely the qualitative aspect of "change." The more discussions of
the concept the prediction covers, and the more these are quantitative rather
than qualitative aspects (among the quantitative ones there is also an order
of precision, ranging from nominal to ratio scales[33]), the more precise the
prediction. The following figure illustrates various degrees of precision in the
change-of-sales example. In addition to the precision of the event, one must
also consider the degree of certainty of its occurrence. There may be complete certainty, there may be a known probability of less than 100 percent of
an event's occurrence, or there may be some degree of certainty attached even
to that probability, and finally there may be complete uncertainty (no basis
for establishing any particular probability) concerning the occurrence of a
change in the value or state of a variable, its direction, and its amplitude.
Although the nature of its subject matter prevents ever achieving this, reaching the upper right-hand cell of Table 7.4 is still the ultimate goal toward
which most marketing research is oriented. Indeed, occupancy of this cell
is the objective of science to be reached by constructing theories having high
explanatory and predictive power.

The degree of certainty attached to the predicted event is largely a func-

Table 7.4   Illustration of the Degree of Precision of a Prediction

	Event	Occurrence of Change	Direction of Change	Amplitude of Change
Degree of Certainty		Sales volume will change next year	Sales volume will increase next year	Sales volume will increase next year by 7%
Decision under certainty	It is certain that . . .			
	There is a probability of $X\%$ that . . .			
Decision under uncertainty	There is a probability of $X\%$ with a chance of error of $Y\%$ that . . .			
	Complete uncertainty that . . .			

[33] Paul E. Green and Donald S. Tull, *Research for Marketing Decisions*, pp. 176–181.

tion of the second area in which precision is relevant, namely the precision of the statements describing the rules of interaction among the system variables. This is very relevant to the problem of scope. The greater the scope of a prediction the greater the degree of precision required in stating the relationships among the independent variables and between these and the dependent variables. As Stinchcombe has observed, "the elegance and power of an explanation can only be as good as the causal connection among variables allows it to be."[34] This is also a reminder that statements of relationships between variables should not only be precise but be causal as well.

The validity of a prediction is important for its precision. *Meaningful* precision can be no more precise than conceptual validity allows it to be. Emphasis is placed on the term "meaningful" simply because one can have rather exact quantitative measurements of relationships between variables in the absence of conceptual relationships. Time is employed frequently in the sciences as a predictor variable and, as such, often is very precise in its relationship with the predicament or dependent variable. A major problem exists, however, concerning the conceptual basis for the prediction. Time is essentially a proxy variable; that is, it serves as an index for other processes, which all too often are not made explicit. Thus precise statements with good explanatory substance are not possible.

ACCURACY

Accuracy in prediction is influenced by the frequency with which factors not included in the prediction interfere with the predicted phenomenon—that is, cause it not to happen exactly as predicted. To some extent there can be a tradeoff between accuracy and precision. The less precise the prediction or, alternatively, the more vague it is, the greater the degree of fluctuation allowed in the phenomenon Q. It is up to the researcher to determine the final tradeoff point.

The accuracy of a prediction is dependent upon the degree of isomorphism between the concepts contained in the predictive premises and the empirical indicators used for a particular prediction. The accuracy of a prediction becomes more of a problem as the concepts become more theoretical and the more the context of application differs from the context(s) in which the hypothesis in the premise originally received its confirmation. From the point of view of the predictive hypothesis, this is the problem of external validity: ". . . to what populations, settings, treatment variables, and measurement variables can this effect be generalized?"[35] When the concepts are theoretical and the operationalization of the variables is new, construct validation procedures are called for.[36]

[34] Arthur L. Stinchcombe, *Constructing Social Theories*, p. 129.
[35] Donald T. Campbell and Julian C. Stanley, *Experimental and Quasi-experimental Design for Research*, p. 5.
[36] Lee J. Cronbach, *Essentials of Psychological Testing*, pp. 142–145.

The example provided in Chapter 6 illustrates the severity of the gap between empathy and the operational definition given to empathy. Using still another example, we can say that low dogmatism is a factor causing the early purchase of innovations.[37] If the empirical indicator of dogmatism is not very isomorphic with the concept of dogmatism, there will probably be a poor association found between dogmatism as theoretically defined and the early adoption of innovations. We may still find a close relationship between the adoption of innovations and the index used as a predictor variable, but the variable in question is not really dogmatism; it may be some other variable or just one particular aspect of dogmatism if the latter has multiple dimensions. Thus the prediction using dogmatism will lack the accuracy based on the theoretical definition of dogmatism. More simply, if dogmatism is not measured in a valid way there can be no accurate empirical prediction made about the impact of dogmatism on the adoption of innovations.

Another illustration of this problem can be given using the concept of an innovator. Some authors define innovators as those people who are among the first 10 percent to adopt an innovation. Others define as innovators people who perceive the item in question as new. This latter definition would very likely group consumers or potential consumers who would be among the first 10 percent to buy with those who would be the last to buy, if ever. The precision or validity of any given set of independent variables in predicting innovativeness would clearly differ in the two situations since the two sample groups differ in important ways.

In addition to the important quality of isomorphism, accuracy is also affected by the reliability of the empirical indicators—that is, the quality of measurements (as opposed to their selection) with which the prediction is made.

Kaplan takes a somewhat different view of accuracy or reliability. He defines reliability as "a measure of the extent to which measurement remains constant as it is repeated under conditions taken to be constant."[38] From this point of view of prediction, reliability is a measure of the correlation between predictions made by repeated use of the same instrument. A reason for low correlations, of course, may be the operation and influence of factors not included in the explanatory variables.

We have already discussed a good example of low accuracy. The different variables intervening between attitude and behavior is an instance where variables not frequently considered by researchers may make the prediction of behavior from attitudes difficult. As intervening variables are introduced into the prediction process, more accurate predictions should result since there is that much less "noise" entering the predictive model.

---

[37] Jacob Jacoby, "Personality and Innovation Proneness."
[38] Kaplan, The Conduct of Inquiry, p. 129.

Attitudes themselves may be intervening variables with cognitive, affective, and action-predisposition subcomponents. This is shown in Figure 7.3. Thus, if one wants to determine how particular stimuli influence the perception of a product or service it becomes necessary to consider the cognitive component of attitudes as mediators between the stimuli and the dependent variable.

Figure 7.3   A schematic conception of attitudes.

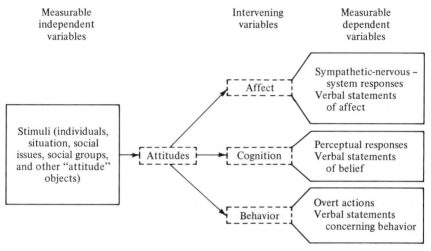

Source: H. Triandis, *Attitude and Attitude Change*, p. 3, © John Wiley & Sons, Inc. Reprinted by John Wiley & Sons, Inc.

Another situation common to consumer behavior is found in a communications context. The initial stimulus may be a particular message meant to influence a specific audience. Intervening variables mediating the impact of this message would likely be the source of the communication and the channels through which it is delivered. More accurately, the affect component of attitudes toward the source and channel would influence the process of decoding the initial stimuli. Thus the accuracy of predictions linking a given product message to particular types of responses must take into account the source and channel effect as reflected by affect components of attitudes.

POWER

Power in prediction is a partial function of the precision of the predictive statement and its scope. The more precise and encompassing of variables a predictive explanation is, the more powerful it is. It is more powerful in the sense that it provides a greater opportunity to control and to control more accurately those variables amenable to control or external manipulation by the researcher or planner.

As was seen earlier, predictions, in order to qualify as scientific predictions, must satisfy a certain number of requirements. Similarly, for factual theories to be regarded as scientific they too must yield predictive formulas satisfying those same requisites. Let us turn now to a more detailed consideration of those requirements.

One obvious condition is that a predictive statement cannot have any practical value if it is *only* logically true—in other words, if it is true only by virtue of its form or if by virtue of the meanings of its components, it has no factual referent. For example, a predictive statement such as "the mere presence of other individuals at sales parties will facilitate or inhibit purchases" has no test value. It is true by itself; that is, it is logically true. This problem has already been treated to some extent.

The following statement about consumer behavior is of mixed power; it is very complete but not very precise: "The consumer's self-image stems from his personality characteristics plus existential social forces such as social learning and communication."[39] The statement is valuable: It possesses causal imagery (patterns of cause and effect) and encompasses broad independent variables. However, the particular personality characteristics and social forces are not stated nor is there any indication as to whether social forces and personality characteristics are additive or multiplicative. Added precision could be obtained by identifying and determining the interrelationship of such variables as self-confidence, need for achievement, dogmatism, control beliefs, reference group dynamics, education, and the like. A more powerful prediction in that it is more precise, is: "Anxiety manifest itself in the purchase behavior in the form of confusion or accelerated search activity, or more deliberate behavior on the part of the purchaser."[39] Specific microlevel phenomena are specified—for example, anxiety-accelerated search and deliberativeness. Some precision is lost, however, since we are not told which of the dependent variables capable of being induced by anxiety is likely to produce particular alternative outcomes.

One problem involving the completeness of power is the issue of prediction as feedback; that is, a stated prediction may affect its own fulfillment. This is largely relevant to social rather than physical contexts. A promotional campaign stressing the virtues of a new nonprescription drug may, through the power of suggestion, cause people actually to experience relief solely on the basis of the prediction that it would provide relief. Studies on placebo effects provide the scientific grounding for such a statement. However, the

[39] Rom J. Markin, *The Psychology of Consumer Behavior*, p. 242.

feedback could be negative if excessive unrealistic expectations were built in the consumer's mind that the product could not match in actual use.

One final dimension of power needs to be addressed. This involves a clarification of the tasks of prediction through making the useful distinction between intrinsic and extrinsic tasks. *Extrinsic predictive tasks* involve qualitative and/or quantitative details of behavior that are objectively correlated with situational facts. The psychological substance that mediates the correlation can often be disregarded. The predictive method can consist entirely of an empirically derived regression equation in some instances.

Extrinsic predictive tasks are geared to answering such questions as the following:

1. What act will occur (among several possible acts)? For example, if the consumer is offered a premium, will he be interested or not?
2. What will be the intensity of the response? Will the consumer be somewhat, or strongly, interested? Will he buy one package or more? Will he generate some word-of-mouth communication?
3. In what situations will a given act be performed at least to some minimum degree? For example, will the consumer be interested by a premium in cases of overabundance?
4. How much pressure is necessary to evoke a response of a specified nature or intensity? How valuable, attractive, and so on should the incentive be?

Intrinsic predictive tasks shift the emphasis away from the outer world and specific behavior toward abstract conceptualization of behavior and to the relatively enduring intrapsychic system. The data essentially involve an endogenous process. Intrinsic predictive tasks refer to questions of the following nature:

1. What kinds of situations or patterns of relationships characterize the individual's buying behavior? Will he be a loyal buyer or not?
2. What patterns of conflicts, attitudes, aptitudes, motives, psychodynamics, defenses, and traits characterize him?

SUMMARY

To summarize, it has been indicated that prediction is an extremely important task in marketing. Consequently, it is very important that marketers have a grasp of the basic elements of prediction. This involves a basic understanding of the nature of prediction and awareness of the distinction between scientific and nonscientific prediction and the structure of scientific prediction. Furthermore, the marketer must be sensitive to the existence of various levels of understanding in prediction and must be conversant with the major predictive techniques. This chapter has attempted to cover those topics and provide the reader with a greater sensitivity to the problems and issues involved in making predictions. Various criteria for evaluating predictions were also presented to enable the reader to be more critical in formulating and using predictions.

CHAPTER 8

METACRITERIA FOR CONTROL

INTRODUCTION

Science has a multiplicity of purposes. Some of these are basic and theoretical, such as explanation and prediction, whereas other purposes are more practical and concerned with control.[1] However, even these varied purposes are interrelated, as evidenced in the preceding chapters on explanation and prediction. Explanation serves a twofold function: (1) to satisfy the human

[1] N. Rescher, *Scientific Explanation*, p. 131.

need to anticipate events (prediction) and (2) to be able to control future events. It is this latter phenomenon, control, that is of concern here. Many scientists claim that control is the central factor in the scientific enterprise. One social scientist philosopher argues that the deductive paradigm of explanation overemphasizes the logical properties of scientific theories and ignores such considerations as the purposes of inquiry and the use made of scientific theories and their constituent explanations.[2] Kelman[3] and Warwick[4] are two of the relatively few social scientists seriously concerned with such issues.

THE CONCEPT OF CONTROL

What does it mean to say that a company controls its market share? And what does "control" mean in the following question: "How can top management secure better control over the operation of the company's marketing subsystem?"[5] In other words, under what conditions can we say that *A* controls *B*?

The sense in which we intend to use "control" here has been best expressed by Skinner: "When we discover an independent variable which can be controlled, we discover a means of controlling the behavior which is a function of it."[6] Note that Skinner uses the concept of control twice: once in reference to the independent variable and once in reference to the dependent variable. Essential to this use of the concept of control is the idea of an intervention in the environment—that is, the creation of a change. A company "controls" its promotional program; that is, it designs, creates, and releases certain stimuli that, to some extent, in turn "control" the behavior of consumers exposed to the stimuli. On some occasions it would seem odd to talk about control of independent variables, particularly when they are close to us, such as speech and gesturization. Nevertheless, the only essential difference to the control of more remote variables is the number of links involved (counted from what we perceive to be the origin of the control chain).

Control as used in this chapter is the systematic manipulation of some element related to or contained within a system so as to effect a change in one or more elements in that system. Control over a particular event can be achieved if the relations specified in the explanation may be manipulated; manipulation of relationships requires manipulation of variables identified in explanations and used in predictions. The definition of control also permits an external state—that is, the environment of a system—to be a source of

[2] E. J. Meehan, *Explanation in Social Science: A System Paradigm.*
[3] Herbert Kelman, *A Time To Speak.*
[4] Donald Warwick and Herbert Kelman, "Ethical Issues in Social Intervention," in *Processes and Phenomena of Social Change.*
[5] Philip Kotler, *Marketing Management: Analysis, Planning, and Control,* 2d ed., p. 755.
[6] B. F. Skinner, *Science and Human Behavior,* p. 227.

causal forces. Control over an event is achieved if endogenous and/or exogenous variables contained in an explanation are manipulated so that a desired result is obtained.

This use of the concept of control renders it equivalent to the concept of cause, and Skinner actually seems to use them interchangeably: "Any condition or event which can be shown to have an effect upon behavior must be taken into account. By discovering and analyzing these causes we can predict behavior; to the extent that we can manipulate them, we can control behavior."[7] Hence, "*A* controls *B*" is equivalent to "*A* causes *B*." Another psychologist employs the concept of causality in the same sense: "Of all of the correlations observable in the social environment, we are interested in those few which represent manipulable relationships, in which by intervening and changing one variable we can affect another."[8]

Consequently, the conditions under which we say that *A* controls *B* are the same under which we say that *A* causes *B*. The latter conditions have already been discussed elsewhere (Chapters 3 and 6). Here it is important to emphasize the difference between *intended* and *actual* control. Intended control is manipulation of independent variables with the intention of controlling some dependent variable(s). Whether actual control is achieved is not at all obvious. For even if the desired results were to be obtained they could be due to other controlling variables. In order to determine whether actual control has taken place—that is, in order to establish the internal validity of the control strategy—experimental and quasi-experimental procedures are required.[9]

THE USES OF CONTROL

There are two basic uses of control. One views it as a *means*, the other as a *goal*.

The first use refers to the theory of knowledge and considers control as a necessary activity in accruing knowledge. Control of the dependent variable(s) is not sought as a goal in itself but primarily as a means for testing propositions and theories. Experimentation is the most prominent vehicle for achieving this cognitive goal. Its function has been clearly expressed by Selltitz *et al.*: "The entire design of an experiment has the function of providing for the collection of evidence in such a way that *inferences of a causal relationship* between the independent and the dependent variables can legitimately be drawn."[10] The logic of control in an experiment is to manipulate

[7] Skinner, p. 23.
[8] Donald T. Campbell, "Methods for the Experimenting Society," p. 14.
[9] See Donald T. Campbell and Julian C. Stanley, *Experimental and Quasi-experimental Design for Research*.
[10] C. Selltitz, M. Jahoda, M. Deutsch, and S. W. Cook, *Research Methods in Social Relations*, p. 97. Italics added.

all those independent variables that are known to control the dependent variables in order to find out whether another variable—the experimental variable —also has controlling force. In other words, the relationships between the variables that one "controls for" in an experiment and the dependent variables have to be truly plausible rival hypotheses—that is, ". . . laws with a degree of scientific establishment comparable to or exceeding that of the law our experiment is designed to test."[11] Hence, one *"controls for" controlling variables.*

The second use of control views it as a goal rather than as a means. Inference about the existence of a causal relationship is not sought but rather assumed and exploited. Instead of controlling for other controlling conditions, following the principle of redundancy all of the available manipulable antecedents are brought to bear so as to maximize the chances of actually controlling the dependent variables. By doing this, however, causal inference as to what actually effected control is made difficult. The desire for valid inference, however, ought not to stifle action. The fallacy that experiments "may become substitutes for action or excuses for inaction"[12] ought to be avoided.

METATHEORETICAL ASPECTS OF CONTROL

This chapter discusses metatheoretical aspects of control from the viewpoint of the marketer who wishes to bring about change and is only secondarily concerned with the accrual of knowledge. The alternative perspective, that of the experimenter using the concept of control as an experimental device for improving explanation and prediction, is not treated here.

In what way is metatheory relevant to the control problem of a marketer? The control problem can be stated as a question: What is the best way of going about controlling a certain (number of) event(s)? We suggest that metatheory is extremely relevant (1) as a source of criteria for selecting the best strategy (or plan of action), and (2) for evaluating the strategy after its implementation. The reason for this is that any strategy recommendation is based on assumptions about the behavior of social units. (Although it is not possible to develop the topic of strategies *per se*, the reader may find Table 8.1 of interest. This table presents a brief summary of major strategy typologies. Figure 8.1 presents an outline of selected criteria influencing strategy development.)[13] If the strategy is to be successful these assumptions ought to be either derived from available behavioral science knowledge or at least be compatible with it. In other words, we maintain that the design of

[11] Donald T. Campbell, "Prospective: Artifact and Control."
[12] Alice M. Rivlin, *Systematic Thinkings for Social Action*; see also Donald T. Campbell, "Prospective," Methods for the Experimenting Society," p. 11.
[13] For a full discussion, see Gerald Zaltman, Philip Kotler, and Ira Kaufman, eds., *Creating Social Change.*

Table 8.1   Typology of Change Strategies

Coercive strategies[a]	Nonmutual goal setting and one-sided deliberativeness
Normative strategies[a]	Compliance achieved through the issuance of directives based on values internalized as proper and legitimate
Utilitarian strategies[a]	Control over the allocation of resources serving as rewards and punishments
Empirical-rational strategies[b]	Provision of rational justification for action
Normative-reeducative strategies[b]	Change of attitudes, values, skills, and significant relationships
Power-coercive strategies[b]	Application of moral, economic, and political resources to achieve change
Power strategies[c]	Use and/or threat of force
Persuasive strategies[c]	Bias in the structuring and presentation of a message; use of reasoning, urging, inducement based on rational and/or emotional appeals
Reeducative strategies[c]	Communication of fact and relearning through affective and cognitive change
Individual change strategies[d]	Use of change among individuals as a means toward social or organizational change
Data-based strategies[d]	Collecting and presenting data in order to initiate problem-solving activity and to provide a basis in which to root decision
Organizational development[d]	Creating a supportive climate or culture for organizational change
Violence and coercive strategies[d]	Actions designed to inflict personal injury or property damage
Nonviolence and direct-action strategies[d]	Attempts to change attitudes and/or behavior

[a] Garth N. Jones, *Planned Organizational Change.*
[b] Robert Chin and Kenneth Benne, "General Strategies for Effecting Changes in Human Systems."
[c] Gerald Zaltman, Philip Kotler, and Ira Kaufman, eds., *Creating Social Change.*
[d] Harvey A. Hornstein *et al., Social Intervention: A Behavioral Science Approach.*

control is very much a theoretical activity in that it involves—with varying degrees of awareness on the part of the practitioner—the application and testing of theories or theoretical statements. In this special sense, control is a theoretical function even though the purpose of exercising control may be unrelated to its potential contribution to knowledge. A fully articulated systematic metatheory of applied behavioral science does not currently exist. However, the control function of knowledge is of such great importance in

Figure 8.1 Outline of selected metacriteria influencing strategy development.

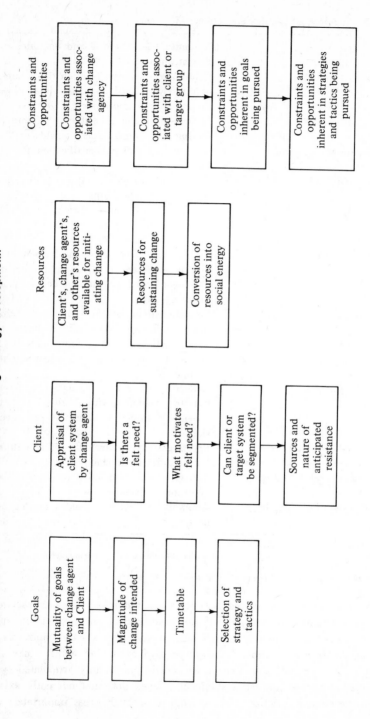

applied activities, such as marketing, as well as in theory development,[14] that we shall proceed to introduce various metacriteria and guidelines for exercising control and evaluating control efforts.

The basic assumption of this chapter, then, is that planned control is, in effect, a process of testing and utilizing behavioral theories. A theory of planned control—as opposed to general theories of behavioral control—is a theory of the implementation and utilization of behavioral theory. The various criteria discussed pertaining to the implementation of change intentions through control activities are appropriately considered metatheoretical criteria. The reader will find, however, that the "flavor" of this chapter is more pragmatic than that of the previous chapters. Even so, pragmatism is not exclusive of theory. This is an important and generally unrecognized point. Kiesler has expressed this well: "But any statement whatsoever of a way to implement an objective *of a social change program is a theoretical statement whether explicitly* recognized or not."[15]

THE CONTROLLER AND THE CONTROL SYSTEM

There are a variety of terms designating the person or group of persons who intend to control: among them are "change agent" and "interventionist." We think that "change agent" is somewhat restrictive, for control is not only concerned with change but also with the maintenance of existing conditions that are satisfactory to the controlling agents. The term "interventionist" seems unsatisfactory for the same reason. Instead, we propose the term "control agent," which encompasses all kinds of control situations and objectives.

A control agent may be part of the system which he attempts to control or he may be operating in the environment of the system. By a system we mean "An entity which is composed of at least two elements and a relation that holds between each of its elements and at least one other element in the set."[16]

The environment of a system is defined as "a set of elements and their relevant properties, which elements are not part of the system but a change in any of which can produce a change in the state of the system."[17] Note that there is a certain arbitrariness involved in differentiating between a social system and its environment. A psychologist notes that "Too frequently concepts of 'system' or 'homeostasis' or 'dynamic structure' are made axiomatic and lose their status as testable hypotheses. Too frequently such concepts are used in a way which provides an infinite flexibility in *ad hoc* explana-

---

[14] See Campbell, "Prospective: Artifact and Control."
[15] Charles Kiesler, "Evaluating Social Change Programs."
[16] Russell L. Ackoff, "Toward a System of Systems Concepts," p. 662.
[17] Ackoff, pp. 662–663.

tions."[18] He suggests a number of determinants of the perception of systems and system boundaries, such as common fate and similarity.[18]

The problem of the boundary between a system and its environment and the position of the control agent with respect to the system is of importance since it determines to some extent the kinds of controlling variables that the control agent may use. In addition, the target's perception of the control agent's position ("inside" or "outside") might influence his reaction to the control attempts. For example, one might ask whether television is seen as belonging to the family system or as an intrusion from outside, and how the differential perception of the boundary influences the reaction to TV commercials.

Let us use the system-environment distinction to discuss a particular control situation, namely, where change is attempted. The prime example of such a situation in consumer behavior research is the new-product problem. Two dimensions are of importance in such a situation: first, the origin of the new-product concept—inside or outside a certain social system (for example, a household consumption system)[19]—and, second, the recognition of the need for change. Both considerations are outlined in Table 8.2. This shows four possible types of change: immanent change; selective change; motivated contact change; and directed contact change.

Table 8.2 Typology of Change Situations

Recognition of the Need for Change	Origin of New-Product Idea	
	Internal to the Social System	External to the Social System
Internal—by members of the social system	Immanent change	Selective contact change
External—by agents	Motivated immanent change	Directed contact change

Source: Adapted from Modernization among Peasants: The Impact of Communication, by Everett M. Rogers in association with Lynn Svenning. Copyright © 1969 by Holt, Rinehart and Winston, Inc. Reprinted by permission of Holt, Rinehart and Wintson, Inc.

Immanent change and motivated immanent change are the least relevant situations to marketing. The most important action marketing can take in these two instances is to observe the more or less spontaneous and independent solution or response to the felt need that originates with the consumers and attempt to improve upon it and then market this new item.

[18] Donald T. Campbell, "Common Fate, Similarity and Other Indices of the Status of Aggregates of Persons as Social Entities."

[19] See Harper W. Boyd, Jr., and Sidney J. Levy, "New Dimensions in Consumer Analysis."

DESIGN OF CONTROL

In order to design an optimal control strategy the control agent should utilize behavioral science knowledge. In order to avail himself of the relevant knowledge we propose that the control agent effect a 'translation' of his practical problem into a more theoretical language. The reader should recall that the basic deductive model is one in which an explanans is sought for an explanandum under certain necessary constraints. In parallel fashion, Argyris sees merit in translating practical problems into theoretical issues.[20] The client's problems become empirical illustrations of more general theories from which the empirical problem phenomena can be deduced. An illustration is shown in Table 8.3.

Table 8.3   Problems as Instances of General Theories

Client's Diagnosis	Interventionist's Conceptualization
1. How can we introduce product planning and program review into the organization?	1. How can we institute a basic change in the living system?
2. How can we make product-planning meetings more effective?	2. How can we determine and increase group effectiveness?
3. How can we get other groups to cooperate with product planning?	3. How can we understand the relationship of small-group dynamics to the large environment in which it is embedded? How can we overcome destructive intergroup rivalries?
4. How can management get more commitment from the employees?	4. What is the differential impact of various leadership styles upon the subordinates?

Source: C. Argyris, *Intervention Theory and Method: A Behavioral Science View,* 1970, Addison-Wesley, Reading, Mass.

If the client's problems are translated into theoretical issues, the problems come into contact with a wealth of concepts and findings in other settings that may be generalizable to the specific situation of the client. Unless the particular problems are first translated into theoretical issues, the new suggestions and insights introduced into control strategies might otherwise be missed. Marketing has benefited considerably from this process. For example, the translation of brand selection and loyalty problems into learning-theory and small-group-theory issues has proved very fruitful; the recasting of salesman-prospect relations into an exchange-theory issue has provided new guidelines for the recruitment, training, and assignment of salesmen; the

[20] Chris Argyris, *Intervention Theory and Method: A Behavioral Science View.*

treatment of new-product purchase behavior in light of innovation adoption and diffusion theory has significantly shaped behavioral research in new-product marketing; light has been shed on market segmentation problems by viewing them from the broader perspectives of personality theory and subculture analysis; translating sales promotion problems into attitude theory issues has been very valuable. This list could be extended to great length.

The metaprocess involved in the iteration between practical problems and theoretical issues is shown in Figure 8.2. Given a marketing problem, the first step is to generalize to a more abstract theoretical issue as defined by the current state of knowledge in the discipline(s) contributing information to the particular issue. Exploration of the theoretical issue *at* a theoretical level can contribute insight and marketing strategy clues directly to the marketing problem. The marketing problem is viewed simply as an explanandum, —that is, as an empirical manifestation of the theoretical issue. Additional insight and guidelines may be derived by examining the implications of a theory in its application in areas traditionally considered as nonmarketing settings.

Figure 8.2   Iteration between problems and theoretical issues.

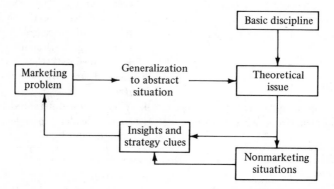

Arndt has suggested a similar process or series of steps useful in borrowing concepts from the behavioral sciences.[21] Briefly, these are: (1) the identification of a marketing problem; (2) translation of the problem in behavioral terms; (3) the search for and evaluation of relevant knowledge; (4) the collection of additional information as necessary; and (5) making the necessary calculations.

One fundamental problem raises itself in any discussion of "borrowing," such as those of Arndt[21] and Zaltman.[22] The problem is that conceptual and methodological tools relevant to one situation are not necessarily relevant

[21] Johan Arndt, "Applications of the Behavioral Sciences."
[22] Gerald Zaltman, "Marketing Inference in the Behavioral Sciences."

to another, despite seeming parallels between the two situations. Kassarjian addresses this in the context of personality and consumer behavior: "The variables that lead to the assassination of a president, confinement in a mental hospital, or suicide may not be identical to those that lead to the purchase of a washing machine, a pair of shoes, or chewable gum . . . consumer behavior researchers must develop their own definition and design their own instruments. . . ."[23] As an example of the application of theoretical knowledge to a marketing problem consider the problem of the adaptation of the *content*,—that is, the promotional appeals—and the *channel* of persuasive communications in international marketing. The theoretical issues involved are: (1) the factors that influence the differential response to promotional appeals cross-culturally, and (2) the factors that influence the differential response to communication channels cross-culturally.

Figure 8.3 presents a proposition that addresses itself to the first problem. Two concepts are linked in a proposition suggesting a (positive) causal relationship: Literacy produces empathy, without the need for changes in other variables. A plausible explanation as to how literacy causes or produces empathy might be the following: Higher degrees of mastery over symbols in written form (literacy) widen experiences through meaningful encounters with the print media and unlock mental abilities, allowing one to encompass these new experiences. This, in turn, increases the ability to project oneself into the role or situation of another (empathy). Presumably consumers in less literate societies have a weaker capacity to empathize or identify with individuals unlike themselves or to project themselves into situations unlike their own. One marketing implication of this proposition concerns our problem of the adaptation of promotional appeals. Successful advertising copy in the United States is often based on the ability of one type of consumer to identify with a different type of consumer or to project himself into a novel situation, either or both of which may be specified in an advertisement. If the empirical generalization proved credible, the following proposition could be used as a guideline for marketing strategy formulation: The lower the level of literacy in a market, the fewer should be the promotional cues involving unfamiliar roles or situations. This would be true even if the message required no reading ability.

Note that prediction is implicit in the above discussion. We predict that under circumstances of low literacy the use of unfamiliar promotional cues will not yield desirable levels of identification among consumers. The marketer must adapt his promotional cues to be compatible with the mental set of potential consumers. He cannot alter their mental set, at least within the relevant future.

The restrictive impact empathy has on the structuring of messages

---

[23] Harold H. Kassarjian, "Personality and Consumer Behavior: A Review."

Figure 8.3   Deduction of a control strategy.

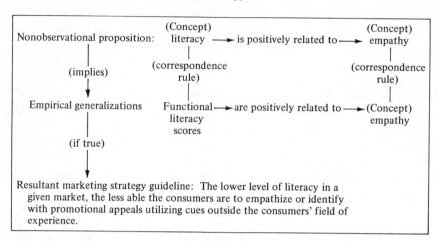

Resultant marketing strategy guideline: The lower level of literacy in a given market, the less able the consumers are to empathize or identify with promotional appeals utilizing cues outside the consumers' field of experience.

directed to consumers in less literate societies may be compensated somewhat through a different communication channel. Consider another proposition, which addresses itself to our second problem: Literacy is negatively associated with eidetic ability. Eidetic ability is the photographic ability to remember visual stimuli.[24] Assume that the generalization involving literacy and eidetic ability has been tested and proved credible and that a plausible law of interaction has been established relating the two variables. There are two marketing implications in the theoretical statement involving the dimensions of time and complexity. Less literate consumers may remember relatively complex visual messages better and longer than more literate consumers. In less literate societies nonwritten advertising may be structured in more complex ways than in highly literate societies and scheduled on a less frequent basis since less reinforcement is necessary as a result of high visual-retentive abilities. Thus, the literacy-empathy statement provides a guideline for selecting the content of advertising and the literacy-eidetic relationship provides guidelines for the channel decision in persuasive communication and the frequency with which it should appear.

EVALUATION OF CONTROL

The control strategy has to be assessed both before and after its implementation. An important consideration in the evaluation is the level of understanding of the relationship between the independent variables and the control target, and the discussion will focus on this issue. Following this, we shall deal with the problems of evaluation after the implementation of the strategy.

[24] For a discussion of eidetic ability see Ralph N. Haber, "Eidetic Images," and Leonard W. Doob, "Eidetic Imagery: A Cross-Cultural Will-o'-the Wisp?"

LEVELS OF UNDERSTANDING IN CONTROL

Presented in Table 8.4 are four different levels of understanding in the control process. At the first level there is the simple identification of the criterion variable(s) and the noting that a certain condition can be wrought by the change agent. The second level involves the identification of manipulable causal factors (the X's) capable of bringing about the phenomenon Q. The third level represents a still higher level of knowledge about the control situation. It identifies the strategies and tactics (the Y's) to be used to alter existing relational patterns among X's and between X's and the condition out of which Q is to emerge. The final level is the specification of the reasons (W's) why strategy Y_1 and so on can affect the relations among X's and between X's and the criterion variables. This involves identifying facilitating factors in the system or in the system's environment.

Table 8.4   Levels of Understanding in Control

Levels of Understanding in Control	Control
Level 1	A certain phenomenon can be brought about with the interventionist being the immediate causal factor.
Level 2	The phenomenon can be made to be of the nature Q as a result of the manipulation of causal factors $X_1, X_2, \ldots, X_n$.
Level 3	The interaction among factors $X_1, X_2, \ldots, X_n$ and between these factors and Q can be manipulated in manner $Y_1, Y_2, \ldots, Y_n$ to produce Q.
Level 4	Factors $X_1, X_2, \ldots, X_n$ can interact for reasons $W_1, W_2, \ldots, W_n$, thus causing Q.

At level 1 the criterion variable is identified. In the illustration used here this variable will be product quality perception. It is ascertained that this is a manipulable variable—that is, within the deliberate control of the change agent. The next level of understanding permits the marketer to say that the product will have a perceived quality Q as the result of his manipulating price and channel of distribution. It has been argued—by Stafford and Enis, for example—that price and price interacting with store image influence perceived product quality.[25] At level 3 the marketer knows, through adequate research, that for his product class and market segment there is a certain price range within which there is a relatively high positive association between price and perceived product quality. Presumably, consumers reason that a high price signifies good workmanship and/or more durable and functional features, thus enhancing the objective quality of the product. There may also be an interaction between causal factors, which has an additional effect on

[25] J. E. Stafford and B. M. Enis, "The Price-Quality Relationship: An Extension."

perceived product quality. The imputed relationship between price and quality and the added causal impact of the interaction effect between price and store images would presumably lead to a strategy of setting a relatively high price and distributing through outlets having favorable images. At a still higher level of understanding, the marketer would base this action on certain reasons $(W_1, W_2, \ldots, W_3)$, such as the income level of the relevant market segment, the importance of quality, and so forth.

EX POST EVALUATION OF CONTROL

The terms evaluation and evaluative research are used interchangeably here to refer to the use of the scientific method for collecting data concerning a situation in which some specified activity is to achieve some desired effect.[26] The terms do not cover the process of assessing the social worth of social cost of a program.[27] Evaluative research, like basic research, utilizes the scientific method and theory is intimately intertwined with it.[28] Evaluative research, however, is concerned with problems having administrative consequences, whereas basic research focuses attention on theoretical problems.[29] The criteria and principles involved in the sound conduct and utilization of evaluative research are somewhat less abstract than those involved in the proper development and use of explanation and prediction discussed earlier. They are also somewhat less abstract than metatheoretical considerations relative to concepts, hypotheses, and theories. They are still, however, important in the process of evaluating the application or testing of a theory.

The complexity of the focal situation of evaluative research is shown in Figure 8.4. There are many interrelated preconditions affecting the formulation and implementation of the marketing program, which itself may be a complex of interrelated variables. The program functions through and among a host of interconnected intervening variables and events and manifests some effect or set of effects. The intervening events may also have multiple independent effects on the program. The program in turn may have a variety of consequences.

The basic question which evaluative research is supposed to answer is: How successful was the control strategy in achieving its objectives? To answer this three steps are essential; each will be discussed further:

1. The objectives have to be specified in advance.
2. The effort expended in the implementation of the strategy and the actual effects have to be measured.
3. A causal analysis should be performed.

[26] Edward H. Suchman, *Evaluative Research*, p. 15.
[27] Unfortunately, this very important problem of assessing social worth and cost cannot be treated within the scope of this book.
[28] Kiesler, "Evaluating Social Change Programs."
[29] Francis G. Caro, ed., *Readings in Evaluative Research*, p. 8.

Figure 8.4   Precondition-consequence continuum of control programs.

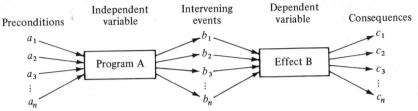

Source: Edward Suchman, *Evaluative Research*, Russell Sage Foundation, 1967.

OBJECTIVES

Suchman has raised several general considerations involved in the specification of objectives.[30] The first concerns *what* the nature is of the content of the objective. Is the objective to change attitudes toward a particular brand? Behavior concerning a particular brand? Is the objective to establish awareness? Interest? The next consideration asks, "*Who* is the target of the program?" Who is the appropriate market segment? How many segments are involved? Is the adoption unit a single member or multimember in nature? Is the target a subset of some market segment,—for example, innovators, opinion leaders, and so forth? Third, "*When* is the desired change to take place?" Is the program a long-run educational one or an immediate-response program? How long is the effect intended to last? How soon is it intended to begin? How permanent is the change intended to be? The fourth consideration asks whether the objectives are *unitary* or *multiple*. Is there a single intended change or a multiple chain of changes? Do the objectives vary by consumer category or market segment? The fifth consideration concerns the *magnitude* of the desired effect. What degree of effectiveness qualifies a program of control to be called a success? Are there specified standards of accomplishment that must be met? Finally, *how* is the objective to be attained? What is the marketing mix?

MEASUREMENT OF IMPLEMENTATION

The first variable to be measured is *effort*. This involves what was done and how well it was done and uses such criteria as the quantity and quality of an occurring activity. Emphasis is on input rather than output. This is one of the easiest evaluative tasks. The number of dollars invested in advertising is easy to assess in detailed ways, such as by market segment, by media, and others. The approximate number of consumer exposures to advertising can also be known with a high degree of accuracy. Similarly, the number of sales calls made and the number of customers entering a store can also be determined, either obtrusively or unobtrusively.

[30] Suchman, *Evaluative Research*, pp. 39–45.

Next the results of effort,—that is, its effects—rather than the effort itself have to be measured. Suchman breaks effects into the following: (1) unitary or multiple effects, (2) unintentional or side effects, (3) duration of effects, and (4) type of effects, including (a) cognitive, (b) attitudinal, and (c) behavioral. Rogers and Shoemaker add manifest versus latent consequences and direct versus indirect consequences.[31] Such questions as the following are asked: What changes occurred? Were these the intended changes? Was it of the desired magnitude? Did the advertising create positive images? Did it reach the intended audience? What was the purchase response rate? Given that many programs involve a hierarchy of objectives, performance criteria can be applied at different levels. For example, performance criteria could be applied at each level of the adoption decision process in campaigns promoting innovations.[32] Were awareness, interest, and the like achieved? Reliability problems are very important in performance ratings. It is known that different consumer groups or segments go through the overall innovation adoption decision process at different speeds. Moreover, consumers also vary with regard to particular stages in ways not consistent with their overall decision-making rate. Consequently, it is necessary to identify clearly the consumer group being tested for the effectiveness of a campaign intended to bring these consumers along this process.

After the *actual* effects have been measured, they can be compared with the intended effects. A promotional campaign intended to precipitate trial of a product can hardly be adjudged adequate if it only succeeds in stimulating interest; it is less adequate still if it only stimulates awareness; it is least adequate when it only reminds consumers of the product's existence. Both exposure and impact must be considered as essential elements of adequacy; as Bigman notes,

> We must distinguish between effectiveness and *impact*. By the latter term I mean the strength of the influence upon exposed individuals. A program or activity may have considerable impact, affecting markedly the thoughts and actions of those it touches; it will be necessarily judged ineffective if it is so designed that this impact is confined to a small fraction of the group it is intended to reach and influence.[33]

In addition to effectiveness, the *efficiency* of the strategy has to be assessed. Efficiency is "concerned with the evaluation of alternative paths or methods in terms of costs. . . . In a sense, it represents a ratio between effort

[31] Everett M. Rogers and Floyd F. Shoemaker, *Communication of Innovations: A Cross-Cultural Approach.*
[32] Martin Trow, "Methodological Problems in the Evaluation of Innovations"
[33] S. K. Bigman, "Evaluating the Effectiveness of Religious Programs."

and performance—output divided by input."[34] This is one of the central features of operations research. Operations research concepts and techniques have been applied to marketing quite successfully and need not be elaborated upon here.

CAUSAL ANALYSIS

Causal analysis involves the analysis of the means whereby a marketing program achieves whatever effects it may have. It calls for an overview and analysis of the impact of particular sequences in the control program. It is concerned, in other words, with overall program and with the interaction among parts of the program or elements in the system. Are particular components interacting in such a way as to produce dysfunctional effects? Are there bottlenecks in the process?

Suchman specifies four main dimensions involved in the analysis of process. The first consists of the specification of the attributes of a program accounting for its degree of success. This involves decomposing the component parts of a process and attributing to them their role in the success or failure of the process or program of control.

The conditions under which the program is more or less successful are also important. Although we have extensive inventories of strategies and tactics, we know relatively little about the circumstances mediating their impact or influence.

PROSPECTS FOR A METATHEORY OF CONTROL

The control objective has in the past been somewhat of a stepchild for metascientists. Although there is an abundance of material relating to explanation and prediction, there is a dearth of comparable discussions of control. Consequently, the material that we have presented in this chapter is of a somewhat more tentative nature than that of the preceding chapters. With control being an important objective of consumer behavior research, however, progress in this area should be of great interest to our field. We shall, therefore, discuss some of the requirements of an improved metatheory of control.

A future metatheory of control will have to move in two distinct directions: first, toward a development of metatheoretical criteria adapted to control; second, toward a methodology for the evaluation of control attempts.

In Chapter 5 we asserted that the variety of criteria for the evaluation of scientific knowledge has to be approached selectively. Researchers with different aims will rank-order the criteria differently. As a consequence, the theories they build will differ too. Ideally, one ought to be able to determine which criteria are most appropriate for each objective. That is to say, there should

---

[34] Suchman, *Evaluative Research*, p. 64.

be a list of criteria relevant for explanation, a second one for prediction, and a third for control.

Following Bunge, we shall briefly discuss two of the differences in the importance of criteria and corresponding theories for explanation-prediction on one hand and for control on the other hand.[35]

Representativeness of theories is less important for control purposes: ". . . the practical man, to whom they are devoted, is chiefly interested in net effects that occur and are controllable on the human scale: he wants to know how things within his reach can be made to work *for him*, rather than how things of any kind really are."[36] There will be an optimal size of the black box for control purposes. Researchers with an interest in explanation and prediction, on the other hand, will always tend to look inside the black box and discover its internal workings.

Related to the problem of representativeness is the degree of *confirmation*. Decomposing the black box into smaller units will in general lead to a better degree of confirmation of predictions. For control purposes, however, the increase in accuracy may not warrant the likely increase in cost involved. The criterion of efficiency is at stake here, and Bunge argues that theories for practical applications ought to be "yielding much with little."[37]

The second major domain for the application of metatheory in control is in the evaluation of control attempts. A psychologist concerned with the evaluation aspects of social programs argued that in governmental and industrial planning, "there is detailed use of available science but no use of the implemented program as a check on the validity of the plans or of the scientific theories upon which they were based. Thus economists, operations researchers, and mathematical decision theorists trustingly extrapolate from past science and conjecture, but in general fail to use the implemented decisions to correct and expand that knowledge."[38] Ideally, this evaluation should be experimental, with random assignment of treatments to the control targets. Since true experimentation is not always feasible in field settings, quasi-experimentation will sometimes have to do.[39] Advances both in methods of experimental and quasi-experimental designs as well as in statistical analysis[40] should increase the relevance of metatheory to the evaluation of control in the future.

---

[35] Mario Bunge, *Scientific Research II: The Search for Truth*, pp. 123–129.
[36] Bunge, p. 123.
[37] Bunge, p. 125.
[38] Campbell, "Methods for the Experimenting Society, p. 4.
[39] See Campbell and Stanley, *Experimental and Quasi-experimental Design for Research*; Donald T. Campbell, "Reforms as Experiments"; and Campbell, "Methods for the Experimenting Society."
[40] See, for example, Hubert M. Blalock, Jr., ed., *Causal Models in the Social Sciences.*

GLOSSARY

Abstract theory. A set of sentences none of whose terms is meaningful.

Abstraction. In traditional logic, the process of deriving a universal from particulars.

Accuracy. The extent of agreement between predicted and observed values.

Analogue prediction. The associative technique whereby a correspondence is set up between two sets of events.

Analytic propositions. Propositions that can only be logically true or false but not factually.

Associative prediction. The technique whereby a variable is predicted from one or more other variables.

Auxiliary hypothesis. A correspondence rule used in the deduction of test implications from nonobservational propositions.

Axiom. See *Postulate*.

Bridge principle. See *Correspondence rule*.

Causal imagery. A conceptualization of cause and effect among two or more variables.

Causal statement. A statement that there exists environments in which a change in the value of one variable can produce a change in another variable without the necessity of changes in still other variables in the environment.

Cause. A factor that makes a designated phenomenon occur.

Cognitive status of theories. Refers to the question of whether theories have real referents or not.

Concatenated theory. A theory whose component propositions enter into a network of relations so as to constitute an identifiable system.

Concept. The basic unit of thought.

Conceptual unity. The property that demands that the components of the theory refer to the same set of phenomena, and that the various propositions are related and stem from the same set of assumptions.

Concurrent validity. A subtype of criterion-related validity in which the criterion and the predictor concepts are measured at the same time.

Confirmation (degree of). The extent to which a proposition or set of propositions is confirmed by experience.

Connotation (of a concept). The set of all the properties common to the elements of the denotation of the concept.

Consistency. A logistic system is said to have consistency when no contradiction can be derived in it.

Construct validity. The extent to which an operationalization measures the concept that it purports to measure; consists of convergent, discriminant, and nomological validity.

Content validity. The degree to which an operationalization represents the concept about which generalizations are to be made.

Contextual definition. A definition that introduces a term by giving synonyms for certain expressions containing it but not for the term itself.

Control. The systematic manipulation of some element related to or contained within a system so as to effect a change in one or more elements in that system.

Convergent validity. Represented by the correlation between two attempts to measure the same concept through maximally different methods.

Correspondence rule. A proposition relating nonobservational to observational concepts.

Correspondence theory of truth. According to this theory, a proposition is true or false if it coheres or fails to cohere with a deductively related system of propositions.

Corroboration (degree of). See *Confirmation.*

The covering-law theory of explanation. The thesis that explanations in science are analyzable in terms of the "nomological-deductive model" and the "probabilistic model."

Criterion-related validity (or pragmatic validity). The degree to which the concept under consideration enables one to predict the value of some other concept, which constitutes the criterion.

Crucial test (or experiment). A test (experiment) in which it is possible to choose among two rival hypotheses H_1 and H_2 concerning the same phenomenon because the test implications of the two hypotheses are conflicting; that is, they are mutually exclusive.

Deducibility. A syntactical property of a set of sentences referring to the fact that some of the sentences follow deductively from others.

Deduction. The process by which one passes from general assertions (universal propositions) to particular instances (singular propositions).

Deductive nomological explanation. An explanation in which the explanans asserts universal deterministic relationships.

Deductive statistical explanation. An explanation in which the explanandum is an empirical generalization involving probabilities.

Deductively complete theory. A theory that is completely formalized.

Defined terms. Those terms of a system defined by other terms of that system.

Definiendum. That which is to be defined.

Definiens. That which is used to define.

Definition. An operation that introduces a new term on the basis of already existing terms.

Definitional operationism. A school of thought that, at its extreme, requires total reducibility of concepts to observations.

Degree of a predicate. The number of places of a predicate. (See also *One-place* and *Two-place predicate.*)

Denotation. The set of objects that possess the properties included in the intension of a concept.

Description. Assertion(s) about the characteristics (attributes) of phenomena.

Designation (rule of). A rule that attaches a name to a concept or set of concepts.

Discriminant validity. The extent to which a concept *differs* from other concepts.

Disposition concept. A concept that refers to a tendency to display specific responses under specifiable conditions.

Empirical generalization. A universal proposition containing only relatively observational concepts.

Empirical interpretability. See *Testability in principle.*

Empirical significance. See *Testability in principle.*

Epistemic gap. The gap between a concept and its operationalization.

Evidence (scientific). Data used to evaluate the truth or falsity of a proposition.

Evidential strength of an explanation. The strength with which the explanans implies the explanandum.

Evidential support of hypotheses. The support derived from comparing its predictions with the actual evidence obtained.

Existential proposition. A proposition that holds for at least one member of the universe of discourse.

Existential quantifier. A linguistic sign read "there exists."

Explanandum. That which is to be explained.

Explanans. That which explains.

Explanation. An answer to a why question of the form "why p?" where p designates a proposition that supposedly is true and refers to some fact, event, or state of affairs.

Explanatory power of an explanation. The extent to which the explanation renders the phenomenon to be explained more likely than other alternative phenomena.

Explicit definition. A definition in which an expression E_2 is stipulated to be synonymous with an expression E_1.

Extension. The set of possible objects, past or future, known or unknown, that if they existed would belong to the concept's denotation.

External consistency. The extent to which a theory is compatible with a sizable segment of existing tested knowledge in other fields as well as its own.

Extrapolation. The technique whereby a variable is predicted from itself.

Extrinsic predictive tasks. Tasks involving qualitative and/or quantitative details of behavior that are objectively correlated with situational facts. The psychological substance that mediates the correlation is disregarded.

Factual truth. The degree of agreement between what a proposition says and the actual state of affairs to which it refers.

Fallacy. An argument that seems to be valid but really is not.

Fallacy of affirming the consequent. A deductively invalid mode of reasoning of the form

$$\text{if } A \text{ is true, then so is } B$$
$$\underline{B \text{ is true}}$$
$$A \text{ is true}$$

(where A and B are propositions).

Falsifiability. The extent to which a proposition or set of propositions is capable of being refuted by experience.

Formal analogy. Analogy of structure between two systems.

Formal concept. A concept defined within systems that are not intended to refer to any objects of the real world.

Formalization of a theory. The explicit and complete formulation of a theory's axioms, and the statement of its presuppositions and rules.

Formation (grammatical) rule. A rule, specifying which sign combinations are permissible within a linguistic system.

Functional or teleological explanations. An explanation in which the "why" question about a phenomenon is answered by specifying a goal or end toward the attainment of which the phenomenon is a means.

Generality of a proposition (degree of). The size of the extension of the concepts contained in the proposition.

Generic concept. A concept that refers to characteristics held in common by *more than one* object.

Genetic explanation (or historicist explanation). An explanation that accounts for a particular state or condition of some unit in terms of some prior state or, more frequently, in terms of a sequence of some prior states.

Ground of a proposition. The extent to which a proposition is based on existing scientific knowledge.

Heuristic power. The capacity for suggesting and directing new research.

Hierarchical theory. A theory in which the component propositions are deducible from a small set of basic principles.

Historicist explanation. See *Genetic explanation.*

Hypothesis. A specific type of proposition that (1) refers to facts that are unexperienced or in principle unexperientiable and (2) is corrigible in view of fresh knowledge.

Hypothetical construct. See *Theoretical concept.*

Independence (principle of). The "primitive" concepts of a theory and its axioms must be mutually independent.

Individual concept. See *Proper concept.*

Induction. The process by which one passes from particular instances (singular propositions) to more general assertions (universal propositions).

Inference valid. An inference the joint assertion of whose premises and the denial of whose conclusion is a contradiction.

Instrumentalism. A position according to which theories are mere instruments, tools, or calculating devices.

Intension (of a concept). The list of all the properties that a concept possesses.

Intensional and extensional vagueness. The degree of precision in the definition of a concept's intension and extension.

Internal consistency. The degree to which within a conceptual system there are no logical contradictions.

Interpretation. An entity is an interpretation of a concept when it embodies the properties listed in the intension of the concept.

Interpreted theory. A set of sentences all of whose terms are meaningful.

Interpretive sentence. See *Correspondence rule.*

Intersubjective corroboration of a proposition (principle of). The results of one observation must be verifiable by subsequent observations by different observers.

Intervening variable. A factor intervening between and connecting the independent and dependent variables.

Intrinsic predictive tasks. The emphasis is not on the outer world and specific behavior but on abstract conceptualization of behavior and to the relatively enduring intrapsychic system.

Isomorphism. See *Formal analogy.*

Language. A system of linguistic signs (terms).

Latitudinal scope of a prediction-explanation. The number of dependent variables included in a prediction-explanation.

Laws. Here, hypotheses that are empirically corroborated to a degree regarded as satisfactory at a certain point in time.

"Laws" of thought. (1) The "law" of contradiction: nothing can be both P and not P; (2) the "law" of excluded middle: anything must be either P or not P; (3) the "law" of identity: if anything is P, then it is P.

Linguistic exactness. The extent to which a concept exhibits minimum intensional and extensional vagueness.

Logic. The study of the validity of different kinds of inference.

Logical truth. The extent to which a proposition follows logically from other propositions in a conceptual system.

Longitudinal scope of a prediction-explanation. The number of independent variables included in a prediction-explanation.

Material (substantive) analogy. Similarity between the properties (one-place predicates) of two systems.

Metatheory. The investigation, analysis, and the description of (1) the technology of building theory, (2) the theory itself, and (3) the utilization of theory.

Meaning. (1) That which a term refers to or the relation between the term and its referent (referential theory), (2) that idea which a term stands for (ideational theory), (3) that response which a term evokes (stimulus response theory).

Methodological simplicity. The ease with which a theory can be built and tested.

Middle-range theory (or hypothesis). A theory (hypothesis) that applies to a limited set of phenomena found in relatively narrowly defined circumstances.

Model. Any system whose study is useful for the understanding of some other system.

Monotonicity. A function is monotone if for any values x_1, x_2, with $x_1 > x_2$, either $f(x_1) > f(x_2)$ or $j(x_2) < j(x_2)$.

Necessary and sufficient condition. A condition of the form: "A is always present whenever B is present and vice versa."

Necessary but not sufficient condition. A condition of the form: "A is always present whenever B is present, but B need not always occur when A is present."

Nominal definition. A definition that arbitrarily introduces an alternative notation for a given linguistic expression.

Nomological validity. The extent to which predictions based on the concept that an instrument purports to measure are confirmed.

Nonformal concept. A concept that is defined within an interpreted system.

Nonobservable entities. Those to which one-place attributes are not ascribed in relatively observational propositions.

Nonobservational propositions. Propositions containing only nonobservational concepts.

Object. Understood, here, to be equivalent to referent.

Object variable. The individual objects to which predicates are attributed.

Observability (degree of). The extent to which the use of a concept is prompted by environmental events as contrasted with intraverbal contexts.

Observable entity. An entity is observable when one-place attributes are ascribed to them in relatively observational statements.

Observation proposition. A singular proposition or a finite conjunction of singular propositions containing only relatively observational concepts that are inductively derived from facts. Their linguistic expression is called a protocol sentence.

Observation validity. The degree to which a concept is reducible to observations.

Observational concept. A concept whose intension refers to attributes of objects, whose presence or absence in a given instance can be intersubjectively ascertained, under suitable conditions by direct observation.

Observational proposition. A proposition that contains only relatively observational concepts and grammatical or logical connectives.

One-place predicate. A one-place predicate designates a property.

One-to-one correspondence. A relation R such that for every member a of its domain, there is only one object b that is a member of its domain such that bRa.

Operational code. The associative technique wherein behavioral norms are used in order to predict behavior.

Operational definition. A definition wherein the use of a term is specified by a set of operations.

Operational interpretation (or operationalization). The process by which one establishes correspondences between concepts and controlled operations or their results.

Operatonalization. See *Operational interpretation.*

Ostensive interpretation (of a concept). An interpretation that points out something to which the concept applies.

Postulate or axiom. Those sentences of a system that are not derivable from other sentences of the system.

Power. The degree of control over the dependent variable that a prediction-explanation provides.

Pragmatics. The systematic study of the uses of signs in social life.

Pragmatic validity. See *Criterion-related validity.*

Precision. The degree of specification of the events or variables involved and of the relationships between those events or variables in a proposition.

Predicate. A syntactic unit expressing the action performed by or the state attributed to the subject of the sentence.

Prediction. (1) A deduction from known to unknown events within a conceptually static system; (2) an assertion about future outcomes generally based on the observation of regularities among sequences of events of the past.

Predictive validity. A subtype of criterion-related validity in which the criterion measure is separated in time from the predictor concept.

Premise. A member of the set of statements assumed for the course of an argument, from which a conclusion is inferred.

Primitive terms. Those terms of a system not defined by other terms of the system.

Probabilistic explanation. An explanation in which the explanans contains probabilistic relationships.

Proper (or individual) concept. A concept that refers to the characteristics of one object only and is applicable only to it.

Proposition. A sequence of concepts; alternatively, the meaning of a sentence.

Propositional function. A proposition whose universe of discourse or attributes are unspecified.

Protocol sentence. A sentence derived from "facts" or "data," which must satisfy two conditions. First, it must be possible to reach a decision as to their truth or falsity in a finite number of observations. Second, they must be intersubjectively corroborated, which means that the empirical truth or falsity of the proposition must be agreed upon by different observers. See *Observation proposition.*

Purely confirmable proposition. A proposition that can be only confirmed but not refuted.

Purely refutable proposition. A proposition that can be only refuted but not confirmed.

Quantifier. Specifies the universe of discourse of a proposition.

Quasi-deductive theories. There are three varieties: (1) theories containing probabilistic statements, (2) theories in which certain steps in the deduction are left out, and (3) theories relying on relative primitives.

Quasi-ostensive interpretation. The type of interpretation that consists of enumerating objects that are proper interpretations of a concept.

Realism. A position according to which theories consist of true or false statements, referring to "real" or "existing" entities.

Reciprocal causation. A quality by virtue of which change in variable x causes a change in variable y, which in turn causes a change in x at some later time.

Reconstruction. See *Formalization*.

Reductionism. A position that requires that all scientific hypotheses be exhaustively reduced to observation propositions.

Reference (the relationship of). The relationship that assigns an object to a term or a concept.

Referent. That to which a term or a concept refers.

Referential universality of a proposition. The size of the universe of discourse.

Refutability. See *Falsifiability*.

Relative primitive terms. Primitive terms in a system that are only partly established.

Reliability. The degree of agreement between two attempts to measure the same concept through maximally similar methods.

Representativeness. The basicness of the mechanisms involved in a theory.

Scientific explanation. An explanation in which the explanans contains only true propositions, and includes laws, and where the explanandum is a logical consequence of the explanans.

Scientific hypothesis. A hypothesis having the additional characteristics of being (1) well formed, (2) meaningful, (3) empirically testable, and (4) grounded.

Scientific method. A set of prescribed procedures for establishing and connecting general laws about events and for predicting events yet unknown.

Scientific prediction. A set of statements (1) whose premises are true, (2) containing data statements that are true but refer to times no later than the present, and (3) whose conclusion relates to the relative future.

Scientific research. The effort to assess existing relevant knowledge and to extend it by developing concepts and testing integrated hypotheses through the acquisition and analysis of meaningful data, and the critical evaluation of the original concepts and premises.

Scope. The universe of discourse of a proposition or set of propositions.

Semantic validity. The degree to which a concept has a uniform semantic usage.

Semantically abstract theory. A theory none of whose terms are interpreted or meaningful.

Semantics. The systematic study of the meaning of signs.

Semiabstract theory. A theory some but not all of whose terms are interpreted.

Semiotics. The general theory of signs, which, according to Morris, includes (1) syntactics, (2) semantics, and (3) pragmatics.

Sentence. A sequence of terms.

Sign. Any physical thing that stands in conventional correspondence to other things (physical or abstract).

Singular proposition. Refers to a definite spatiotemporal region—that is, to some perceptual object or state of affairs located in space and time.

Spatiotemporal universality of a proposition. The specification of the spatial and temporal boundaries of the universe of discourse.

Stability. The extent to which a system is able to accommodate new evidence.

Strength. The extent to which a system entails other systems.

Structural certainties. The associative technique wherein structural variables of a given system are used in order to predict a particular system behavior.

Sufficient but not necessary condition. Whenever A is present B occurs, but A need not always be present when B occurs.

Syllogism. A valid deductive argument having two premises and a conclusion.

Syntactics. The systematic study of the relations of signs to signs.

Syntax. The systematic study of the structure of sign systems.

Synthetic propositions. A proposition that can be factually true or false.

System. An entity composed of at least two elements and a relation that holds between each of its elements and at least one other element in the set.

Systematic presuppositions. There are two major instances: (1) The theory contains formulations that presuppose a body of theory that itself is complete; this is an elliptic formulation. (2) The theory from which the presuppositions are derived is itself incomplete.

Systemic validity. The extent to which a concept enables the integration of previously unconnected concepts and/or the generation of a new conceptual system.

Tautology. A compound proposition that is formally true no matter what truth values are assigned to its constituent propositions.

Term. A linguistic sign.

Testability in principle. It is possible to derive from a set of propositions (sentences) test implications of the form: "If test conditions C are realized, then outcome E will occur."

Theorem. A well-formed formula of a given logistic system for which there is a proof in the system.

Theoretical attempts. (1) Systems that can partially be rendered into formal structure. (2) Verbal systems that cannot be partially formalized without substantial modifications.

Theoretical concept (or hypothetical construct). A concept that derives its meaning from its role in the theory in which it is embedded and the purposes of the theory.

Theory. A set of propositions (sentences) with the following characteristics: (1) There is more than one proposition (sentence), (2) the set contains nonobservational propositions (sentences), (3) the propositions (sentences) are deductively connected, and (4) the nonobservational propositions (sentences) must be testable in principle.

Token. A specified utterance of a given linguistic expression or a written occurrence of it.

Two-place predicate. Designates a relation.

Unifying power. Refers to the ability of a theory to relate previously unrelated areas.

Universal proposition. A proposition that holds for all the elements of the universe of discourse.

Universal deterministic relationship. A relationship of the form: "In all cases when conditions of kind F are realized, conditions of kind G are realized as well."

Universal quantifier. A sign read "for all."

Universe of discourse of a proposition. The domain of elements referred to by the proposition.

Well-formedness. The extent to which a theory obeys the rules of "formation" and "transformation" (elementary logic).

BIBLIOGRAPHY

Aaker, D., "Using Buyer Behavior Models To Improve Marketing Decisions." *Journal of Marketing*, **34**, July 1970, pp. 52–57.

Abell, P., *Model Building in Sociology*. New York: Schocken Books, 1971.

Achinstein, P., *Concepts of Science: A Philosophical Analysis*. Baltimore: The Johns Hopkins Press, 1968.

Ackoff, R. L., "Toward a System of Systems Concepts." *Management Science*, **17**, 1971, pp. 661–671.

Alston, W. P., "Logical Status of Psychoanalytic Theories," in *Encyclopedia of Philosophy*, P. Edwards (ed.). New York: Macmillan, 1967.

Argyris, C., *Intervention Theory and Method: A Behavioral Science View.* Reading, Mass.: Addison-Wesley, 1970.

Arndt, J., "Applications of the Behavioral Sciences," in *Insights into Consumer Behavior*, J. Arndt (ed.). Boston: Allyn and Bacon, 1968, pp. 1–18.

Assael, H., and Day, G. S., "Attitude and Awareness as Predictors of Market Share." *Journal of Advertising Research*, 8, 1968, pp. 3–10.

ATV House, *Opinion Leaders, A Study in Communication.* London: ATV House, 1969.

Axelrod, J. N., "Attitude Measures that Predict Purchase." *Journal of Marketing Research*, 8, 1968, pp. 3–18.

Ayer, A. J., *Language, Truth and Logic.* London: V. Gollancz Ltd., 1936.

Barnett, H. G., *Innovation: The Basis of Cultural Change.* New York: McGraw-Hill, 1953.

Bartels, R., "Can Marketing Be a Science?" *Journal of Marketing*, 15, 1951, pp. 319–328.

———, "The General Theory of Marketing." *Journal of Marketing*, 32, January 1968, pp. 29–33.

———, *Marketing Theory and Metatheory.* Homewood, Ill.: Irwin, 1970.

Bass, F. M., "Testing vs. Estimation in Simultaneous-Equation Regression Models." *Journal of Marketing Research*, 8, 1971.

Bauer, R. A., "Self-Confidence and Persuasibility: One More Time." *Journal of Marketing Research*, 7, 1970, pp. 256–258.

Baumol, N. J., "On the Role of Marketing Theory." *Journal of Marketing*, 21, 1957, pp. 413–418.

Bechtoldt, H. P., "Construct Validity: A Critique." *American Psychologist*, 14, 1959, pp. 619–629.

Bennett, P. D., and Mandell, R. M., "Prepurchase Information-Seeking Behavior of New Car Purchasers—The Learning Hypothesis." *Journal of Marketing Research*, 6, November 1969, pp. 430–433.

Berelson, B., and Steiner, G. A., *Human Behavior: An Inventory of Scientific Findings.* New York: Harcourt, 1964.

Bergmann, G., *Philosophy of Science.* Madison, Wis.: University of Wisconsin Press, 1957.

Berlyne, D. E., "Motivational Problems Raised by Exploratory and Epistemic Behavior," in *Psychology: The Study of a Science*, Vol. 5, Sigmund Koch (ed.). New York: McGraw-Hill, 1963.

Berlyne, D. E., "Curiosity and Exploration." *Science*, 153, no. 3731, 1966, pp. 284–364.

Bigman, S. K., "Evaluating the Effectiveness of Religious Programs." *Review of Religious Research*, 2, 1961, p. 113.

Blalock, H. M., Jr., *Causal Inferences in Nonexperimental Research.* Chapel Hill, N.C.: University of North Carolina Press, 1964.

Blalock, H. M., Jr., "The Measurement Problem: A Gap Between The Languages of Theory and Research, in *Methodology in Social Research,* H. M. Blalock, Jr. and A. B. Blalock (eds.). New York: McGraw-Hill, 1968.

Blalock, H. M., Jr., ed., *Causal Models in the Social Sciences.* Chicago: Aldine-Atherton, 1971.

Blau, P. M., *Exchange and Power in Social Life.* New York: Wiley, 1964.

Bohrnstedt, G. W., "Reliability and Validity Assessment in Attitude Measurement," in *Attitude Measurement,* G. F. Summers (ed.). Skokie, Ill.: Rand McNally, 1970.

Boone, L. E., "The Search for the Consumer Innovator." *Journal of Business,* **43,** April 1970.

Bourne, L. E., and Restle, F., "Mathematical Theory of Concept Identification." *Psychological Review,* **66,** 1959, 278–296.

Boyd, H. W., Jr., and Levy, S. J., "New Dimensions in Consumer Analysis." *Harvard Business Review,* **41,** Nov.–Dec., 1963, pp. 129–140.

Braithwaite, R. B., *Scientific Explanation.* New York: Cambridge, 1953.

Brandt, L. W., and Metzger, W., "Reality: What Does It Mean?" *Psychological Reports,* **25,** 1969, pp. 127–135.

Bridgman, P. W., *The Logic of Modern Physics.* New York: Macmillan, 1927.

Brodbeck, M., "Models, Meaning and Theories," in *Readings in the Philosophy of the Social Sciences,* M. Brodbeck (ed.). New York: Macmillan, 1968, p. 583.

Bross, I. D. J., *Design for Decision.* New York: Macmillan, 1953.

Brown, R., *Explanation in Social Science.* Chicago: Aldine-Atherton, 1963.

Bruck, M., *Empathy and Ideology: Aspects of Administrative Innovation.* Skokie, Ill.: Rand McNally, 1966, pp. 21–47.

Bruner, J. S., Goodnow, J. J., and Austin, G. A., *A Study of Thinking.* New York: Wiley, 1956.

Brunner, J. A., and Mason, J. L., "The Influence of Driving Time upon Shopping Center Preference." *Journal of Marketing,* **32,** April 1968, pp. 57–61.

Bunge, M., *Metascientific Queries.* Springfield, Ill.: Charles C. Thomas, 1959.

Bunge, M., *Causality: The Place of the Causal Principle in Modern Science.* New York: Meridian, 1963.

Bunge, M., *Scientific Research I: The Search for System.* Berlin: Springer, 1967.

Bunge, M., *Scientific Research II: The Search for Truth.* Berlin: Springer, 1967.

Buzzell, R. D., "Is Marketing a Science?" *Harvard Business Review,* **14,** 1963.

Campbell, D. T., "Methodological Suggestions from a Comparative Psychology of Knowledge Processes." *Inquiry,* **2,** 1959, pp. 175–179.

Campbell, D. T., "Common Fate, Similarity and Other Indices of the Status of Aggregates of Persons as Social Entities," in *Decisions, Values and Groups*, Vol. I, D. Willner (ed.). New York: Pergamon, 1960, p. 185.

Campbell, D. T., "Recommendations for APA Test Standards Regarding Construct, Trait, or Discriminant Validity." *American Psychologist*, 15, 1960, pp. 546–553.

Campbell, D. T., "Distinguishing Differences of Perception from Failures of Communication in Cross-Cultural Studies," in *Cross-Cultural Understanding: Epistemology in Anthropology*, F. S. C. Northrop and H. H. Livingston (eds.). New York: Harper & Row, 1964.

Campbell, D. T., "Reforms as Experiments." *American Psychologist*, 24, 1969, pp. 409–429.

Campbell, D. T., "Prospective: Artifact and Control," in *Artifact in Behavioral Research*, R. Rosenthal and R. L. Rosnow (eds.). New York: Academic Press, 1969, pp. 351–382.

Campbell, D. T., "Definitional versus Multiple Operationism." *Et Al.*, 2, 1969, pp. 14–17.

Campbell, D. T., "Methods for the Experimenting Society." Working Paper, Dept. of Psychology, Northwestern University, 1971.

Campbell, D. T., and Fiske, D. W., "Convergent and Discriminant Validation by the Multitrait-Multimethod Matrix." *Psychological Bulletin*, 56, 1959, pp. 81–105.

Campbell, D. T., and Stanley, J. C., *Experimental and Quasi-experimental Design for Research*. Skokie, Ill.: Rand McNally, 1963.

Carnap, R., *Introduction to Semantics*. Cambridge, Mass.: Harvard University Press, 1942.

Carnap, R., *Meaning and Necessity*. Chicago: University of Chicago Press, 1947.

Carnap, R., "The Methodological Character of Theoretical Concepts," in *Minnesota Studies in the Philosophy of Science*, vol. I, H. Feigl and M. Scriven (eds.). Minneapolis: University of Minnesota Press, 1956.

Carnap, R., *Introduction to Symbolic Logic and Its Applications*. New York: Dover, 1958, pp. 4–5.

Caro, F. G., ed., *Readings in Evaluative Research*, New York: Russell Sage, 1971.

Caws, P., *The Philosophy of Science: A Systematic Account*. Princeton, N.J.: Van Nostrand, 1965.

Chaffee, S. H., and MeLeod, J. M., "Consumer Decision and Information Use," in *Consumer Behavior: Theoretical Sources*, S. Ward and T. Robertson (eds.). Englewood Cliffs, N.J.: Prentice-Hall, 1973.

Chin, R., and Benne, K., "General Strategies for Effecting Changes in Human Systems," in *The Planning of Change*, W. G. Bennis, K. D. Benne, and R. Chin (eds.). New York: Holt, Rinehart and Winston, 1969.

Church, A., *Introduction to Mathematical Logic*, Vol. I. Princeton, N.J.: Princeton University Press, 1956.

——, "Propositions and Sentences," in *The Problem of Universals*, I. M. Bochenski *et al.* (eds.). Notre Dame, Ind.: University of Notre Dame Press, 1956.

Church, A., "Propositions," in *Encyclopedia Britannica*, 14th ed., Chicago, 1958.

Cohen, A. R., Brehm, J. W., and Latané, B., "Choice of Strategy and Voluntary Exposure to Information under Public and Private Conditions," *Journal of Personality*, **27**, 1959, p. 63.

Cohen, J. B., "An Interpersonal Orientation to the Study of Consumer Behavior." *Journal of Marketing Research*, **4**, August 1967, pp. 270–278.

Cohen, M. S., and Nagel, E., "Measurement," in *The Structure of Scientific Thought*, E. H. Madden (ed.). Boston: Houghton Mifflin, 1960.

Copi, I. M., "On Crucial Experiments," in *The Structure of Scientific Thought*, E. H. Madden (ed.). Boston: Houghton Mifflin, 1960.

Copley, T. P., and Callom, F. L., "Industrial Search Behavior and Perceived Risk," in *Proceedings of the 2nd Annual Conference of the Association for Consumer Research*, D. M. Gardner (ed.). University of Illinois, Urbana, Ill., 1971, pp. 208–231.

Corey, L. G., "People Who Claim To Be Opinion Leaders: Identifying Their Characteristics by Self-Report." *Journal of Marketing*, **35**, October 1971, pp. 48–58.

Costner, H. L., "Theory, Deduction, and Rules of Correspondence." *American Journal of Sociology*, **75**, 1969, pp. 245–263.

Cox, D. F., ed., *Risk-Taking and Information Handling in Consumer Behavior*. Cambridge, Mass.: Harvard University Press, 1967.

Cox, R., Alderson, W., and Shapiro, S. J., *Theory in Marketing*. Homewood, Ill.: Irwin, 1964.

Cronbach, L. J., *Essentials of Psychological Testing*, 3d ed. New York: Harper & Row, 1971.

Cronbach, L. J., and Meehl, P. E., "Construct Validity in Psychological Tests." *Psychological Bulletin*, **52**, 1955.

Cronkhite, G., *Persuasion: Speech and Behavior Change*. Indianapolis: Bobbs-Merrill, 1969.

Davis, H. L., "Measurement of Husband-Wife Influence in Consumer Purchase Decisions." *Journal of Marketing Research*, **8**, August 1971.

Day, G., "Theories of Attitude Structure and Change," in *Consumer Behavior: Theoretical Sources*, S. Ward and T. Robertson (eds.). Englewood Cliffs, N.J.: Prentice-Hall, 1973.

De Groot, A. *Methodology: Foundations of Influence and Research in the Behavioral Sciences*. The Hague: Mouton, 1969.

Deutscher, I., "Words and Deeds: Social Science and Social Policy." *Social Problems*, **13**, Winter 1966, 235–254.

Doby, J. T., "Logic and Levels of Scientific Explanation," in *Sociological Methodology*, E. F. Borgatta (ed.). San Francisco: Jossey-Bass, 1969.

Dodd, S. C., "Systemmetrics for Evaluating Symbolic Systems." *Systematics*, **6**, 1968, pp. 27–49.

Doob, L. W., "Eidetic Imagery: A Cross-Cultural Will-o'-the-Wisp?" *Journal of Psychology*, **63**, 1967, pp. 13–34.

Dubin, R., *Theory Building*. New York: Free Press, 1969.

Engel, J. F., Kollat, D. T., and Blackwell, R. D., *Consumer Behavior*. New York: Holt, Rinehart and Winston, 1968.

Engel, J., Kollat, D., and Blackwell, R., *Consumer Behavior*, 2d ed. New York: Holt, Rinehart and Winston, in press.

Evans, F. B., "Psychological and Objective Factors in the Prediction of Brand Choice." *Journal of Business*, **32**, October 1959, pp. 340–369.

Farley, J. U., Howard, J. A., and Lehmann, D. R., "After Test Marketing, What?" *Proceedings of the Business and Economic Statistics Section*, American Statistical Association Annual Meeting, Detroit (December 27–30, 1970, Washington, pp. 288–296.

Farley, J. U., and Ring, L. W., "An Empirical Test of the Howard-Sheth Model of Buyer Behavior." *Journal of Marketing Research*, November 1970, pp. 427–438.

Feigl, H., "The Scientific Outlook: Naturalism and Humanism," in *The Philosophy of Science*, H. Feigl and M. Brodbeck (eds.). New York: Appleton, 1953, pp. 8–18.

Feigl, H. and Brodbeck, M., eds., *The Philosophy of Science*. New York: Appleton, 1953.

Findlay, J. N., *Meinong's Theory of Objects*. New York: Oxford, 1933.

Fishbein, M., "The Relationships Between Beliefs, Attitudes, and Behavior," in *Cognitive Consistency*, S. Feldman (ed.). New York: Academic Press, 1966.

Fishbein, M., "Attitude and the Prediction of Behavior," in *Readings in Attitude Theory and Measurement*, M. Fishbein (ed.). New York: Wiley, 1967.

Frege, G., "The Thought." *Mind*, **65**, 1956.

French, C. L., "Correlates of Success in Retail Selling." *American Journal of Sociology*, **66**, September 1960, pp. 128–134.

Galtung, J., "An Inquiry into the Concepts of 'Reliability,' 'Intersubjectivity' and 'Constancy.'" *Inquiry*, **2**, 1959, pp. 107–125.

Galtung, J., *Theory and Methods of Social Research*. New York: Columbia University Press, 1967.

Gensch, D. H., and Staelin, R., "The Appeal of Buying Black." *Journal of Marketing Research*, **9**, 1972.

Green, P. E., and Tull, D. S., *Research for Marketing Decisions*, 2d ed. Englewood Cliffs, N.J.: Prentice-Hall, 1970.

Greenberg, B. G., "Evaluation of Social Problems." *Review of the International Statistical Institute*, **36**, no. 3, 1968, pp. 260–277.

Greer, S., *The Logic of Social Inquiry*. Chicago: Aldine-Atherton, 1969.

Guskin, A., and Chesler, M., "Partisan Diagnosis of Social Problems," in *Perspectives on Social Change*, R. Schwartz and G. Zaltman (eds.). New York: Wiley-Interscience, 1973.

Haber, R. N., "Eidetic Images." *Scientific American*, **220**, April 1969, pp. 36–44.

Halbert, M., *The Meaning and Sources of Marketing Theory*. New York: McGraw-Hill, 1965.

Hall, E. T., *The Silent Language*. New York: Fawcett, 1961.

Hamlyn, D. W., "Analytic and Synthetic Statements," in *Encyclopedia of Philosophy*, P. Edwards (ed.). New York: Macmillan and The Free Press, 1967, pp. 105–109.

Hampshire, S., "Ideas, Propositions and Signs." *Proceedings of the Aristotelian Society*, **40**, 1939–40.

Harré, R., "History of Philosophy of Science," in *Encyclopedia of Philosophy*, P. Edwards (ed.). New York: Macmillan and The Free Press, 1967.

Harré, R., *The Principles of Scientific Thinking*. Chicago: University of Chicago Press, 1970.

Harvey, D., *Explanation in Geography*. London: E. Arnold, 1969.

Hayakawa, S. I., *Language in Thought and Action*. New York: Harcourt, 1949.

Hempel, C. G., "Fundamentals of Concept Formation in Empirical Science." in *International Encyclopedia of Unified Science*, Vol. 11. Chicago: University of Chicago Press, 1952.

Hempel, C. G., *Aspects of Scientific Explanation*. New York: Free Press, 1965.

Hempel, C. G., *Philosophy of Natural Science*. Englewood Cliffs, N.J.: Prentice-Hall, 1966.

Hempel, C. G., "Confirmation: Qualitative Aspects," in *Encyclopedia of Philosophy*, P. Edwards (ed.). New York: Macmillan and The Free Press, 1967.

Hempel, C. G., and Oppenheim, P., "Studies in the Logic of Explanation." *Philosophy of Science*, **15**, 1948, pp. 135–175.

Herrmann, R. O., and Beik, L. L., "Shoppers' Movements Outside Their Local Retail Area." *Journal of Marketing*, **32**, October 1968, pp. 45–51.

Hesse, M., "Laws and Theories," in *Encyclopedia of Philosophy*, P. Edwards (ed.). New York: Macmillan and The Free Press, 1967.

Hesse, M., "Models and Analogy in Science," in *Encyclopedia of Philosophy*, P. Edwards (ed.). New York: Macmillan and The Free Press, 1967.

Hesse, M., "Is There an Independent Observation Language?" in *The Nature and Function of Scientific Theories*, D. G. Colodny (ed.). Pittsburgh: University of Pittsburgh Press, 1970.

Homans, G. E., *Social Behavior: Its Elementary Forms*. New York: Harcourt, 1961.

Hornstein, H. A., *et al.*, *Social Intervention: A Behavioral Science Approach*. New York: Free Press, 1971.

Howard, J. A., *Marketing: Executive and Buyer*. New York: Columbia University Press, 1963.

Howard, J. A., *Marketing Theory*. Boston: Allyn and Bacon, 1965.

Howard, J. A., and Sheth, J. N., *The Theory of Buyer Behavior*. New York: Wiley, 1969.

Hughes, G. D., and Guerrero, J. L., "Automobile Self-Congruity Models Re-examined." *Journal of Marketing Research.* **8**, 1971, pp. 125–127.

Hull, C. L., *Principles of Behavior*. New York: Appleton, 1943.

Hull, C. L., *A Behavior System*. New Haven, Conn.: Yale University Press, 1952.

Hunt, E. B., *Concept Learning: An Information-Processing Problem*. New York: Wiley, 1962.

Hunt, S. D., "The Morphology of Theory and the General Theory of Marketing." *Journal of Marketing*, **35**, April 1971, pp. 65–68.

Hunt, S. D., *et al.*, "Price, Brand Name, and Product Composition Characteristics as Determinants of Perceived Quality." *Journal of Applied Psychology*, **55**, no. 6, 1971, pp. 570–579.

Jacoby, J., "Personality and Innovation Proneness." *Journal of Marketing Research*, **8**, 1971, pp. 244–247.

Jones, G. N., *Planned Organizational Change*. New York: Praeger, 1969.

Kanter, D. L., "The Way You Test Advertising Depends upon the Approach the Advertising Itself Takes, Says Researcher." *Advertising Age*, July 15, 1957.

Kaplan, A., *The Conduct of Inquiry: Methodology for Behaviorial Science*. New York: Intext Educational Publishers, Chandler Publishing Company, 1964.

Kassarjian, H. H., "Personality and Consumer Behavior: A Review." *Journal of Marketing Research*, **8**, November 1971, pp. 409–419.

Kelman, H., *A Time To Speak*. San Francisco: Jossey-Bass, 1968.

Kemeny, J. G., *A Philosopher Looks at Science*. Princeton, N.J.: Van Nostrand, 1959.

Kendler, T. S., "Concept Formation." *Annual Review of Psychology*, 1961, pp. 447–472.

Kidder, L. H., and Campbell, D. T., "The Indirect Testing of Social Attitudes," in *Attitude Measurement*, G. I. Summers (ed.). Skokie, Ill.: Rand McNally, 1970, pp. 333–385.

Kiesler, C., "Evaluating Social Change Programs," in *Processes and Phenomena of Social Change*, G. Zaltman (ed.). New York: Wiley-Interscience, 1973.

Kinnear, T. C., and Taylor, J. R., "Multivariate Methods in Marketing Research: A Further Attempt at Classification." *Journal of Marketing Research*, **8**, October 1971.

Kneale, W., and Kneale, M., *The Development of Logic*. New York: Oxford, 1962.

Koehler, B., Beres, M. B., and Zaltman, G., "A Simulation of Invisible Colleges." Working Paper, Northwestern University, Graduate School of Management, 1972.

Kollat, D. T., Engel, J. F., and Blackwell, R. D., "Current Problems in Consumer Behavior Research." *Journal of Marketing Research*, **7**, August 1970, pp. 327–332.

Kotler, P., *Marketing Management: Analysis, Planning and Control*, 2d ed. Englewood Cliffs, N.J.: Prentice-Hall, 1972.

Kuhn, T. S., *The Structure of Scientific Revolutions*, 2d ed. Chicago: University of Chicago Press, 1962.

Kunkel, J. H., and Berry, L. L., "A Behavioral Conception of Retail Image." *Journal of Marketing*, **32**, October 1968, pp. 21–27.

Labovitz, S., and Hagedorn, R., *Introduction to Social Research*. New York: McGraw-Hill, 1971.

Lachman, R., "The Model in Theory Construction." *Psychological Review*, **67**, no. 2, 1960, pp. 113–114.

Langer, S. K., *An Introduction to Symbolic Logic*, 3d rev. ed. New York: Dover, 1967.

Lazarsfeld, P. F., "Concept Formation and Measurement in the Behavioral Sciences: Some Historical Observations," in *Concepts, Theory, and Explanation in the Behavioral Sciences*, G. J. Di Renzo (ed.). New York: Random House, 1966, pp. 144–202.

Lehmann, D. R., Farley, J. U., and Howard, J. A. "Testing of Buyer Behavior Models," *Proceedings of the 2nd Annual Conference of the Association for Consumer Research*, D. M. Gardner (ed.). University of Illinois, Urbana, Ill. 1971, pp. 232–242.

Lerner, D., *The Passing of Traditional Society*. New York: Free Press, 1958.

Leventhal, H., "Fear Appeals and Persuasion: The Differentiation of a Motivational Construct." *American Journal of Public Health*, **61**, June 1971, pp. 1208–1224.

Levy, S. J., "Promotional Behavior," in *Managerial Analysis in Marketing*, F. D. Sturdivant *et al.* (ed.). Glenview, Ill.: Scott, Foresman, 1970, pp. 372–435.

Lin, N., and Zaltman, G., "Dimensions of Innovations," in *Processes and Phenomena of Social Change*, G. Zaltman (ed.). New York: Wiley-Interscience, 1973.

MacCorquodale, K., and Meehl, P. E., "On a Distinction between Hypothetical Constructs and Intervening Variables." *Psychological Review*, **55**, 1948, pp. 95–107.

Maddi, S. R., ed. *Perspectives on Personality: A Comparative Approach*. Boston: Little, Brown, 1971.

Maloney, J., "Separate Parts Bin for a New Social Psychology." *Journal of Contemporary Psychology*, in press.

Mandler, G., and Kessen, W., *The Language of Psychology*. New York: Wiley, 1959.

Margenau, H., *The Nature of Physical Reality.* New York: McGraw-Hill, 1950.

Markin, R. J., *The Psychology of Consumer Behavior.* Englewood Cliffs, N.J.: Prentice-Hall, 1969.

Martilla, J. A., "Word-of-Mouth Communication in the Industrial Adoption Process." *Journal of Marketing Research,* **8,** 1971.

Marx, M. H., "The Dimension of Operational Clarity," in *Theories in Contemporary Society,* M. H. Marx (ed.). New York: Macmillan, 1963, pp. 187–202.

McConnel, J. D., "The Price-Quality Relationship in an Experimental Setting." *Journal of Marketing Research,* **5,** 1968, pp. 300–303.

McGuire, W. J., "The Nature of Attitudes and Attitude Change," in *Handbook of Social Psychology.* Reading, Mass.: Addison-Wesley, 1969.

Meehan, E. J., *Explanation in Social Science: A System Paradigm.* Homewood, Ill.: The Dorsey Press, 1968.

Merton, R., *Social Theory and Social Structure.* New York: Free Press, 1968.

Miller, S. J., Mazis, M. B., and Wright, P. L., "The Influence of Brand Ambiguity on Brand Attitude Development." *Journal of Marketing Research,* **8,** November 1971, pp. 455–459.

Montgomery, D. B., "Consumer Characteristics Associated With Dealing: An Empirical Example." *Journal of Marketing Research,* **8,** 1971, pp. 118–120.

Montgomery, D. B., and Ryans, A. B., "Stochastic Models of Consumer Choice Behavior," in *Consumer Behavior: Theoretical Sources,* S. Ward and T. Robertson (eds.). Englewood Cliffs, N.J.: Prentice-Hall, 1973.

Montgomery, D. B., and Urban, G., *Management Science in Marketing.* Englewood Cliffs, N.J.: Prentice-Hall, 1969.

Moore, G. E., "The Nature of Judgment." *Mind,* **8,** 1899.

Morgenbesser, S., "Scientific Explanation," in *International Encyclopedia of the Social Sciences,* D. L. Sills (ed.). New York: Crowell-Collier-Macmillan, 1968.

Myers, J. H., Stanton, R. R., and Haug, A. F., "Correlates of Buying Behavior: Social Class vs. Income." *Journal of Marketing,* **35,** October 1971, pp. 8–15.

Nagel, E., *The Structure of Science.* New York: Harcourt, 1961.

National Research Council, *The Behavioral and Social Sciences.* Englewood Cliffs, N.J.: Prentice-Hall, 1969.

Newman, J. W., *Motivation Research and Marketing Management.* Cambridge, Mass.: Harvard University Press, 1957.

Nicosia, F. M., *Consumer Decision Processes: Marketing and Advertising Implications.* Englewood Cliffs, N.J.: Prentice-Hall, 1966.

Nicosia, F. M., and Rosenberg, B., "Substantive Modeling in Consumer Attitude Research: Some Practical Uses." *Proceedings of the 4th Attitude Research Conference,* November 1971.

O'Brien, T. V., "Tracking Consumer Decision Making." *Journal of Marketing*, **35**, January 1971, pp. 34–40.

Osgood, C. E., "A Behavioristic Analysis of Perception and Language as Cognitive Phenomena," in *Contemporary Approaches to Cognition*. Cambridge, Mass.: Harvard University Press, 1957.

Osgood, C. E., "Motivational Dynamics of Language Behavior," in *Nebraska Symposium on Motivation*, vol. 5, Marshall R. Jones (ed.). Lincoln, Neb.: University of Nebraska Press, pp. 348–424.

Osgood, C. E., Suci, G. J., and Tannenbaum, P. H., *The Measurement of Meaning*. Urbana, Ill.: University of Illinois Press, 1957.

Ostland, L., "Role Theory and Group Dynamics," in *Consumer Behavior: Theoretical Sources*, S. Ward and T. Robertson (eds.). Englewood Cliffs, N.J.: Prentice-Hall, 1973.

Oxenfeldt, A. R., *Executive Action in Marketing*. Belmont, Calif.: Wadsworth Publishing Co., Inc., 1966.

Phillips, B. S., *Social Research: Strategy and Tactics*. New York: Macmillan, 1966.

Pinson, C., and Roberto, E., "Simplicity, Parsimony, and Model Building." *Proceedings 1972 Midwest Conference, American Institute for Decision Sciences*, J. M. McKinney, R. T. Riley (eds.), pp. 31–34.

Pinson, C., Angelmar, R., and Roberto, E., "An Evaluation of the General Theory of Marketing." *Journal of Marketing*, **36**, July 1972.

Platt, J. R., "Strong Inference." *Science* **146**, no. 3642, December 1964, pp. 347–353.

Plummer, J. T., "Life Style Patterns and Commercial Bank Credit Card Usage." *Journal of Marketing*, **35**, pp. 35–41, 1971.

Popper, K. R., *The Logic of Scientific Discovery*. New York: Science Editions, 1961.

Popper, K. R. *Conjectures and Refutations: The Growth of Scientific Knowledge*. New York: Harper & Row, 1965.

Quine, W. V. O., *From A Logical Point of View*. Cambridge, Mass.: Harvard University Press, 1953.

Ray, M. L., and Wilkie, W. L., "Fear: The Potential of an Appeal Neglected by Marketing." *Journal of Marketing*, **34**, January 1970, pp. 54–62.

Rescher, N., *Scientific Explanation*. New York: Free Press, 1970.

Reynolds, F. D., and Darden, W., "Construing Life Style and Psychographics," in *Life Style and Psychographics*, W. D. Wells (ed.). New York: American Marketing Association, in press.

Rivlin, A. M., *Systematic Thinkings for Social Action*. Washington, D.C.: Brookings, 1971.

Robertson, T., and Kennedy, J. N., "Prediction of Consumer Innovators: Application of Multiple Discriminant Analysis," *Journal of Marketing Research*, **5**, February 1968, pp. 64–69.

Robertson, T., and Ward, S., "Consumer Behavior Research: Promise and Prospects," in *Consumer Behavior: Theoretical Sources*, S. Ward and T. Robertson (eds.). Englewood Cliffs, N.J.: Prentice-Hall, 1973.

Robertson, T. S., *Innovative Behavior and Communication*. New York: Holt, Rinehart and Winston, 1971.

Rogers, E. M., *Diffusion of Innovations*. New York: Free Press, 1962.

Rogers, E. M., *Modernization among Peasants: The Impact of Communication*. New York: Holt, Rinehart and Winston, 1969.

Rogers, E. M., and Shoemaker, F. F., *Communication of Innovations: A Cross-Cultural Approach*. New York: Free Press, 1971, pp. 347–385.

Rokeach, M., "Attitude Change and Behavior Change." *Public Opinion Quarterly*, **30**, Winter 1967, pp. 529–550.

Rosenberg, M., *Occupations and Values*. New York: Free Press, 1957.

Rozeboom, W. W., "Mediation Variables in Scientific Theories." *Psychological Review*, **63**, 1956, pp. 249–264.

Rudner, R. S., *Philosophy of Social Science*. Englewood Cliffs, N.J.: Prentice-Hall, 1966.

Russell, B., *An Inquiry into Meaning and Truth*. New York: Norton, 1948.

Rychlak, J. F., *A Philosophy of Science for Personality Theory*. Boston: Houghton Mifflin, 1968.

Ryle, G., "Meaning and Necessity," *Philosophy*, vol. 24, 1949.

Sackstedter, W., " 'Theories' and Usage." *The Journal of Philosophy*, **59**, June 7, 1962.

Scheffler, I., *The Anatomy of Inquiry*. New York: Knopf, 1963.

Schuessler, R., "Prediction," in *International Encyclopedia of Social Sciences*, D. L. Sills (ed.). New York: Crowell-Collier-Macmillan, 1968.

Schutz, A., "Common Sense and Scientific Interpretation of Human Action," *Philosophy of the Social Sciences: A Reader*, Maurice Natanson (ed.). New York: Random House, 1963, pp. 302–346.

Schwartz, G., *Development of Marketing Theory*. Cincinnati: South-Western Publishing Company, 1963.

Scriven, M. S., "Definitions, Explanations, and Theories," in *Theories and the Mind–Body Problem*, H. Feigl, M. Scriven, and G. Maxwell (eds.), Minnesota Studies in the Philosophy of Science, 11. Minneapolis: University of Minnesota Press, 1958, pp. 477–482.

Seipel, C., "Premiums—Forgotten by Theory." *Journal of Marketing*, **35**, April 1971, pp. 26–34.

Selltitz, C., Jahoda, M., Deutsch, M., and Cook, S., *Research Methods in Social Relations*. New York: Holt, Rinehart and Winston, 1959.

Sheth, J., and Talarzyk, W. W., "Perceived Instrumentality and Value Importance as Determinants of Attitudes." *Journal of Marketing Research*, **9**, 1972, pp. 6–9.

Sheth, J. N., "A Review of Buyer Behavior." *Management Science*, **13**, 1967, pp. B718–B756.

Sheth, J. N., "The Multivariate Revolution in Marketing Research." *Journal of Marketing*, **35**, January 1971.

Silk, A. J., and Geiger, F. P., "Advertisement Size and the Relationship between Product Usage and Advertising Exposure." *Journal of Marketing Research*, **9**, February 1972, pp. 22–26.

Simon, H. A., and Newell, A., "The Uses and Limitations of Models," *Theories in Contemporary Psychology*, M. H. Marx (ed.). New York: Macmillan, pp. 89–104.

Singer, J., "Motivation for Consistency," in *Cognitive Consistency*, S. Feldman (ed.). New York: Academic Press, 1966.

Skinner, B. F., *Science and Human Behavior*. New York: Free Press, 1953.

Sommers, M. S., "Problems and Opportunities in the Development of Consumer Behavior Theory," in *Consumer Behavior*, R. Holloway, R. Mittelstaedt, and M. Venkatesan (eds.). Boston: Houghton Mifflin, 1971, pp. 14–22.

Stafford, J. E., and Enis, B. M., "The Price-Quality Relationship: An Extension." *Journal of Marketing Research*, **6**, 1969, pp. 456–458.

Stinchcombe, A. L., *Constructing Social Theories*. New York: Harcourt, 1968.

Suchman, E. H., *Evaluative Research*. New York: Russell Sage, 1967.

Summers, G. F., ed., *Attitude Measurement*. Skokie, Ill.: Rand McNally, 1970.

Taylor, C., "Psychological Behaviorism," in *Encyclopedia of Philosophy*, P. Edwards (ed.). New York: Macmillan, 1967.

Taylor, W. J., " 'Is Marketing a Science?' Revisited." *Journal of Marketing*, **29**, 1965, pp. 49–53.

Torgerson, W. S., *Theory and Methods of Scaling*. New York: Wiley, 1958.

Triandis, H., *Attitude Change*. New York: Wiley, 1971, p. 3.

Trow, M., "Methodological Problems in the Evaluation of Innovation." Paper read at the Symposium on Problems in the Evaluation of Instruction, Los Angeles, December 15, 1967.

Tucker, W. T., and Painter, J. J., "Personality and Product Use." *Journal of Applied Psychology*, **45**, 1961.

U.S. Dept. of Health, Education and Welfare, Public Health Service, Publication No. 413, 1925, p. 610.

Venkatesan, M., "Cognitive Consistency and Novelty Seeking," in *Consumer Behavior: Theoretical Sources*, S. Ward and T. Robertson (eds.). Englewood Cliffs, N.J.: Prentice-Hall.

Vinacke, W. E., *Psychology of Thinking*. New York: McGraw-Hill, 1952.

Wallace, W. W., *The Logic of Science in Sociology*. Chicago: Aldine-Atherton, 1971.

Ward, S., and Robertson, T. S., eds., *Consumer Behavior: Theoretical Sources*. Englewood Cliffs, N.J.: Prentice-Hall, 1973.

Wartofsky, M. W., *Conceptual Foundations of Scientific Thought*. New York: Macmillan, 1968.

Warwick, D., and Kelman, H., "Ethical Issues in Social Intervention," in *Perspectives on Social Change*, R. Schwartz and G. Zaltman (eds.). New York: Wiley-Interscience, 1973.

Webb, E. J., Campbell, D. T., Schwartz, R. D., and Sechrest, L., *Unobtrusive Measures: Nonreactive Research in the Social Sciences*. Skokie, Ill.: Rand McNally, 1966.

Wells, W. D., and Beard, A., "Personality and Consumer Behavior," in *Consumer Behavior: Theoretical Sources*, S. Ward and T. S. Robertson (eds.). Englewood Cliffs, N.J.: Prentice-Hall, 1973.

Wells, W. D., and Tigert, D. J., "Activities, Interests, and Opinions." *Journal of Advertising Research*, 11, August 1971, pp. 27–35.

White, A. R., "Coherence Theory of Truth," in *Encyclopedia of Philosophy*, P. Edwards (ed.). New York: Macmillan, 1967.

Wiseman, F., "A Segmentation Analysis on Automobile Buyers During the New Model Year Transition Period." *Journal of Marketing*, 35, April 1971, pp. 42–49.

Woodman, J. J., "The Pupil Response as a Measure of Social Attitudes," in *Attitude Measurement*, Gene F. Summers (ed.). Skokie, Ill.: Rand McNally, 1970, pp. 514–533.

Zaltman, G., *Marketing: Contributions From the Behavioral Sciences*. New York: Harcourt, 1965.

Zaltman, G., "Marketing Inference in the Behavioral Sciences." *Journal of Marketing*, 34, July 1970, pp. 27–32.

Zaltman, G., Angelmar, R., and Pinson, C., "Metatheory in Consumer Behavior Research." *Proceedings of the 2nd Annual Conference of the Association for Consumer Research*, D. M. Gardner (ed.), University of Illinois, Urbana, Ill., 1971.

Zaltman, G., Kotler, P., and Kaufman, I., eds., *Creating Social Change*. New York: Holt, Rinehart and Winston, 1972.

Zaltman, G., and Vertinsky, I., "Health Service Marketing: A Suggested Model." *Journal of Marketing*, 35, July 1971.

Author Index

Subject Index